Multiculturalism and the
Foundations of Meaningful Life

Andrew M. Robinson

Multiculturalism and the Foundations of Meaningful Life: Reconciling Autonomy, Identity, and Community

UBCPress · Vancouver · Toronto

16 15 14 13 12 11 10 09 08 07   5 4 3 2 1

Printed in Canada on ancient-forest-free paper (100% post-consumer recycled) that is processed chlorine- and acid-free, with vegetable-based inks.

Library and Archives Canada Cataloguing in Publication

Robinson, Andrew M. (Andrew Mackenzie), 1966-
    Multiculturalism and the foundations of meaningful life : reconciling autonomy, identity, and community / Andrew M. Robinson.

    Includes bibliographical references and index.
    ISBN 978-0-7748-1313-6

    1. Multiculturalism. 2. Multiculturalism – Case studies. 3. Multiculturalism – Canada. 4. Multiculturalism – Canada – Case studies. I. Title.

HM1271.R63 2007   305.8   C2007-900345-1

Canada

UBC Press gratefully acknowledges the financial support for our publishing program of the Government of Canada through the Book Publishing Industry Development Program (BPIDP), and of the Canada Council for the Arts, and the British Columbia Arts Council.

This book has been published with the help of a grant from the Canadian Federation for the Humanities and Social Sciences, through the Aid to Scholarly Publications Programme, using funds provided by the Social Sciences and Humanities Research Council of Canada.

UBC Press
The University of British Columbia
2029 West Mall
Vancouver, BC V6T 1Z2
604.822.5959 / Fax 604.822.6083
www.ubcpress.ca

Contents

Acknowledgments

As those who have done it must know, writing a book takes a lot time and a lot of one's attention: time and attention that would otherwise be spent with other people, doing other things. My first debt of gratitude is therefore to my wife, Barbara, without whose support and patience this project would never have come to fruition. I would also like to thank my parents for their unconditional love and support and my sons, William and James, for putting it all in perspective.

There are a number of others I should thank. Foremost among them is Richard Vernon at the University of Western Ontario, who supervised the dissertation out of which this book developed. Others who read and commented on papers, parts of which have made their way into this book, are Joseph Carens, Marc Doucet, Richard Sigurdson, Diane Lamoureax, and Peter Kulchyski. I thank the anonymous reviewers at UBC Press whose comments helped make this a much better book. I would like to express my appreciation for colleagues whose support and interest in my work helped bring it to fruition. These include Marty Westmacott and Michael Southern at the University of Western Ontario, Howard Leeson and Joyce Green at the University of Regina, and Rob Feagan, Kathryn Carter, and Leo Groarke at Laurier Brantford. Finally, I thank Emily Andrew at UBC Press, who was incredibly helpful in shepherding this manuscript through the review and funding processes.

Small portions of this book have appeared previously in print, although most have been rewritten. Arguments in Chapter 7 first appeared in "Would International Adjudication Enhance Contextual Theories of Justice? Reflections on the UN Human Rights Committee, *Lovelace, Ballantyne,* and *Waldman," Canadian Journal of Political Science* 38, 2 (June 2006): 271-91 (© Cambridge University Press), and some of the evidence and arguments concerning the Pueblo in Chapters 5 and 6 first appeared in "Cultural Rights and Internal Minorities: Of Pueblos and Protestants," *Canadian Journal of Political*

Science 36, 1 (March 2003): 107-27. The relevant extracts are reproduced with permission.

I also wish to recognize the financial support this project has received from the Canadian Federation for the Humanities and Social Sciences, through the Aid to Scholarly Publishing Programme, and from Wilfrid Laurier University through a book preparation grant from the Research Office.

Multiculturalism and the
Foundations of Meaningful Life

Introduction

The extension of special rights and privileges to ethnocultural minorities is almost universally practised in liberal-democratic societies, yet it has not been satisfactorily reconciled with liberal principles, either in theory or in the popular imagination. Francophones and First Nations in Canada, Welsh and Scottish in the United Kingdom, Basques and Catalonians in Spain, Maori in New Zealand, Aborigines in Australia, Corsicans in France, Amish and Indians in the United States, and ethnic and immigrant groups in all of these countries receive rights, privileges, or exemptions not available to other citizens. For those of us who believe in the value and legitimacy of such rights, this is a cause for concern.

Lacking clear theoretical justification, these rights can appear to constitute anomalous violations of an otherwise consistent and appealing liberal conception of distributive justice. This impression is reinforced when claims for special treatment are handled in ways that do not appear to reflect consistent underlying principles. Together these perceptions suggest that different treatment is unjust treatment because it violates the basic principle that all citizens be treated with equal respect. This is a serious charge; it demands a response.

At least since Will Kymlicka published *Liberalism, Community, and Culture*, political philosophers have debated the compatibility of liberal principles of justice and claims for special treatment based on cultural difference.[1] Some, like Kymlicka, have argued that liberal principles can be reconciled with respect for cultural communities; others have critiqued this project in defence of traditional liberal principles;[2] still others have argued that proper respect for cultural difference may require a move away from liberal principles.[3]

This book develops an argument of the first variety: it seeks to reconcile liberal principles with the accommodation of cultural and other communities. As with all such arguments, the very logic of the values I seek to reconcile requires navigating a course between the Scylla of cultural relativism and the Charybdis of liberal universalism. On the one hand, cultural relativism, if based on an interpretation of equal respect that requires uncritical acceptance of all cultures people have created, can provide no basis for critiquing the way communities treat their members. On the other hand, liberal universalism, if based on an interpretation of equal respect that requires identical treatment for all individuals, closes off the possibility of adjusting rights and privileges to accommodate differences between communities. These competing tensions are illustrated by Desmond Clarke and Charles Jones:

> Liberal societies are committed, in principle, to the ideal of equal opportunities for all citizens. When apparently fair procedures and structures are implemented, it is always open to individuals to argue that they are burdened unequally because of their special circumstances. If the claim of unfairness or inequality is to be addressed, it must be possible to find some impartial principle by reference to which the dispute may be resolved. However, if each person is entitled to appeal to their own "culture" as the exclusive source of values or principles for conflict resolution, and if the concept of culture is sufficiently broad to include almost all value differences that are likely to arise in a society, then the possibility of a principled resolution of any disagreement seems to be precluded by cultural relativism.[4]

This poses a challenge to those who feel the attraction of both liberal universalism and cultural difference. Joseph Carens describes it as a "challenge ... to find a critical perspective which is at the same time open to the possibility of genuine differences among people's values and commitments."[5] For Avigail Eisenberg, the "challenge ... is to develop an approach that systematically and fairly incorporates the cultural and historical circumstances of different people into analysis, without giving everything away to context."[6]

This book takes up this challenge by developing a theoretical approach that incorporates and builds on the insights of leading theorists sympathetic to both liberal democracy and the interests of ethnocultural minorities. (I follow Kymlicka in referring to such writers collectively as "liberal culturalists."[7]) It takes as its point of departure the co-existence of a high level of consensus among liberal culturalists on *advocacy positions* ("the moral stand or policy one adopts") with great diversity in the *ontological assumptions* ("what you recognize as the factors you will invoke to account for social life") to which they appeal to justify their advocacy positions.[8] Its key contribution is to suggest that we might answer the challenge of finding a systematic and principled reconciliation to the apparent conflict between liberal universalism and communal particularism by returning to questions of ontological, or what I will call foundational, assumptions.

The Liberal Culturalist Consensus

The broad liberal culturalist consensus on advocacy positions can be summarized in six claims, which I describe in fairly general language, as the consensus does not carry over into all of the details. The first two claims form a basic starting point. First, it is reasonable to speak of groups of individuals that can be defined in terms of culture. Second, justice, properly understood, requires liberal-democratic conceptions of justice that equate equal treatment with identical treatment to be modified, or even transformed, to facilitate the recognition or accommodation of cultural groups.

The third and fourth claims concern the nature of accommodations: different types of groups warrant different types of recognition or accommodation, and the exact nature of recognition or accommodation must be determined contextually – that is, there are no universal, cookie-cutter solutions. Recognition and special accommodation have primarily been argued for four types of groups. National majorities are cultural nations that constitute the majority, or at least the dominant, group within a state or sub-state unit. It is generally suggested that it is both legitimate and inevitable that national majorities will use the state to promote the interests and survival of their cultures. National minorities are groups that have a strong sense of collective ethnocultural identity and live on their homeland within the territory of the state in question. It is generally claimed that such groups can legitimately demand the conditions necessary to ensure their survival as distinct peoples or societies, for example, group representation in political institutions, exclusions from laws or obligations that apply to other citizens, and self-government arrangements, including federalism. Indigenous peoples and traditional or premodern minorities are similar to national minorities in that they have a strong sense of collective identity, some may aspire to exercise powers of self-government, and, at least in the case of indigenous peoples, they may share ethnocultural features and live on their traditional homeland. These groups are distinguished from national minorities, however, by the fact that their present ways of life, or their origins as a group, or both, are not products of modernity. As for special accommodations, those associated with indigenous peoples are typically most extensive, usually including self-government, while those claimed for other minorities, such as Amish and Hutterite religious communities, are usually restricted to special exemptions that would permit them to survive as communities. Finally, unlike national and indigenous minorities, ethnic and immigrant groups are typically not concentrated on traditional homelands but arrived in the state as immigrants. Further, unlike premodern minorities, who often arrived in the state as a group, ethnic or immigrant minorities typically arrived as individuals or familial units. The accommodations suggested for these groups tend to be significantly less extensive than those suggested for the other groups. It is generally agreed that while they cannot justify claims to self-government, they can, in justice, exercise rights to use their language and live according to their traditions in their private lives as well as expect alterations of the society's public culture so that they can integrate without having to abandon their identity.

The final two claims concern intergroup relations and the bases of social unity. The fifth is that intercultural dialogue is both an appropriate means for making and resolving claims for recognition and accommodation and the vehicle through which social unity is to be fostered and sustained. Sixth, it is suggested that accommodating legitimate claims (and the dialogue through which this is to occur) is likely to enhance social unity, while denying legitimate claims is likely to undermine it. Liberal culturalists generally claim that any threats recognizing diversity may pose to state unity cannot be any worse than those arising from attempts to impose uniformity. The outcome of intercultural dialogue, it is often suggested, will be the development of a shared identity that can sustain the strong "sense of common purpose and mutual solidarity" that no mere modus vivendi between groups ever could.[9]

Two things are striking about this consensus. One is that it has not been accompanied by a similar consensus at the level of foundational assumptions. The other is the lack of interest some liberal culturalists have shown in attempting to address these disagreements by focusing on foundational assumptions. For example, Kymlicka has written that he has doubts about the usefulness of "a more high-level abstract theory that starts from first premises about the nature of reason, knowledge, and personhood,"[10] and Joseph Carens has written a very interesting book that considers how the ideals of fairness as neutrality and fairness as even-handedness might be reconciled in practice despite having "not yet worked out a general theoretical account of how this would work and how the two ideals might be reconciled in principle."[11]

A key supposition of this book is that much is to be gained by focusing on such foundational assumptions. Consider, for example, Carens' explanation of his reluctance to provide precise definitions for culture or identity: "Such definitions are rarely helpful, in part because they sometimes exclude things that are morally and theoretically relevant, in part because the limiting implications of the precise definition are often lost sight of in subsequent arguments."[12] While I think he is right in his description of what can go wrong, I think the appropriate response is not to eschew defining axiomatic terms but to be careful about getting definitions right and to be rigorous in applying them.

Overview of the Book

The book is divided into three parts. In Part 1, Inspecting the Foundations, I discuss important contributions to the multiculturalism debate and identify a number of issues and questions that, I believe, necessitate a return to foundational questions about the nature of identity, autonomy, and community. The chapter is organized according to these issues and questions. My aim is not so much to critique or evaluate the arguments I discuss as to suggest why we are pressed towards these fundamental questions. The reasons vary. Sometimes they are found in disagreements between particular authors, sometimes in the different ways in which authors address the same issues. At other times, the reasons are suggested by loose ends within the work of a single author. The overall aim is to justify a return to foundational assumptions and to identify issues that such a return should enable us to address. These issues include the nature and value of the relationship between individuals and communities; how communities are defined; the role of socialization; the social units with which cultural interests should be associated; what to make of the distinction between modern and premodern or traditional cultures; and finally, the relationship between state borders, social unity, and intercultural dialogue.

In Part 2, The Foundations of Meaningful Life, I suggest that by placing meaningful life, defined as the pursuit of subjectively significant purposes, at the centre of a theory of justice, definitions of identity, autonomy, and community can be reconfigured in ways that permit their theoretical reconciliation. The approach I adopt, which owes much to those theorists I consider in Part 1, involves three major moves. The first, which I make here, is to place the inquiry in a broadly liberal context by stating two axiomatic assumptions: one, all individuals have equal moral worth and, thus, must be treated with equal respect; and two, the only interests that should matter in a theory of justice are those of individuals.

The second move, which is made in Part 2, is the development and defence of a conception of the person who has an essential interest in meaningful life. The reference to meaning or meaningful life, as anyone familiar with the authors canvassed in Part 1 will know, is nothing new. What is different is the way I position this value as underlying and explaining the significance of other key normative values. Most important, this use of meaningful life allows the development of a conception of the person that suggests how we might integrate, without ranking, our beliefs in the importance of personal autonomy and identification with community. To achieve this, I utilize a distinction drawn by John Rawls between a general concept and particular conceptions of that concept.[13] This permits the development and explication of conceptions of personal autonomy and community that, while being reconfigured in ways that reveal how they may be mutually supportive, remain true to their general concepts. In so doing, I hope to demonstrate the usefulness of shifting discussion from advocacy positions to foundational assumptions: while many particular conceptions of personal autonomy and identification with community may be irreconcilable, the concepts of personal autonomy and identification with community need not be.

Since the term "meaningful life" means different things to different people, Chapter 2 begins by defining it. I argue that defined as a life characterized by the pursuit of subjectively significant purposes, meaningful life is general enough to be compatible with many different ways of life but substantive enough to escape the charge of radical relativism. The conception of the person for whom meaningful life is an essential interest is used to generate an account of human agency that in turn leads to a conception of a fluid-yet-fragile self-identity, a conception of community as context of value, and a conception of personal autonomy as situated autonomy.

These reconfigured conceptions are distinguished by the way they work together to sustain meaningful lives. Situated autonomy is reconcilable with the value of identification with community because it presupposes that people govern themselves by reference to values that they access in the communities with which they identify. In recognizing that autonomy requires such identifications, we find reasons to resist defining autonomy in ways that would threaten the development of such identifications. The conception of a fluid-yet-fragile self-identity permits us to recognize that self-identities can be based on identifications with multiple and often conflicting communities. Finally, the association of community with traditions that connect their members with contexts of value provides the basis for a defence of a much wider range of communities than cultural nations or societal cultures. I refer to these assumptions collectively as the foundations of meaningful life.

Chapter 3 applies the conceptions of fluid-yet-fragile self-identity and community as context of value to explain why special accommodations for particular communities can be justified, why people who are not members of these communities might reasonably be expected to accept the burdens such accommodation may impose on them, and the bases of social unity in culturally diverse states. Finally, Chapter 4 considers the implications of situated autonomy for how we should evaluate and address the role of socialization. This requires defending situated autonomy as a conception of personal autonomy, even though it rejects the ideal of the examined life.

The argument's third and final move is made in Part 3, A Politics of Liberal Multiculturalism. Here the theoretical foundations of meaningful life laid in Part 2 are used to ground a principled and systematic account of the practice of liberal multiculturalism. Part 3 aims to demonstrate three broad points: that the foundations of meaningful life can generate principles to inform substantive thinking about public policy; that these principles are internally consistent; and that the principles can support the main points of the liberal culturalist consensus. Each chapter addresses a different set of practical questions and builds on the preceding chapters.

Chapter 5 addresses two related issues. It begins by discussing the problem of defining communities. This is illustrated by considering *R. v. Powley*, a Canadian Supreme Court case that raised issues of Métis identity. It then moves on to consider when claims for special protection can be justified by revisiting criteria introduced in Chapter 3. It explores these criteria in more detail through case studies that cover a range of minority communities represented in the liberal culturalist consensus: national minorities (francophones in Quebec, Welsh speakers in Wales), indigenous peoples (the Pueblo of New Mexico, the Coast Salish of British Columbia), non-indigenous premodern communities (the Amish in Wisconsin), and ethnic immigrant groups (Muslims in Ontario).

Chapter 6 suggests principles to govern the design of communal accommodation. Four key principles are identified, and the cases introduced in Chapter 5 are used to illustrate how they might apply in particular circumstances. The chapter concludes by considering the case of Pueblo Indians who converted to Protestantism in order to illustrate how these principles might help address issues raised by conflict *within* communities.

Finally, Chapter 7 completes the development of advocacy positions by considering the implications of the foundations of meaningful life for state-community relations. It considers two key aspects of state-community relations that a theory of liberal multiculturalism must address. One concerns the initiation and evaluation of claims for special accommodation. The case of Mi'kmaq demands for logging and fishing rights is introduced to demonstrate how the principles developed here might apply in practice as well as how they might help us sort out conflicts *between* communities. In the course of discussing these claims, the potential benefits and drawbacks of international adjudication are also assessed. The second aspect of state-community relations concerns state intervention in the internal practices of communities. Principles to guide practice are suggested, and their usefulness illustrated through case studies of the Amish in Wisconsin and Muslims in Ontario.

The book concludes by summarizing its main contributions to the wider debate: that a return to ontological assumptions is a useful way to advance thinking about liberal multiculturalism; that the foundations of meaningful life provide a compelling account of the relationship between individuals and communities; and that the theory of liberal multiculturalism erected on these foundations can provide a cogent response to those who believe that communal accommodations are never justified.

Part 1:
Inspecting the Foundations

1
Why Return to Foundational Assumptions?

To build a country for everyone, Canada would have to allow for second-level or "deep" diversity, in which a plurality of ways of belonging would also be acknowledged and accepted. Someone of, say, Italian extraction in Toronto or Ukrainian extraction in Edmonton might indeed feel Canadian as a bearer of individual rights in a multicultural mosaic. His or her belonging would not "pass through" some other community, although the ethnic identity might be important to him or her in various ways. But this person might nevertheless accept that a Quebecois or a Cree or a Dene might belong in a very different way, that these persons were Canadian through being members of their national communities. Reciprocally, the Quebecois, Cree, or Dene would accept the perfect legitimacy of the "mosaic" identity.

Charles Taylor, "Shared and Divergent Values," 1993

Much has been accomplished since Will Kymlicka suggested in his *Liberalism, Community, and Culture* that the interests of ethnocultural minorities could be reconciled within a liberal theory of justice. In fact, as noted in the Introduction, the positions of a number of prominent theorists have converged on a general set of advocacy positions that I am calling the liberal culturalist consensus. My aim in this chapter is to demonstrate three claims I made in the Introduction: that the emerging consensus on advocacy positions is not accompanied by a similar consensus on foundational assumptions, that these underlying differences have significant implications for matters of practical policy, and thus, that a return to ontological or foundational assumptions is warranted. To establish these claims, I consider the work of a number of prominent theorists who have taken positions in the ongoing conversation on liberal multiculturalism. In discussing their contributions, my aim is not so much to critique or evaluate their arguments as to describe the implications they have for questions of foundational assumptions. Sometimes this involves considering disagreements between authors; at other times, it involves comparing how different authors address the same issues; and at other times still, it involves focusing on loose ends within the work of a single author.

As the purpose of this chapter is to raise questions that open up a space for the argument of the rest of the book, no linear argument runs through its various sections. Each stands alone, united only by a common purpose. While more issues could probably have been raised, I have chosen to focus on six: the nature and value of the relationship between individuals and communities; how the membership and substance of communities are defined; the role of socialization; the social units with which cultural interests should be associated; what to make of the distinction between modern and premodern or traditional cultures; and finally, the relationship between state borders, social unity, and intercultural dialogue. The chapter concludes by indicating how the matters it raises are addressed in the rest of the book.

Conceptualizing the Individual-Communal Nexus

It is impossible to discuss obligations of the state with respect to cultural communities without making assumptions, implicit or explicit, about the nature and value of the relationship between individuals and communities. Without some significant relationship between individuals and communities, it is difficult to justify accommodating communities within a liberal state. Once this is allowed, however, basic questions present themselves: What is the nature of the relationship between individual and community, and why is the relationship worth preserving? How these questions are answered will determine, in part, the policies advocated to accommodate such communities. For example, while no liberal culturalist would advocate policies that would disrupt the relationship between individuals and communities or undermine the values that make communities worthy of protection, what constitutes such policies will depend on how the relationship and its value are conceived. In this section I canvass three such conceptions under the broad headings of cultural monism, radically fluid self-identity, and fluid identities/constitutive communities. These conceptions raise foundational issues, both by virtue of their irreconcilability and for reasons specific to each, which I note along the way.

Cultural Monism

Cultural monism refers to the assumption that, under most circumstances, individuals have a significant relationship with only one cultural community, and that, under normal circumstances, this will be the cultural community in which they were born and initially socialized. I discuss this assumption as illustrated in the work of Will Kymlicka and Charles Taylor. While these theorists share a similar cultural monist view on the nature of the relationship, they differ in their assumptions about its value: for Kymlicka, its value lies in its contribution to personal autonomy; for Taylor, in its contribution to collective goods that inform personal identity. Both the cultural monist account itself and the comparison of Kymlicka's and Taylor's accounts of its value raise questions that lead us back to foundational assumptions.

The liberal-communitarian debate of the 1980s provided the context within which Kymlicka located his seminal work, *Liberalism, Community, and Culture*. While no doubt an oversimplification, this debate can be viewed as pitting liberals, whose commitment to individual choice and personal autonomy did not permit adequate recognition of community, against communitarians, whose assumption of a constitutive relationship between the individual and his or her community did not allow for adequate recognition of personal autonomy. Just how was the relationship between individuals and communities conceived from these perspectives?

Ronald Dworkin provides an example of a liberalism that provides little or no basis for accommodating communities, cultural or otherwise. For Dworkin, whether any end or conception of the good will have enough of a society's resources to be viable is simply a matter of luck:[1]

> Numbers will indeed count ... [People] who need a community of other committed believers in which to flourish, may find that enough other people share their convictions to enable them to join together in creating a special religious community without benefit of the criminal law. Nor is any minority, whether religious, sexual, or cultural, assured of social requirements ideal for them. Numbers count for them as well: they would plainly be better off ... if more people shared their views, or had tastes that made their own activities less expensive. Their prospects ... will depend on the opportunity costs to others.[2]

Where members of a cultural minority find their "just" share insufficient to sustain their community, Dworkin counsels them to accept this as bad luck, abandon any appeals for sufficient space, and ask themselves, "What is a good life for someone entitled to the share of resources I am entitled to have?"[3] Dworkin can suggest this because he assumes that people are related to their communities in such a way that they are able to exercise choice over their identities and the communities in which their identities are grounded. This is reflected, for instance, when he writes that "it is part of each person's ethical responsibility to decide an ethical identity for himself – to decide for himself whether it is a parameter of his life that he is an aristocrat or talented or whether these properties are only opportunities or limitations he faces in leading a life properly defined in some quite different way."[4] Dworkin draws the implications of this quite starkly when, after entertaining the possibility that a person's personality may "disintegrate" if it becomes "detached from formerly unquestioned convictions," he asks, "Why should people not be able to reassemble their sense of identity"?[5]

To avoid this refusal to accommodate communities, Kymlicka must adopt a conception of the nature of the relationship between individuals and communities that can set limits to the individual's capacity for choice and thus explain why it is not always reasonable to expect people to reassemble their identities. While the communitarian conception of this relationship offers to circumscribe choice in the way that Kymlicka requires, it is not available to him for other reasons. Michael Sandel's "constitutive community" is representative of this communitarian approach. It suggests that the self is situated or embedded in inherited communal social practices that play an inextricably constitutive role in constructing the individual's identity. This self is typically defined in contrast to the liberal self, which Sandel describes as radically disembodied (that is, not determined by its circumstances; free to become whatever it chooses).[6] The self who finds him- or herself situated in a constitutive community presupposes a conception of human agency that is more a matter of discovery than of choice. The individual first recognizes that she is "indebted in a complex variety of ways for the constitution of identity – to parents, family, city, tribe, class, nation, culture, historical epoch, possibly God, Nature, and maybe chance,"[7] and then, through self-reflection, differentiates among those unchosen and thus limited attributes the ones that are "mine" (that "I have") from those that are "me" (that "I am"). Viewed in this way, community "describes not just what [people] *have* as fellow citizens but also what they *are,* not a relationship they choose (as in a voluntary association) but an attachment they discover, not merely an attribute but a constituent of identity."[8] From the perspective of this conception of the relationship between individual and community, Dworkin's "why should people not be able to reassemble their sense of identity[?]" cannot arise.

While the communitarian conception of the relationship between individual and community offers to circumscribe choice in the way Kymlicka requires, he cannot accept it because it presents this relationship as so strong and enduring that it undermines his commitment to individual choice and autonomy. Kymlicka's key achievement is to develop a subtle and ingenious argument that suggests the possibility of an alternative to both approaches. He begins by treating a liberal conception of justice that promotes individual freedom and equality by privileging a conception of personal autonomy (defined as "the capacity to rationally reflect on, and potentially revise, our conceptions of the good life")[9] as foundational. Concern for cultural community is introduced instrumentally in the suggestion that personal autonomy can be exercised only within a specific kind of community, a societal culture. This is "a culture which provides its members with meaningful ways of life across the full range of human activities, including social, educational, religious, recreational, and economic life, encompassing both public and private spheres. These cultures tend to be territorially concentrated, and based on a shared language."[10] As contexts of choice, societal cultures support their members' capacity for personal autonomy by providing them with options and with resources such as narratives, traditions, and conventions that inform their sense of identity and enable them to make "intelligent judgements about how to lead [their] lives."[11] Given the further assumptions that people do not choose their membership in societal cultures and that people cannot reasonably be expected to renounce it,[12] Kymlicka suggests that liberals should agree that justice requires "special political rights ... to remove inequalities in the context of choice which arise before people even make their choices."[13]

Thus, Kymlicka seeks to reconcile liberalism and cultural community by reconceptualizing the relationship between cultural community and personal autonomy while avoiding the extremes of both. On the one hand, associating contexts of choice with community enables recognition of a special relationship between the individual and his or her cultural community. On the other hand, associating the value of community with its capacity to support personal autonomy facilitates the extension of protection to cultural communities without threatening liberal freedoms within the community. This is reflected in his call for "*freedom within* the minority group, and *equality between* the minority and majority groups," and in his now famous endorsement of 'external protections' (measures that protect the community against the actions of outsiders) and rejection of 'internal restrictions' (measures designed to preserve the community's character and which can stifle internal dissent).[14] This distinction is reflected, for example, in his suggestion that while the Quiet Revolution of the 1960s transformed the character of Quebec's cultural community – from traditional, agrarian, and religious to modern, industrial, and secular – the community never ceased to exist as a context of choice for its members.[15] Where communities are protected as societal cultures, and not as communitarian constitutive communities, the cultural marketplace, to use Kymlicka's term, continues to function; "decisions about which particular aspects of one's culture are worth maintaining and developing should be left to the choices of individual members."[16]

While Kymlicka's view of the relationship between individuals and communities represents a genuine advance, its reliance on cultural monist assumptions is problematic. To see why, we need to reconsider the idea of a societal culture. Societal cultures are said to perform two distinct functions for their members: provide them with meaningful options, which Kymlicka calls a "context of choice," and provide them with a sense of identity and intellectual resources that they rely on to make important decisions about their lives.[17] The latter, which provide individuals with standards that inform their choices, I call a context of value.

It is essential for Kymlicka's defence of minority cultural communities within a liberalism that privileges personal autonomy that we presume that both of these functions are performed exclusively by societal cultures; this is the substance of his cultural monism. To see why, consider the alternatives. If an individual's context of choice exceeded the bounds of her societal culture, her capacity for personal autonomy could conceivably survive if she lost access to it. If, however, the contexts of value that informed her capacity for choice were located in sub-communities within her societal culture, it is not clear that protecting the societal culture would necessarily preserve her capacity for choice, and if these contexts of value were located in transnational communities that extended across societal cultures, it is not clear that her capacity for choice would necessarily be threatened if she lost access to her societal culture.

Once these possibilities are admitted, we are pressed to confront foundational questions about the nature of the relationship between individual and community. Is it reasonable to assume that individuals' societal cultures and contexts of *choice* overlap? I think this is what James Nickel was getting at when he wrote in a review of *Liberalism, Community, and Culture* that the "key problem for choice [for Inuit adolescents] is how to combine or integrate ... options from two different cultural frameworks into a meaningful life plan that fits contemporary circumstances."[18] Conversely, is it reasonable to assume that individuals' societal cultures and contexts of *value* overlap? To cite a personal example, while I am sure that I do draw on my identification with Canada in making some choices, I more often draw on my membership in communities that exist within and across societal cultures – religious, familial, and professional communities, for example.[19] Such questions press us towards even more basic ones. Is cultural monism a reasonable account of the relationship between individuals and communities?[20] And if not, what would a better account look like?

Further questions are raised if we look at a difference between Kymlicka's approach and Charles Taylor's. The difference does not lie in their general assumptions about the nature of the relationship between individuals and communities. Like Kymlicka's, Taylor's account reflects cultural monist assumptions. This is reflected most recently in his focus on the historically developed collective state of consciousness of a civilization, which he calls its social imaginary. Similar to societal culture, a social imaginary includes "the ways people imagine their social existence, how they fit together with others, how things go on between them and their fellows, the expectations that are normally met, and the deeper normative notions and images that underlie these expectations."[21] While limited in time and space, a social imaginary "constitutes a horizon we are virtually incapable of thinking beyond."[22]

The difference that I want to consider concerns the value that each associates with this relationship. For Kymlicka, the value lies in how the relationship contributes to individuals' personal autonomy. For Taylor, it lies in the way that communities can embody important collective goods that contribute to their members' identities. Indeed, he thinks this is so valuable that it can justify placing limits on individuals' personal autonomy. This is exemplified in his discussion of the laws in Quebec that restrict the use of languages other than French on commercial signs. Taylor says that while such laws limit individual freedom, the Quebec government can legitimately pass such legislation because it is designed to preserve and promote the French language as a collective good that is constitutive of the authentic identities of members of the Québécois nation. He goes so far as to describe the preservation of the identity of the French Canadian cultural community as the Quebec state's raison d'être.[23] The implication is clear: the interest of a cultural community in preserving its character/collective goods may sometimes legitimately outweigh the autonomy interests of individuals.

This difference in foundational assumptions leads Taylor and Kymlicka to advocate different policy positions for the treatment of internal dissidents (that is, members of the cultural nation who oppose rules designed to protect its collective goods). Whereas Kymlicka tends to privilege the autonomy of the dissidents,[24] Taylor says that, within the very broad limitations of respect for human rights and democracy, dissidents may be required to comply with such policies. For instance, to the person who objects to having to obey a law with which he or she disagrees, Taylor answers: "Something essential to your identity is bound up in our common laws ... something of the order of cultural identity."[25] Thus, for Taylor, the survival of communities may sometimes require us to resist attempts to maximize personal autonomy.[26] These conflicting policy prescriptions for handling internal dissidents raise questions about the individual-community relationship further: Why is it valuable? Because it promotes personal autonomy? Because it contributes to member's self-identity? Must we choose between them?

The cultural monist account of the relationship between individuals and communities presses us to consider matters of foundational assumptions for three reasons. First, we must ask whether it captures the true nature of this relationship. Second, disagreements persist among its advocates about its value and the practical implications. And third, as we are about to see, cultural monism is not the only possible account of this relationship.

Radically Fluid Self-Identity

Chandran Kukathas presents a very different conception of the nature and value of the relationship between individual and community. He is no advocate of the liberal culturalist consensus, but his work raises important questions, especially about the relationship between group identity and political context.

Kukathas says his aim in making his argument is not to deny that people have interests in groups but to argue that they can be accommodated without legitimizing special group rights. Thus, he says it "is not that groups do not matter but rather that there is no need to depart from the liberal language of *individual* rights to do justice to them." All that this requires, he suggests, is respect for freedom of association – the freedom "to form communities and to live by the terms of those associations." This unwillingness to recognize anything special in the relationship between individuals and communities reflects a deeper assumption that self-identity is radically fluid in nature. Observing that group identities appear to mutate over time, he suggests that this "reflects their nature as associations of individuals with different interests." As such, cultural communities are best understood as voluntary associations of individuals who "live according to communal practices each finds acceptable." Kukathas' faith in the capacity of individuals to exercise choice over their communal identifications is reflected when he rejects that states need to insist on "liberal" education, claiming that there "is no more reason to insist that gypsy parents offer their children a 'rational choice' of life-style through public education than there is to require that other parents offer their children the opportunity to become gypsies."[27]

Kukathas' conception of fluid self-identity does not lead him to deny that there is value in the relationship between individuals and communities – he accepts that people have legitimate interests in avoiding the dislocation and anomie that can accompany the disintegration of communities. Instead, it leads him to contest cultural monist assumptions about the relatively enduring nature of the identity of cultural communities by suggesting that all group identities have "a contextual character: Group boundaries 'tend to shift with the political context.'" On this ground, he offers two reasons for resisting policy that would attempt "to answer questions about what political institutions are defensible by appealing to the interests of existing groups." Given his assumptions about the fluidity of identity, such attempts do not so much recognize as create groups: group identities are always mutating, and thus, while "groups may generate entitlements," "entitlements can also generate groups." As well, the real effect of institutionalizing existing groups is to disregard internal dissent and favour "existing majorities."[28]

Kukathas' work suggests difficult questions that any account of multiculturalism must address. In particular, is it possible to maintain that the relationship between individuals and communities is sufficiently important and enduring to warrant special recognition while also recognizing that group identities appear to mutate over time and across contexts, and that some individuals appear to be able to exercise more choice over their communal identifications than cultural monism assumes?

Fluid Identity/Constitutive Community
A third possibility for understanding the relationship between individuals and communities retains both a conception of fluid self-identity and a con-

stitutive role for communities. An example of this is found in Iris Marion Young's idea of social groups.[29]

Contrary to Kukathas' radically fluid self-identity, Young's idea of social groups suggests a relationship between self-identity and groups or communities that could justify special accommodation. This is illustrated when she distinguishes social groups from "aggregates" and "associations." Unlike aggregates, which consist of individuals who share a set of attributes, social groups involve self-identification: it is "identification with a certain social status, the common history that social status produces, and self-identification that defines the group as a group." Unlike associations, such as clubs, political parties, churches, colleges, unions, and corporations in which individuals, conceived as "ontologically prior to the collective," come together to perform specific practices or form certain types of affiliation, social groups "constitute individuals. A person's particular sense of history, affinity, and separateness, even the person's mode of reasoning, evaluating, and expressing feeling, are constituted partly by her or his group affinities."[30]

Contrary to Kymlicka and Taylor, Young suggests that social groups embrace the constitutive nature of communal identifications without embracing cultural monism. For instance, she says that social groups that individuals join later in life can nevertheless be "socially prior to individuals."[31] This is possible, she suggests, because such groups reflect a quality that Martin Heidegger called thrownness, whereby "one *finds oneself* as a member of a group, which one experiences as always already having been. For our identities are defined in relation to how others identify us, and they do so in terms of groups which are always already associated with specific attributes, stereotypes, and norms." Thrownness, Young says, causes membership in social groups to define "one's very identity, in the way, for example, being Navaho might." Events such as heterosexuals becoming gay or young people becoming old "exemplify thrownness precisely because such changes in group affinity are experienced as transformations in one's identity."[32]

Whatever its strengths, and I think they are considerable, Young's approach greatly increases the complexity of the phenomena for which our foundational assumptions must account. The cumulative effect of the personal transformations in identifications she describes is that "most people in modern societies have multiple group identifications … [and] every group has group differences cutting across it."[33] Here again we face difficult questions. Is it possible to conceive a theory of the nature and value of the relationship between individuals and communities that accurately captures the complexity of fluid self-identities and multiple cutting identifications? Even if is possible, could such a theory explain why particular communities might warrant special accommodations? And, finally, could such a theory be operationalized into effective public policy?

Summary

The various accounts we have seen of the nature of the relationship between individuals and communities – cultural monist, fluid self-identity, fluid self-identity/constitutive community – and its value – personal autonomy, collective goods, and identity – are, at least as presented in these formulations, irreconcilable. Besides the other points raised along the way, it is this very fact of irreconcilability that presses us to return to matters of foundational assumptions by leading us to ask, which, if any, presents an accurate account of the nature and value of this relationship?

Communal Definition

Another matter we need to consider is how cultural communities and their membership are to be defined. Much discussion seems to be conducted on the assumption that the substance, and thus the membership, of communities are already known; that is, we know who are members of particular cultural communities and who are not. But matters are more complex than this, with significant implications for public policy.

The relationship between the presumed substance of a community and the people who constitute its membership has an inherent complexity. Consider Kymlicka's suggestion that, in principle, membership in a cultural community be open to anyone "who is willing to learn the language and history of the society and participate in its social and political institutions."[34] Rather than clarifying matters, associating the substance of the community with its language and history merely opens the door to a certain degree of circularity: to determine if someone belongs, we need to know if he or she has learned the society's language and history; to determine this, we need to know the proper form of the language and the correct (or at least not incorrect) version of the history; to do this, we would need to ask members of the community; but, and here the circle is completed, to do this we need to know who belongs to the community. (This is not a fanciful proposition, as the discussion of the Métis in Chapter 5, pp. 100-1, shows.) Two questions reflect the practical significance of this point: How do we know that the "dissenter" who Kymlicka would have a community tolerate isn't really a non-member? And how do we know that the individual Taylor would require to respect communal laws is actually a member of the community? These questions need to be answered correctly, otherwise the character of communities may be altered to suit the preferences of non-members or the autonomy of non-members may be curtailed to promote the interests of communities with which they do not identify.

How communities are defined also affects the nature of the threats they are understood to face. If communities are defined as societal cultures, the main threats they face are those that undermine their ability to sustain the contexts of choice that contribute to their members' autonomy. If communities are defined as social imaginaries, the main threats concern their ability to sustain the collective goods that contribute to members' identities. The threats posed to communities defined as social groups are sometimes those that challenge communities' ability to sustain ways of life and, at other times, where members do not accept how others have identified them, it is group membership itself that appears to be the problem and exit the solution.[35] Which of these characterizations is treated as authoritative will have important implications for public policy.

How should we define the substance and membership of communities? While the answer is not clear, two things are: the answer will have significant implications for the policy positions we advocate, and finding it will involve considering the nature and value of community itself.

The Role of Socialization

How should we address the role of socialization in forming the relationship between individual and community? Reviewing an exchange between Kukathas and Kymlicka about the extent to which an individual's choice to associate with a community in which he or she was born and socialized can be considered free illustrates just what is at stake.

Consistent with his assumptions about fluid and mutable group and self-identities, Kukathas says individuals' choices to associate with such communities can be treated as voluntary where "members recognize as legitimate the terms of association and the authority that upholds them" and express such recognition by choosing to remain in the community.[36] Not surprisingly, given his commitment to personal autonomy and his more constitutive assumptions about the role of community, Kymlicka disagrees. He draws attention to the role of socialization by suggesting that someone deprived of "literacy, education, or the freedom to learn about the outside world ... does not have a substantial freedom to leave because she lacks the preconditions for making a meaningful choice."[37] While Kymlicka accepts that the presence of a society into which to exit is a necessary precondition of free choice, he says it is not sufficient; individuals should also receive a mandatory education that enables them to "acquire an awareness of different views about the good life, and an ability to examine these views intelligently."[38] In responding to this critique, Kukathas seems to assume that there are only two alternatives for addressing socialization: "to leave cultural communities alone to manage their own affairs, whatever we may think of their values ... [or] to champion the claims or the interests of individuals who, we think, are disadvantaged by their communities' lack of regard for certain values."[39] Believing these are the only options, Kukathas thinks he has simply made a hard choice.

This interchange suggests several difficult questions. How much impact should we suppose processes of socialization in communities have on the freedom of individuals' subsequent life choices? Are the alternatives really as stark as Kukathas presents them? And finally, what remedial actions or interventions, if any, do the effects of socialization require of the state?

Social Units and Cultural Interests

Even among theorists who agree on both the legitimacy of cultural accommodations and the supposition that only individuals, and not communities, can bear rights, two positions can be discerned when we consider which social units those cultural interests are associated with: those that associate cultural interests with communities and those that associate them with individuals. Below I describe examples of these approaches and note how the position they adopt on cultural interests and social units affects their attempts to justify their liberal culturalist desire to advocate the accommodation of ethnic and immigrant minorities.

Associating Cultural Interests with Communities

When cultural interests are associated with one type of community, that community becomes the paradigmatic case and the accommodation of other types of communities must be justified as exceptions or by analogy. Kymlicka provides an example of the former, Taylor the latter.

Kymlicka, as we have seen, works within a framework that emphasizes individual rights and associates cultural interests with a specific type of community: the societal culture. While this works well for justifying accommodations for groups, such as national minorities, that qualify as societal cultures, it does not work nearly so well for other groups, such as immigrant communities, that by definition do not form societal cultures.[40] To extend his argument to such groups, Kymlicka employs what we might call an indirect justification. Since individuals, including members of ethnic and immigrant minorities, depend on having access to a societal culture to support their capacity for autonomy, and since the political community does not support *their* societal culture, justice requires that they have access to one that it does sustain. While such a view could justify a policy of assimilation, Kymlicka avoids this by suggesting that the integration of ethnic and immigrant groups must be on "fair terms." This requires ensuring that the "common institutions into which immigrants are pressured to integrate provide the same degree of respect, recognition, and accommodation of the identities and practices of ethnocultural minorities as they traditionally provided for the dominant group."[41] Thus, having associated cultural interests with a particular type of community (societal culture), Kymlicka must invoke a supplemental argument to justify accommodating ethnic and immigrant groups.

While Taylor also associates cultural interests with a specific type of community – the nation – his account of modernity allows him to justify the accommodation of ethnic and immigrant minorities as analogous to this special type. This is facilitated by three ideals he associates with modernity:

authenticity, recognition, and, most important, popular sovereignty. Taylor says the ideal of authenticity – "the idea that each of us has an original way of being human" with which we must live in accordance if we are to "be true and full human beings" – developed in the wake of the "collapse of social hierarchies." Disembedded from the social positions that defined identity in premodern societies, each person's identity became "individualized": without a socially defined identity, the individual had to define her identity for herself. While personal identity is individualized in modernity, it does not, Taylor says, develop in isolation, but rather it develops dialogically in communication with "significant others."[42]

This is where authenticity connects with identity and recognition: equal respect for individuals requires extending equal recognition to the identities they have formed. As I understand it, the emphasis on dialogical relations has two important consequences. The first ties back to authenticity: for an individual to lead an authentic life, others must recognize, and not misrecognize, the identity the individual has actually formed.[43] Second, if we care about the authenticity of individual identities, and if authentic identities are formed and sustained in dialogical relationships with significant others, we should also care about the communities and cultures that foster and sustain these relations. Thus, an acceptable account of justice must prove "willing to weigh the importance of certain forms of uniform treatment against the importance of cultural survival, and opt sometimes in favor of the latter."[44]

For Taylor, liberal concern for individual freedom and equality meets concern for identity, authenticity, and recognition in the ideal of popular sovereignty, which he says requires the realization of "the government of *all* the people."[45] This can be the case only where the people share a political identity that can act as the basis of a collective agency. Under conditions of cultural diversity, if the authenticity of each citizen's identity is to be given equal recognition, the state cannot define this collective agency in terms of just one, even if the largest, of its cultural groups. For if it does, members of its cultural minorities may come to believe that they are "being ruled by some agency that need take no account of [them]." Those who are excluded will feel alienated; "the rule of [the] government [will seem] illegitimate in the eyes of the rejecters, as we see in countless cases with disaffected national minorities."[46]

For the government to be the government of all the people, the state's political identity – which Taylor defines variously as "some strong common purpose or value" and "the generally accepted answer to the What/whom [is a country] for? question" – must be shared.[47] Thus, Taylor suggests, the state balances its needs to recognize its citizens' different identities and to generate a collective identity capable of acting as a sovereign people, through the process of "sharing identity space": "Political identities have to be worked out, negotiated, creatively compromised between peoples who have to or want to live together under the same political roof." Sharing identity space requires more than a nationalism that simply leaves room for minorities to exist.[48] When identity space is shared properly, it seems, the core goals of the minorities contribute to the political identity that exercises popular sovereignty.[49] The practical outcome of such sharing of identity space is the accommodation of ethnic and immigrant minorities. This, as the chapter's epigraph illustrates, is reflected in what Taylor has famously called "deep" diversity. The secondary and derivative nature of the claims of ethnic and immigrant groups is not entirely escaped, however: "Modern nationalist politics," Taylor writes, "is a species of identity politics. Indeed, the original species: national struggles are the site from which the model comes to be applied to feminism, to struggles of cultural minorities, to the gay movement, et cetera."[50]

Associating Cultural Interests with Individuals

Where cultural interests are associated with individuals, however, the accommodation of different types of communities can be justified on a common basis; in this case, differences in the size and substance of communities affect which, and not whether, accommodations can be justified. Carens and Tully provide examples of this approach.

Like Kymlicka, Carens adopts a framework that places more emphasis on rights than on popular sovereignty. Unlike Kymlicka, though, he associates cultural concerns with individual interests that are separate and distinct from their interests in liberal rights. Culture, Carens says, can be a legitimate source of individual interests "because what people regard as their interests often depends on how they think of themselves and on how they think about the identity of their community."[51] This allows him to justify rights for ethnic and immigrant minorities on the very same basis as national minorities. So constructed, culture and identity claims do not appear so much a matter of thresholds (for example, a group is/is not a nation/societal culture) as of a continuum: "As the number of immigrants speaking a given language increases in a given area, the justification for not having public service providers who speak the language decreases."[52]

Tully relies on a similar understanding of the relationship between cultural interests and individuals, but unlike Carens and more like Taylor, he assigns a central role to popular sovereignty. The individual interest that unites culture and popular sovereignty for Tully is freedom: "The primary question is thus not recognition, identity or difference, but freedom; the freedom of the members of an open society to change the constitutional rules of mutual recognition and association from time to time as their identities change."[53] This understanding of freedom reflects assumptions about the importance of culture to individual identity: "The diverse ways in which citizens think about, speak, act and relate to others in participating in a constitutional association ... are always to some extent the expression of their different cultures." A just constitution for Tully, then, would emphasize popular sovereignty by giving "recognition to the legitimate demands of the members of diverse cultures in a manner that renders everyone their due, so that all would freely consent to this form of constitutional association."[54] This has the effect that no type of cultural group has a privileged position in Tully's account; the rights of nations, he writes, "are a subset of the kinds of rights that any member invokes whenever he or she enters into public debate, joins a political party, votes, demonstrates, introduces a bill in parliament, enters into litigation, initiates treaty negotiations, or any other form of participation, with the aim of changing any of the rules of the society."[55]

Summary

As one of the main concerns of this book is to determine whether the cultural accommodations of the liberal culturalist consensus can be justified in a way that does not leave them vulnerable to charges of being unprincipled or arbitrary, it is of supreme importance that the question of the social units with which cultural interests are properly associated be resolved.

Modern versus Premodern or Traditional Cultures

A different set of questions comes to the fore when we consider how different authors deal with the fact that many communities that demand cultural accommodations are not modern, or not liberal, or neither. In this section I discuss four approaches to accounting for the distinction between modern and premodern cultures within broadly liberal theories of justice, noting questions suggested by each approach as well as implications for how and whether certain advocacy positions of the liberal culturalist consensus can be justified.

Modernity as Inescapable

The first account treats the advance of a particular conception of a liberal modernity, and thus the decline of traditional or premodern cultures, as inevitable. Kymlicka and Taylor, both of whom work with conceptions of a liberal modernity influenced by the work of Ernest Gellner, exemplify this approach.

The types of communities that are the primary foci of Kymlicka's and Taylor's theories reflect a particular conception of modernity: they are committed to the liberal ideals of equality and rights, they are democratic, they are organized into bureaucratic welfare states, their economies are industrial, and they "tend to be national cultures."[56] Further, and significantly, both characterize the progress of this modernity and the particular kinds of cultural community it privileges as, in Taylor's words, "becoming inescapable."[57] This renders the status of certain indigenous and premodern and traditional communities problematic.

One approach that has been adopted to square this assumption with the liberal culturalist commitment to accommodating such communities assumes, more often tacitly than expressly, that all cultures will eventually modernize. Taylor is most clear in his attempt to find space for a defence of cultural diversity within a framework that presumes the inescapability of modernity. This is reflected in his discussion of the "'subtraction' account of the rise of modernity," which he describes as suggesting that, for modernity to emerge, we "just needed to liberate ourselves from the old horizons."[58] As I understand it, the problem with the subtraction account is that it encourages the view that the individual, as represented in modern societies, reflects what is universal in human nature after all the trappings of socialization have been removed. Taylor thinks this is wrong and dangerous because it misconceives the nature of modern society; properly understood, the emergence of modernity involved the transformation, not the transcendence, of social orders. Thus, for instance, he says that even in the most individualistic modern societies, individual independence is "a social, and not just a personal, ideal." Taylor attempts to recognize space for cultural diversity by suggesting that while modernization may be inescapable, it is not necessarily homogenizing. Rather, it is a process each society undergoes on its own terms: "It is easy to go on nourishing the illusion that modernity is a single process ... my foundational hunch is that we have to speak of 'multiple modernities.'"[59] Modernity, even liberal conceptions of justice in modernity, is multiple because each cultural group undergoes modernization by "finding resources in their traditional culture to take on the new practices."[60] Kymlicka appears to take a similar tact by placing indigenous people's commitment to "a premodern way of life" in the recent past and describing them as aspiring to "the ability to maintain certain traditional ways of life while nevertheless participating on their own terms in the modern world."[61]

This approach raises several questions. Is it reasonable to treat modernity as inescapable?[62] If the progress of modernity is indeed inescapable, might there still not be good reasons to extend cultural accommodations to particular traditional or premodern communities to help them resist its advance? And if so, how, to what extent, and for how long?

Distinct Moral Foundations

A different account of the relationship between modern and premodern cultures avoids privileging modernity by defending traditional cultures on a separate basis from that which supports liberal modernity and its rights. This approach can stand on its own or, as employed by Kymlicka, can act to supplement the modernity as inescapable account.

The approach is implicit in Kymlicka's discussion of how to deal with illiberal traditional groups such as the Amish and Hutterites. While he believes they should be tolerated, he doesn't try to justify this within his liberal framework of justice. Instead, he appeals to principles external to his autonomy-based framework, such as honouring historic agreements, and to pragmatic considerations, such as the concern that "attempts to impose liberal principles by force are often perceived ... as a form of aggression or paternalistic colonialism" and often "backfire."[63]

While this approach supplements Kymlicka's theory, it rests at the core of Joseph Carens'. Although Carens says that "liberal democracy is the only just political order, at least under modern political conditions,"[64] his general approach is to treat liberal rights and membership in cultural communities as having distinct moral foundations. He does so by assuming that traditional and illiberal cultures may embody genuine human goods.[65] Where conflicts arise between these two distinct moral foundations, Carens says reconciliation requires a "contextual" approach that involves a play back and forth between two conceptions of justice: justice as neutrality, "the idea of a common set of liberal democratic principles" that can be used to assess "claims about the respect due cultural difference"; and justice as even-handedness, the idea that under some conditions "context is morally decisive, that our moral judgements should turn on our understanding of the history and culture of a particular political community."[66] He says that whether a group can justify a claim for special accommodation depends on the balancing of a variety of factors, including "who [members of the group] are and what they care about", the degree of compatibility between their demands and the principle of equal respect, and "political judgements differentiating more fundamental interests from less fundamental ones."[67]

When we ask what principles are to govern the invocation and adjudication of these different sets of principles, however, the answers we receive are not satisfactory. For instance, it is not clear what principles govern Kymlicka's invocation of historic agreements and pragmatic considerations. Similarly, Carens is explicit about the kinds of factors that should be at play in a contextual analysis aimed at resolving such conflict, but he says little about the calculus that is to be applied to these factors to reach a resolution. In fact, he insists that "there is no master principle that enables us to determine when we should respect claims advanced in the name of culture and identity and when we should deny them."[68]

If we accept the general thrust of this approach, then, we are pressed to raise questions about the underlying moral assumptions that are to guide evaluations when conclusions drawn from distinct moral foundations conflict. If concerns about moral arbitrariness are to be addressed, we must ask whether it is possible to develop a principled approach to resolving conflicts between such foundations. And, this, it seems, requires us to ask questions about the nature of the relationship between these different moral foundations. How are they related? Are they commensurable? Incommensurable? Which takes precedence under which circumstances?

Appeal to a Common Underlying Value

Another account of the relationship between modern and premodern cultures suggests that they both derive their value from a common underlying value but realize it in different ways. An example of this is found in Joseph Raz's appeal to the underlying value of well-being.

For Raz, well-being is related to "how good or successful" a person's life is "from his point of view," measured against his "actual goals." While it doesn't matter for well-being how these goals are acquired – they may be the outcome of choice or one "may have drifted into, grown up with, never realized that anyone can fail to have them, etc."[69] – Raz avoids relativism by adopting a perfectionist position that rejects the assumption that something is valuable simply if someone wants it.[70] Having identified a value that lies deeper than and does not presuppose personal autonomy, Raz is able to find value in both modern societies where "personal autonomy is a fact of life" and traditional societies where "each person's course in life (occupation, marriage, place of residence) are [sic] determined by tradition or by his superiors."[71] He achieves this through two main steps. First, he suggests that autonomy is a characteristic of societies, not of individuals. What differentiates modern from traditional societies is not that people make choices in one and not the other but that the societies themselves are constituted in different ways: "The conditions of autonomy do not add an independent element to the social forms of a society. They are a central aspect in the character of the bulk of its social forms."[72] For instance, in autonomy-enhancing societies, marriages are chosen, while in traditional societies they are pre-arranged.[73] Having assumed that it is difficult if not impossible for people to be autonomous in traditional societies, the question becomes whether they can nevertheless experience well-being. Raz's answer is expressed in his rejection of the idea that personal autonomy and choice are valuable in all societies: "To be a universal value it must be the case that people who lack personal autonomy cannot be completely well-off, or have a completely good life ... There were, and there can be, non-repressive societies, and ones which enable people to spend their lives in worthwhile pursuits, even though their pursuits and the options open to them are not subject to individual choice."[74] Thus, by appealing to the underlying value of well-being, Raz can recognize value in societies that do not value autonomy.

The practical implication is that Raz recommends different policies for modern and traditional societies. Within modern autonomy-enhancing societies, he, like Kymlicka, says the state has a duty to sustain the conditions that make autonomy possible.[75] The reason is that socialization in such societies makes the experience of autonomy a prerequisite of well-being.[76] For similar reasons, Raz advocates the toleration or even protection of traditional societies within modern societies if "they are viable communities offering acceptable prospects to their members, including their young."[77] According to Raz, "wrenching" people out of traditional societies "may well make it impossible for them to have any kind of normal rewarding life whatsoever because they have not built up any capacity for autonomy."[78] In short, communities that enable their members to experience well-being should be accommodated.

To round things out, Raz also advocates the accommodation of modern cultural minorities, who by definition have "built up a capacity for autonomy." He does so by making an argument similar to Kymlicka's, with two key differences. One is that Raz's argument is limited to modern societies and does not apply to traditional communities. The other is that his encompassing groups, which play a role very similar to societal cultures and are also conceived in cultural monist terms,[79] are not necessarily territorially concentrated,[80] and thus can be applied more easily than Kymlicka's societal cultures to justify accommodation of ethnic and immigrant groups.[81]

This approach of appealing to underlying values appears capable of providing a principled basis for recognizing that there might be value in both modern and premodern cultures. Some questions it raises concern the nature of this underlying value: What is this underlying value? Why is it important? How, if at all, is this value to serve to prevent radical appeals to cultural relativism that would undermine the very possibility of a principled multicultural politics?

Rejecting the Modern/Premodern Distinction

The final account of the relationship between modern and premodern cultures that I wish to discuss rejects both cultural monism and the moral significance of the distinction between modern and premodern cultures. It is illustrated in James Tully's idea of a "post-imperial view of constitutionalism." Tully's approach is distinguished by his refusal to treat processes of modernization as a constraint on his moral thinking. He adopts a critical perspective towards modernity by attempting to view matters "from the perspective of the struggles of Aboriginal peoples."[82] This offers an important vantage point because, as Carens notes, Aboriginal cultures are not modern and "cannot be understood as the product of modernization."[83] When modern constitutionalism is viewed from this vantage point, Tully says, "unnoticed aspects of its historical formation and current limitations can be brought to light."[84]

This perspective enables Tully to challenge assumptions about the superiority of modernity as well as the tendency to essentialize the West as modern.[85] He argues that the modern view is not the only understanding of constitutionalism in the Western tradition; other elements are "hidden" and available to be recovered.[86] This argument results in a decidedly anti-monist understanding of the relationship between individuals and cultural communities: cultures in diverse societies, Tully writes, "are neither sharply bounded, homogenous nor static; they are a cluster of intercultural relations negotiated and renegotiated over time."[87]

Properly understood, he argues, Western civilization embodies "two dissimilar [constitutional] languages: a dominant, 'modern' language and a subordinate, 'common-law' or simply 'common' language."[88] The dominant modern language embodies key elements largely shared by the approaches of Rawls and Dworkin, Taylor and Kymlicka: "A culturally homogenous and sovereign people ... [who establish a constitution that] founds an independent and self-governing nation state with a set of uniform legal and representative political institutions in which all citizens are treated equally."[89] Theorists in the traditions of modern constitutionalism, he says, respond to demands for recognition of cultural diversity either by assimilating those demands "to the prevailing forms of recognition" or by judging them "unwarranted."[90] The second, or common constitutional language, reflects Tully's anti-monist account of cultures. Within each culture there are competing views on many matters, including constitutionalism; some overlap with perspectives found in other cultures, some do not. Tully describes the overlap as representing a "common language of constitutionalism" that is spoken on the "intercultural common grounds." This dovetails with his thoughts on freedom and popular sovereignty: the only view of constitutionalism to which all might freely consent is the one articulated on this "'common' ground."[91]

An implication of this idea of an intercultural common ground is that it blurs the distinction between modern and premodern cultures. It suggests that the contemporary West *can* recognize the demands of traditional cultures because it shares many of their values; these values have not been left behind in a premodern past but rather have been "elbowed aside" and are merely "hidden."[92] This view also provides a basis for challenging assumptions about the superiority of liberal modernity. Since the intercultural common ground highlights that which is common to, or overlaps, all cultures, it actually marginalizes the very features that distinguish modernity.

The idea of an intercultural common ground underlying and overlapping and thus binding together various cultures in a shared conception of justice is appealing. It seems especially well suited for recognizing both modern and premodern cultures on their own terms. It does, however, raise a couple of questions. What is the content of this common ground and how can we know we've discovered it? And even if we can know it, what, besides its commonality and its fit with a certain conception of popular sovereignty, should convince us to prefer it to other conceptions of justice?

Summary
Here again we are presented with irreconcilable positions that press us to ask questions about foundational assumptions. Either the progress of modernity should be treated as inevitable or it should not. Either the values of liberal

modernity should be applied to all cultures and communities, or they should not. If not, then we must ask how our moral universe must be constructed if both modern and traditional cultures should be respected within their own spheres. And finally we must ask if any moral basis can generate a principled and non-arbitrary approach to adjudicating conflicts across these spheres. If not, then our choice may really be between liberal universalism and moral relativism.

State Borders, Social Unity, and Intercultural Dialogue

While the boundaries of states and sub-state units are often morally and historically arbitrary, their impact sets the context of all debates about multiculturalism: borders determine which groups are present and thus must find a way to live together; they affect which group is in the majority and which the minority; they influence the distribution of power between groups and thus help determine which groups have to request cultural accommodations and which groups are in a position to satisfy or deny such requests. As I noted in describing the liberal culturalist consensus, there is a tendency in this literature to suggest intercultural dialogue as a basis for fostering and sustaining social unity under these conditions.

One problem with the appeal to intercultural dialogue is that, at least within some philosophers' arguments, it lacks a clear purpose. This problem appears most distinctly in the works of Kymlicka and Carens. Although both advocate intercultural dialogue as a means for modern liberal societies to interact with traditional and illiberal societies,[93] both also indicate that they believe liberal conceptions of justice constitute justice, if not universally, at least under modern conditions. My concern can be stated as a question: Where liberal-democratic conceptions of justice are presupposed to constitute justice, what "shared" or "mutual understanding" can be expected to emerge about the substance of justice?[94] Tully captures the essence of my concern when he writes that if one "language or tradition gained ascendancy in a constitutional negotiation, it would cease to be a dialogue at all."[95]

This said, I think it is fair to say that among the approaches canvassed in this chapter, intercultural dialogue has a clearer purpose in those, like Tully's, that put more emphasis on popular sovereignty than on liberal rights. For instance, on Tully's account, the purpose of dialogue is not to discover some pre-existing understanding of justice but to produce or even constitute justice in relations between cultural groups. Tully argues that a constitution that reflected the common language of constitutionalism would "be seen as a form of activity, an intercultural dialogue in which the culturally diverse sovereign citizens of contemporary societies negotiate agreements on their forms of association over time in accordance with the three conventions of mutual recognition, consent and cultural continuity."[96] That is, each group would be recognized by other groups as it understands itself (mutual recognition), and it would be permitted to sustain its present identity (continuity) until such time as it agreed to changes affecting that identity (consent).

Even under conditions where intercultural dialogue has such a clear purpose, I think it is fair to ask whether, other things being equal, either majorities or minorities should be positively motivated to engage in such dialogues. From the majority's perspective, several negative implications may be associated with intercultural dialogue. Successful dialogue may require compromising "hallowed" conceptions of the state-level community; it is likely to entail a lot of work and frustration; and it may be perceived as impeding the majority's ability to "act as a nation."[97] Thus, majorities may feel that the costs associated with successful dialogue outweigh any possible benefits. Intercultural dialogue does not look much better from the minority's perspective. The main reasons for participating are more often to avoid bad outcomes than to achieve good ones. Consider, for example, reasons Kymlicka has suggested for minorities to participate: to demand special accommodations, rights, or privileges; to defend existing accommodations from encroachments; to protect their interests and identities from being marginalized; and to overcome systemic discrimination.[98] But minorities must attempt to achieve these goals by engaging in a dialogue that is likely to be conducted in the majority's language, a language that presupposes its values and conceptions of justice. Again, Tully captures the essence of the problem when he writes: "If there is to be a post-imperial dialogue on the just constitution of culturally diverse societies, the dialogue must be one in which the participants are recognized and speak in their own languages and customary ways. They do not wish either to be silenced or to be recognised and constrained to speak within the institutions of interpretation of the imperial [modern liberal] constitutions that have been imposed over them."[99] Given these concerns, we might ask, as many national minorities do, wouldn't it be better all around to revisit the question of the territorial boundaries of states and, wherever possible, advocate secession?

This being the case, those of us who wish to resist secessionist impulses need to develop answers that face these problems with the arbitrariness of state boundaries head-on. Kymlicka's treatment of secession and social unity in *Multicultural Citizenship* provides a good example of how this problem is often confused by cultural majorities. In the course of two paragraphs he acknowledges that liberalism is not inconsistent with secession in principle, then notes many good and well-known reasons why secession "is not always possible or desirable," and concludes that "we need to find some way to *keep* multination states *together*."[100] The problem is that the conclusion doesn't follow from the premises: if it is meant to apply to situations where secession is not a viable option, the problem, by definition, is not how to keep them together but what to do when they cannot be separated; and, if it is meant to apply to cases where secession is a viable option, it raises the question of why groups should not be allowed to live apart.

In situations such as Quebec in Canada, Scotland in the United Kingdom, and Catalonia in Spain, state borders and intercultural dialogue cannot be justified by appeals to the impossibility of secession. Instead, I think we must accept with Taylor that in such cases the coexistence of different peoples in the same state is "always grounded in some mixture of necessity and choice."[101] Once we accept this, different questions arise. For example, if we accept the moral and historical arbitrariness of existing state borders and their uneven effects on the interests of cultural communities, are there any good reasons to insist on sustaining such political communities where secession is a viable option? And, assuming an answer can be found to the first question, are there any means by which intercultural relations in such states might be made more just?

Conclusion

The purpose of this chapter has been to demonstrate that the emerging consensus on advocacy positions is not accompanied by a similar consensus on foundational assumptions, that these underlying differences have significant implications for matters of practical policy, and thus that a return to ontological or foundational assumptions is warranted. Rather than summarize all the questions that have been raised, I will simply emphasize how the topics canvassed naturally lead to matters of foundational assumptions. The first four topics – the nature and value of the relationship between individuals and communities, how communities are to be defined, the role of socialization, and whether cultural interests should be associated with individuals or communities – all raised questions that can be answered only by considering the nature and formation of individual identity, the nature of community, and the relationship between the two. The fifth topic – modern versus premodern or traditional cultures – requires considering the relationship between justice, liberalism, and a conception of personal autonomy that privileges individual choice and critical reflection. The final topic – state borders, social unity, and intercultural dialogue – requires considering what, if anything, can justify efforts to maintain the unity of existing states, with their arbitrary majorities and minorities. We have also seen that how these questions are answered has implications for how key elements of the liberal culturalist consensus are to be implemented, and for whether others, such as the accommodation of ethnic, immigrant, traditional, and premodern groups, can be justified at all.

Part 2:
The Foundations of Meaningful Life

2
Meaningful Life and the Conception of the Person

A rabbi from Eastern Europe turned to me and told me his story. He had lost his first wife and their six children in the concentration camp of Auschwitz ...

I made a last attempt to help him by inquiring whether he did not hope to see his children again in Heaven. However, my question was followed by an outburst of tears, and now the true reason for his despair came to the fore: he explained that his children, since they died as innocent martyrs, were thus found worthy of the highest place in Heaven, but as for himself he could not expect, as an old, sinful man, to be assigned to the same place.

Viktor Frankl, *Man's Search for Meaning,* 1984

This chapter begins the process of developing a set of foundational assumptions – what I call the foundations of meaningful life – that can form the basis on which the principles of a politics of liberal multiculturalism can be developed. At the core of these assumptions is a conception of the person who has an essential interest in meaningful life.

As we shall see, this conception of the person will be developed in a way that incorporates insights from the approaches discussed in Chapter 1. First, by focusing on the meaningful lives of individuals, it reflects Carens' and Tully's approach of associating cultural concerns with individuals, and not groups, thus avoiding the extreme of communitarian constitutive community. Second, it reflects an account of the relationship between individuals and communities similar to the approach that was described as fluid identity/constitutive community.

Third, this focus on meaningful life facilitates revisiting the meaning of personal autonomy and identification with community. This relies in part on John Rawls' distinction between a general concept and particular conceptions of that concept.[1] The arguments in Part 2 turn on a distinction between the general concepts of personal autonomy and identification with community and the particular conceptions they have been given. I take the general concept of personal autonomy to consist in the ability to pursue one's ends free from coercion and manipulation, and that of identification with a community to consist in a "psychological orientation" as a member of a particular community, "with a resulting feeling of close emotional association."[2] Fourth, as an underlying value, meaningful life does not necessarily privilege any type of culture, modern or traditional, liberal or illiberal. This shares many of the advantages of Raz's account of well-being, while avoiding the drawbacks associated with Raz's cultural monism. Finally, the specific definitions that will be developed of meaningful life and other key terms form the basis of a theory that can answer charges of moral arbitrariness by developing explicit principles that can be appealed to in settling conflicts between values.

Meaningful Life

We will begin by considering the idea of meaningful life. The key move this represents is not the claim that meaningful life is important: many theorists have employed terms such as "meaning," "meaningful life," and "meaningful choice." Rather, this approach is distinguished by giving meaningful life a central role in its justificatory framework, by treating it as having universal and intrinsic value, and by suggesting that it constitutes an essential interest that underlies both the values of personal autonomy and identification with community.

The problem to which meaningful life responds is captured in Alfred Stern's description of man as a citizen of two worlds – "the world of values and the world of value-free physical, causal occurrences [objective reality]." A meaningful life connects with the world of values and thus avoids "axiological emptiness."[3] In a more positive tone, Bhikhu Parekh emphasizes that people need to feel that there is a purpose to particular activities as well as to whole lives: "Human beings seek to make sense of themselves and the world and ask questions about the meaning and significance of human life, activities and relationships. To ask what is the meaning of an activity is to ask questions about its nature and point or purpose; and to ask what is its significance is to ask questions about its worth or value, the kind and degree of importance to be assigned to it, and its place in human life in general."[4] This idea of a relationship between value, purpose, and meaning presents a good place to start. It suggests that we need to consider the nature of that with which one must connect to lead a meaningful life.

Robert Nozick is helpful in this regard. Like Stern he says a life becomes meaningful when a person is able to transcend his or her individual limits and connect "with some things or values beyond [him- or herself]."[5] Nozick has considered several types of meaning, two of which are relevant here.

One, meaning as intrinsic meaningfulness, sets as its standard connection with "objective meaning ... in itself, apart from any connections to anything else." This suggests an unrelenting, Cartesian, approach to meaning: one must reject anything that has meaning only by reference to something else. Another type, meaning as objective meaningfulness, sets a less exacting standard. It suggests that meaning requires only connection with something that is important, non-trivial, or significant.[6] There are good reasons for preferring objective to intrinsic meaningfulness.

While the standard of intrinsic meaningfulness is intuitively appealing, it has inherent drawbacks that justify setting it aside. A fundamental problem is that it requires us to accept nothing less than that which has intrinsic meaning. This threatens an infinite regress that would leave the question of meaning forever in doubt: "However widely we connect and link, however far our web of meaningfulness extends, we can imagine drawing a boundary around all that, standing outside looking at the totality of it, and asking 'but what is the meaning of that, what does that mean?'"[7] The only way to end the regress and secure meaning is to connect with that around which it is impossible to draw a boundary: "the unlimited." The unlimited can be viewed as intrinsically meaningful because there is no ground outside of it from which to question its meaning.[8] But, as Nozick suggests, the ideal of connection with the unlimited might actually undermine, rather than sustain, meaningful lives: one's life may appear meaningless in light of the unlimited, but, given the potentially vast proportions of the unlimited, it may not be obvious what its meaning is.[9]

A related problem with intrinsic meaningfulness is that the scepticism it requires seems unlikely to ever admit of an answer at all. This concern is reflected in Tolstoy's conclusion that "the strictly scientific knowledge, that knowledge which, as Descartes did, begins with a full doubt in everything, rejects all knowledge which has been taken on trust, and builds everything anew on the laws of reason and experience, cannot give any other answer to the question of life than what I received – an indefinite answer ... an identity, $0 = 0$, life is nothing. Thus the philosophical knowledge does not negate anything, but only answers that the question cannot be solved by it."[10] As such radical questioning is unlikely to support meaningful lives, we would do well to abandon intrinsic meaningfulness as a standard for meaning in human life.

Objective meaningfulness recommends itself precisely because it suggests limits to the regress that intrinsic meaningfulness encourages. As Nozick suggests, "It does not follow that the requisite connection must be with something that itself has *meaning*. What bestows meaning by connection must itself be nontrivial, but there are ways of being nontrivial other than having [intrinsic] meaning. Something is nontrivial, also, if it has value. The chain that grounds meaning cannot terminate in something worthless, but it ... can rest upon something valuable. Thus the apparently inexorable regress is stopped."[11] Objective meaningfulness can end the regress by accepting limited transcendence: "The transcending of our limits so as to connect with a wider context of value which itself is limited." This, Nozick says, "does give our lives meaning – but a limited one."[12] In recommending objective meaningfulness as our standard I am not suggesting that there is some objective standard by which an impartial observer could judge a life meaningful or meaningless but rather that from the individual's own perspective the values that sustain meaning in his or her life have a justification independent of his or her preferences. The importance of this approach is suggested when Bernard Williams writes that where the meaningfulness of a person's life is not secured outside of herself (that is, where it is conditional on her existence), she could have no reason for choosing against suicide.[13]

Now, one may ask, how can achieving a limited transcendence by connecting with non-trivial things or values beyond oneself infuse one's life with meaning? The answer, I suggest, is found in the pursuit of subjectively significant purposes. As Paul Edwards writes: "When we ask whether a *particular* person's life has or had any meaning ... we are usually concerned not with cosmic issues but with the question whether certain purposes are to be found *in* his life."[14] Significant purposes play a crucial role in mediating between the world of values and the world of value-free physical, causal occurrences; they can infuse lives with meaning because, through them, we apply the interpretations of objective reality we find in the world of values to that value-free world. Since the transcendence this represents is always limited, it allows for the possibility of purpose *in* life without purpose *of* life.[15]

So far I have suggested that a meaningful life is characterized by the pursuit of subjectively significant purposes, the significance of which is derived from and secured by connections with contexts of value located beyond the self. I now want to suggest that the enjoyment of such a life is intrinsically valuable. How can this be? While I don't think I can offer a knock-out argument for this proposition, I will suggest two reasons for taking it seriously. The first is that I believe this claim resonates at some deep level with our experience as human beings. The second is found in the appeal of the conceptions of autonomy and identification that this conception of meaningful life inspires.

Let's consider how this conception of meaningful life resonates with human experience. Think of the idea of value. Something that is valuable has worth; it is desirable. Anything that makes being alive desirable for a human, then, constitutes a human value. Surely this is also true for anything that by its absence makes being alive undesirable. Something is an intrinsic human value if its presence or absence, in and of itself and not just the consequences of its presence or absence, makes being alive desirable or undesirable.

I propose that subjectively significant purposes are this sort of intrinsic human value. To support this proposition I present an admittedly eclectic and impressionistic collection of observations that bear witness to the negative proposition that a life without purpose is intrinsically worthless. I leave it to the reader to judge if these observations make "the most sense of human life."[16] Viktor Frankl, a psychotherapist and concentration camp survivor, emphasizes the importance of purpose when he writes of those who perished in the Nazi death camps: "Woe to him who saw no more sense in his life, no aim, no purpose, and therefore no point in carrying on."[17] John Stuart Mill, in his autobiography, draws a similar connection between purpose and the value of a life: "All my happiness was to have been found in the continual pursuit of this end [reforming the world according to utilitarian principles]. The end had ceased to charm, and how could there ever again be any interest in the means? I seemed to have nothing to live for."[18] A similar connection is drawn by Leo Tolstoy in his autobiographical writings: "My life came to a standstill. I could breathe, eat, drink, and sleep, and could not help breathing, eating, drinking, and sleeping; but there was no life, because there were no desires the gratification of which I might find reasonable."[19] In a less personal tone, Emile Durkheim draws this connection in his account of "anomic suicide": "All man's pleasure in acting, moving, and exerting himself implies the sense that his efforts are not in vain and that by walking he has advanced. However, one does not advance when one walks towards no goal, or – which is the same thing – when his goal is infinity."[20] For John Rawls, this connection is made in the idea that self-respect includes one's "secure conviction that his conception of his good, his plan of life is worth carrying out ... When we feel that our plans are of little value ... all desire and activity becomes empty and vain, and we sink into apathy and cynicism."[21] While these observations do not amount to an argument, they draw strength to the extent that they resonate with human experience.

When I speak of a meaningful life, then, I refer to a life characterized by the pursuit of subjectively significant purposes, the meaning of which is drawn from some context of value secured beyond the self. Conversely, a meaningless life lacks significant purposes or is experienced in a context within which the pursuit of such purposes is impossible. While this conception of a meaningful life obviously attests to the influence of Kymlicka's work, there is a key difference: where Kymlicka's account associates meaning with meaningful choice and contexts of choice, this account associates it with meaningful lives and contexts of value.

Another feature of this conception of meaningful life is that it is anti-perfectionist; it only describes the general features of a life, not its particular substance. Thus, we can accept that the purposes that sustain meaning in one person's life might be experienced as meaningless in another's. This prevents us from judging the meaningfulness of a person's life by assessing its substance, but it does enable us to judge it by its form, facilitated by the conceptions of autonomy and identification it generates.

Self-Identity and Contexts of Value

I have suggested that meaningful lives involve connections with contexts of value. We can continue to flesh out this model of personhood by considering the origin of these contexts as well as how people connect with them. This requires introducing three important concepts: situation, self-identity, and governing assumptions. A person's situation is the totality of his or her unchosen attributes. These range from physical appearance to membership in groups, communities, and traditions. David Archard says that situation comprises three interrelated sets of facts: "First, there are those facts pertaining to an individual's biological endowment; second, those having to do with the conditions of an individual's education and rearing; third, those defining the present social and historical setting for an individual's life."[22] Thus, the self is *thrown*, to use Heidegger's term, into a life characterized by membership in groups and communities that are experienced as "always already having been."[23] Self-identity emerges, as Michael Sandel has usefully suggested, out of a situation when the agent identifies with some of his attributes and not others, differentiating those which he is from those which he merely has.[24] Those which he believes he is constitutes his self-identity.

Certain identifications that constitute self-identity are more important to meaning than others. The subset most important to meaning I call governing assumptions.[25] These assumptions are the part of self-identity, to use Charles Taylor's phrase, that describes "who we are, 'where we're coming from' ... [they are] the background against which our tastes and desires and opinions and aspirations make sense."[26] They include a person's values and principles as well as the person's understanding of the relationship between his or her values and principles – for example, which are most important, which apply in which circumstances. While we treat them as authoritative (consciously or otherwise) when considering how to act or which purposes to adopt, they need not be especially coherent or law-like. In recognizing that a person's identifications usually evolve during his or her life, I call the first set of governing assumptions to emerge out of one's situation his or her moral starting point.[27]

Governing assumptions connect a person's contexts of value to her purposes. Michael Sandel illustrates this connection when he writes: "If my fundamental values and ends are to enable me, as surely they must, to evaluate and regulate my immediate wants and desires, these values and ends must have a sanction independent of the mere fact that I happen to hold them with a certain intensity."[28] This raises two further questions: Where are contexts of value located, and how do we tap into them?

Contexts of value are located in communities. More specifically, they are located in the traditions that unite and define communities. Traditions and communities are analytically distinct. Consider the Catholic tradition. While we can sensibly speak of one Catholic tradition, this one tradition is embodied in thousands of separate communities. Further, each of these communities differs in the way the tradition is practised, depending, in part at least, on its members' other identifications. For example, the Catholic tradition is practised differently in Italian, Irish, and Pueblo communities. Individuals access contexts of value that inform their personal governing assumptions, then, by identifying with communities that embody traditions. Parekh provides a useful illustration of how values can be so embedded: "Respect for human life, for example, does not remain an abstract moral principle but gets embodied in such things as the customs and rituals surrounding how we dispose of the dead, what we wear and how we conduct ourselves at funerals, how we treat strangers, help the old and the poor, and celebrate the birth of a child."[29] When a community embodies a tradition in this way, it functions as a context of value in much the same way as I associated with Kymlicka's societal cultures in Chapter 1, pp. 17-19 (that is, it acts as a focus of identification, which individuals call on when considering how to act). This I call a community-as-context-of-value.

We can draw a useful distinction between types of community-as-context-of-value by differentiating two types of tradition that such communities may embody. This distinction relies on definitions provided by John Kekes. A purposive tradition is "an association of people guided by a specific and common goal ... [that] provides the framework in which [its members] aim to achieve whatever this goal happens to be."[30] The values with which these traditions connect their members include the shared good the tradition aims to achieve, as well as the various virtues and vices understood to contribute to or detract from it. The other type of tradition, which Kekes calls moral tradition, "does not aim to achieve a specific goal ... [but rather] to create a context in which specific goals can be achieved. Legal, political, managerial, and law enforcement traditions are examples of it ... [They] are ground-clearing rather than architectural; enabling rather than productive; protective rather than venturesome. A moral tradition has achieved its purpose if no one in a society needs to be aware of its existence."[31] Moral traditions are important for two reasons: they help sustain purposive traditions existing within them, and they can embody their own contexts of value.[32]

These distinctions are useful. They provide us with a language to compare the kinds of community Kymlicka and Taylor champion – societal culture, nation – with some of those championed by communitarians – church, ethnicity, neighbourhood. This new language permits us to see that while these types of community have something important in common – all can connect their members with contexts of value – there is also a significant difference: societal cultures and nations tend to embody moral traditions, the other communities tend to embody purposive traditions. The importance of this distinction will become evident in subsequent chapters.

These distinctions also can help us distinguish groups that do not represent communities-as-contexts-of-value. Interest groups, for example, whose members "seek a particular goal, or desire the same policy, or are similarly situated with respect to some social effect,"[33] embody neither purposive nor moral traditions. People typically join interest groups to pursue purposes they have already formed, not to connect with contexts of value. Similarly, ideological groups – collectives "of persons with shared political beliefs"[34] – are best understood as representing competing perspectives within broader, often moral, traditions. American liberals and conservatives, for example, promote conflicting interpretations of the moral tradition of the wider American political community.

As for how people tap into contexts of value, identifications with communities-as-contexts-of-value can inform a person's purposes in several ways. For instance, they can inspire purely individual purposes. They can also contribute to individual purposes understood in collective terms. This is illustrated by Sandel's "intersubjective conception of the self" where the "subject of possession is 'we' rather than 'I.'": "Where this sense of participation in the achievements and endeavours of (certain) others engages the reflective self-understandings of the participants, we may come to regard ourselves, over the range of various activities, less as individuated subjects with certain things in common, and more as members of a wider (but still determinate) subjectivity, less as 'others' and more as participants in a common identity, be it a family or community or class or people or nation."[35] Such identifications can provide people with what Taylor calls moral frameworks that tell them where they stand in relation to their conception of the good and help them determine purposes by indicating how particular options might move them in relation to that good.[36]

Identifications with contexts of value do not, however, determine people's choices. People's governing assumptions can be, and often are, plural and fluid, and as a result idiosyncratic. There are good reasons for believing this. Different people can develop different purposes from identifications with the same tradition. At the same time, since people, especially in modern plural societies, may identify with many, often competing, communities and traditions, their governing assumptions will be distinguished by how they integrate (or fail to integrate) those identifications.

This limiting yet not determinative nature of identifications can be illustrated with an example. Consider someone whose inherited situation has the following attributes: woman, Paul's daughter, Catholic, Pueblo, American, liberal. First, note that many different self-identities could emerge from this one situation. A person might believe she is a Catholic Pueblo who happens to have American citizenship, or she might think she is a liberal American woman who has Pueblo ancestry. Second, the same could be said of the governing assumptions that might arise from this self-identity. Third, two people might apply the same authoritative identifications differently.

Someone for whom being a Catholic liberal is authoritative might respond to abortion as a Catholic, a liberal, or both. Finally, a person could treat the same identifications as authoritative in similar situations and still come to different conclusions. The limiting effect of identifications, at least over the short term, is illustrated by the surprise we would feel if this person were to suddenly adopt the purposes of a Polynesian, a Buddhist, or a Mormon.

I have suggested that lives are meaningful when they are characterized by the pursuit of subjectively significant purposes. The significance of purposes, in turn, is defined by reference to contexts of value secured outside of the self. Individuals access such contexts of value by identifying with communities-as-contexts-of-value that embody purposive or moral traditions. Self-identity emerges from a person's unchosen situation when the person distinguishes the elements of her situation that define who she is from those which she merely has; those elements that she is constitute her self-identity. Those elements of her self-identity that she refers to when determining her subjectively significant purposes are her governing assumptions.

Human Agency: Normal and Meta-Agency

The model of human agency developed here has two elements: normal agency and meta-agency. These are ideal types; in practice, they often overlap.

Normal agency, accounting for the bulk of human deliberation, proceeds *from* a person's governing assumptions that the person takes as given. It is through normal agency that people transform their connections with contexts of value into significant purposes, as well as engage in their pursuit. A person initiates normal agency, for example, by asking herself, "What should I, as a liberal Catholic, do in this situation?" Of course, for most people most of the time, normal agency will be neither this intellectualized nor this transparent. A person may simply believe certain things to be good or bad, right or wrong. For example, a person might reason, "Abortion is wrong; therefore I should not have an abortion." No explicit connection need be drawn between this belief and identification as a Catholic.

In meta-agency, conversely, one's governing assumptions *are* the subject of deliberation. A person may ask, for example, "Given my dissatisfaction with the outcome of my previous decisions, should I reconsider, reinterpret, or reject my identifications as a liberal, a Catholic, or both?" Meta-agency is typically initiated when circumstances conspire to threaten the meaningfulness of a person's life by revealing shortcomings in his or her governing assumptions. For instance, a person may be unable to construct governing assumptions from her situation; her purposes may fail too often when put into practice; or previously unrecognized inconsistencies within her governing assumptions may be revealed.

Such meaning-threatening experiences create dissonance. Dissonance presents a problem and an opportunity. It is a problem since it threatens the meaningfulness of a person's life and can lead, ultimately, to anomie. It is an opportunity to the extent that its successful resolution often refines a person's governing assumptions and so improves her reasons for having confidence in them. However unlikely, a person who never experiences dissonance would never need to exercise meta-agency.

Meta-agency may usefully be conceptualized as following the dialectic pattern of thesis, antithesis, synthesis.[37] The thesis in meta-agency is a person's present governing assumptions. I called one's first such thesis his or her moral starting point. Antithesis arises from dissonance. The agent responds to dissonance by engaging in critical reflection. In critical reflection a person considers the identifications that constitute her governing assumptions, her perceptions of objective reality, and her understanding of the relationship between the two, in the hopes of locating the cause of dissonance. Synthesis is reached, if it is reached, when the source of dissonance is addressed and meaning recovered. Meta-agency can, of course, fail: just as societies collapse and traditions die, some people who experience dissonance never fully recover a sense of meaning in their lives. Typically, though, one escapes dissonance by transforming one's governing assumptions – by prioritizing, reinterpreting, compartmentalizing, rejecting, or adopting identifications to increase internal consistency or consonance with objective reality – or by acting on external circumstances, where possible, to remove the source of dissonance. Presuming synthesis is achieved, the person exercises normal agency again on the basis of new or transformed governing assumptions and, perhaps, a transformed self-identity.

Of course, this account is idealized. Often, a person exercises normal agency in many spheres of his life while exercising meta-agency in others. Also, normal and meta-agency may overlap: in choosing one purpose rather than another through normal agency, a person may strengthen his commitment to one governing assumption or weaken his commitment to another – actions more akin to meta-agency.

Philyp Rosser's introspective essay "Growing through Political Change" illustrates this model of agency. Rosser's unchosen moral starting point was a Labour-supporting Welsh community. The communities into which he found himself *thrown* presented him with competing contexts of value. His Welsh community was "Welsh in terms of language and ethos," while the Labour Party he was committed to in the 1960s and 1970s was "seemingly devoid of roots and belonging." Despite such incongruities, he was able to create and maintain governing assumptions by compartmentalizing his identifications:

> As long as I retained a perspective of politics which was unquestionably British that tension never really surfaced. Nothing was easier than for me to live out my Welsh existence, to speak the language in the home, in

everyday conversation in the village and listen to Welsh sermons in chapel on Sundays. But it stopped there. Politics, was, after all, different. Socialism contained that transcendent quality which welded the struggle of industrial south Wales to the same struggle which was taking place in other parts of Britain, from London's East End, to Tyneside and the west of Scotland. Loyalties needed to be flung far beyond the confines of Wales.

A source of dissonance in his life was the realization that in doing nothing to prevent the decline of the Welsh community, he was losing a part of his self-identity: "[I had] experiences accumulated on returning to Wales at periodic intervals and seeing a community, my own community, dying ... [and] the realisation that the decline of this community was not something extraneous to myself but was becoming increasingly personalised – that in the balance was not only the survival or extinction of a community but really it was the life or death of my own identity, my own specific Welsh consciousness." Rosser responded to this by exercising what I am calling meta-agency. He determined that the root of his crisis was the irreconcilability of two key identifications: "The Labour Party's socialism is so heavily imprinted with British statism that it cannot come to terms with the community and cultural needs of a distinctive Welsh national identity." He resolved the dissonance by rejecting the Labour dimension of his self-identity (in his words, "discarding the maladjusted ethos of British socialism") and integrating his socialism directly into his Welsh identification, to create a socialism "rooted in the Welsh situation."[38]

This discussion of identity and agency suggests that self-identity can be both fluid and fragile: fluid to the extent that people may radically transform the identifications that constitute their self-identity through meta-agency; fragile to the extent that meta-agency may fail, leaving connections to important contexts of value severed but generating no new identifications that could motivate significant purposes to replace them. This conception of a fluid-yet-fragile self-identity offers an alternative to the cultural monist conception of the relationship between individual and community discussed in Chapter 1. The implications of this conception of self-identity for distributive justice are explored further in Chapters 3 and 4.

Situated Autonomy

As has been noted, the general concept of personal autonomy as the ability to pursue one's ends free from coercion and manipulation is consistent with a wide variety of particular, and often conflicting, conceptions. The conception of personal autonomy suggested by the conception of the person who has an essential interest in meaningful life I call situated autonomy. I discuss it in terms of three key aspects of agency: the pursuit of purposes, the formation of purposes, and the nature of governing assumptions.

The pursuit of purposes necessitates the freedom to lead our lives, as

Kymlicka has said, from the inside. This raises the matter of positive and negative liberty. Least contentious is negative liberty: the freedom from coercive interference with the pursuit of one's purposes. This liberty is clearly consistent with situated autonomy. To lead meaningful lives, people must be free to pursue their purposes. To deny them this is to demonstrate a lack of respect for meaningful life itself. Although there may be circumstances in which interference is warranted, it always represents harm.

More contentious is positive liberty. People lack positive liberty when they are prevented from pursuing their purposes because they lack resources, capacities, or opportunities. Its provision often requires a redistribution of resources, making it more burdensome, and more transparently burdensome, than negative liberty. Given that our central focus is on meaningful life and not an abstract conception of equality of opportunity, we can be open to the possibility that justice may require the unequal treatment in the distribution of resources that positive liberty may require. Therefore, meaningful life, through the derivative value of situated autonomy, is compatible with liberalism's long-standing commitment to negative and positive liberty.

The second key aspect of agency, the formation of purposes, raises two issues concerning the normal agency by which people form purposes. The first turns on the idea of personal autonomy as self-governance. This contrasts the idea of governance with caprice: for the self to govern, it must treat something as authoritative. This requires the ability to form second-order or higher-order preferences or desires: "Lower-order desires ... have as their object actions of the agent: a desire to *do* X or Y; higher-order desires ... however, have as their object other, lower-order desires; a desire to desire to do X or Y."[39] In forming higher-order preferences, people "reflect upon and adopt attitudes towards their first-order desires, wishes, intentions."[40] Without this capacity, a person could not be self-governing at all. This is reflected in our idea of governing assumptions.

Those who lack governing assumptions are not autonomous. They are usually described in one of two ways. One type of non-autonomous person is like Benn's *inner-impelled* who lacks autonomy because he behaves like an automaton, responding "uncomprehendingly to drives or attractions" that he cannot control. This person suffers from "natural" deficiencies in the skills required to self-govern (for example, neurosis or psychosis).[41] A second type is like Harry Frankfurt's *wantons* and Benn's *anomic choosers* who pursue whichever course of action they are most strongly inclined to follow at the time. Such a person "does not care which of his inclinations is the strongest;"[42] he makes no attempt to live consistently and acts on "impulse not because he is impelled but because he acknowledges nothing as a reason for doing otherwise."[43] Wantons simply do not govern themselves. Such people are incapable of determining and pursuing significant purposes, and thus cannot lead meaningful lives.

Although people must be able to form second-order preferences to exercise situated autonomy, there is no presumption that these governing assumptions must be so clear and consistent that their self-identities become "unified, free, and self-made," as Iris Marion Young suggests, or that their lives are "ordered according to a plan or conception which fully expresses one's will," as Robert Young proposes.[44] In fact, situated autonomy can provide a justification for self-governance where people's governing assumptions are not unified and even where they conflict. The reason: only the person him- or herself is likely to have the self-knowledge necessary to sustain meaning while managing multiple and conflicting identifications.[45]

The second issue with the formation of purposes through the exercise of normal agency concerns the conditions under which this occurs. Situated autonomy requires the processes by which people form their purposes to be free of undue external influences. This condition is not respected where, as Gerald Dworkin has suggested, people are influenced by hypnotic suggestion, manipulation, coercive persuasion, or subliminal influence.[46] This is also true of any influences that, as Christman suggests, "were the agent to be made aware of their presence and influence, she would be moved to revise her desire set."[47] This condition reflects concern for meaningful lives in two ways. First, purposes based on false, incomplete, or misleading information, or that do not reflect a person's own governing assumptions, are more likely to fail or prove meaningless because of these influences. Second, those who exert such influences fail to show respect for meaning in the lives of those they manipulate.

The third key aspect of agency concerns the nature of governing assumptions. This raises the issue of the impact of socialization identified in Chapter 1: Are the governing assumptions from which purposes are formed the person's own? We can distinguish two cases in which people develop governing assumptions: when adults exercise meta-agency, and when children are socialized to form moral starting points. The first case is fairly straightforward; respect for meaningful life requires that people not be subjected to the kinds of illegitimate influences noted above. In the case of children, two matters must be addressed: the nature of the processes by which socialization occurs and how the children should respond to their socialization as they mature. Our model of agency suggests that the socialization of children must be treated differently from meta-agency in adults. While, as a general rule, coercion and manipulation are inconsistent with personal autonomy, the formation of the secure identifications on which situated autonomy depends may be consistent with some coercion and manipulation to steer children away from certain influences and towards others. Nevertheless, distinctions must be made between legitimate socialization that respects meaningful lives and illegitimate socialization that does not. This will be taken up more fully in Chapter 7 by developing a principled alternative to the dichotomy

Kukathas presents between always interfering with processes of socialization and always leaving them alone.

The second issue children and socialization raises concerns how people should respond to the fact that no one ever chooses his or her moral starting points. It is useful to consider this as a problem of the role of critical reflection in the autonomous life. The role of critical reflection is a central aspect of the debate about community and justice. As we saw in Chapter 1, Kymlicka suggests that everyone should be provided with a liberal education so that they will be able to critically reflect on their inherited beliefs, while Kukathas thinks this is unnecessary. Raz suggests that whether one needs a capacity for choice and critical reflection is determined in part by the type of society into which one is socialized; some liberals assume people can exercise critical reflection to reconstruct their lives in the face of failed communities; and some communitarians assume that no amount of critical reflection can allow individuals to ever fully escape constitutive communities.

Three positions can be taken on the role of critical reflection in personal autonomy: the "examined life," the "dogmatic" or "unreflective" life, and the "life of open-minded conviction." Those who lead the examined life engage in critical reflection as a matter of principle. They do not wait to experience dissonance to question their governing assumptions. They live by Socrates' credo in the *Apology* that "the unexamined life is not worth living for man." Robert Young exemplifies this view when he writes: "We may accept that our socialization precludes our adopting motivations *de novo*, but believe as well that we have the choice of making them our own by identifying with them in our reflective judgings or rejecting them. Once privy to such awareness it does not matter so much how one came to have one's particular first-order desires, but whether or not on reflection one desires to have such desires."[48] On this view, governing assumptions can only be the person's own if he or she consciously makes them so by comparing them with available alternatives and critically reflecting on them. Autonomy is reconciled with socialization, this suggests, through a process of self-awareness in which one accepts or rejects previously unrecognized elements in one's socialization.[49]

At the other end of the spectrum, someone who leads the dogmatic or unreflective life is either unwilling or unable to engage in critical reflection, even when faced with circumstances that would typically cause dissonance in others. Examples include people who act "according to a program implanted by someone else," the hypnotized, the brainwashed, and those who cannot disobey an authoritarian parent.[50] To such people, the idea that their governing assumptions may not be their own is incomprehensible.

Intermediate between these two types of life are those who lead lives of open-minded conviction. Such people act on beliefs they hold firmly and sincerely as either true or as their best account so far. They are comfortable with objective (as opposed to intrinsic) meaning. Their lives are autonomous in at least two ways. First, they exercise normal agency and so determine their subjectively significant purposes. Second, while they are not especially motivated to seek information that challenges their beliefs, their lives are distinguished from the dogmatic by their ability to articulate "good reasons" for their adherence to their beliefs, and by their willingness to engage in meta-agency if and when they experience dissonance. On this view, a person's governing assumptions are her own so long as she can identify them and give an account of their validity.

Situated autonomy adopts the life of open-minded conviction as the most reasonable characterization of the role of critical reflection in meaningful lives. This position is defended in Chapter 4 by arguing against treating the examined life as a standard for autonomy and by arguing that the life of open-minded conviction can be distinguished from the dogmatic life.

To draw together the three key aspects of agency in a definition of situated autonomy: A person exhibits situated autonomy if, in her day-to-day life, she exercises normal agency in accordance with governing assumptions that are her own in the sense that she can identify them and give an account of their validity, and she is willing, if she experiences dissonance, to exercise meta-agency. This definition makes three claims. First, a person must exercise normal agency to be autonomous. This means she must have governing assumptions, which rely, in turn, on self-identity and identifications with communities. Second, these governing assumptions must be her own. Third, she need only be willing to exercise meta-agency when and if she experiences dissonance.

Thus, situated autonomy sets a credible minimum standard for autonomous life while stopping short of the examined life. This is something it must do if it is to be open to premodern communities and illiberal traditions. Its insistence on normal agency excludes the wanton and inner-impelled, but its endorsement of the life of open-minded conviction allows it to suggest, contrary to the conception of the examined life, that meta-agency, and thus critical reflection, have only contingent value. While not as heroic as some conceptions of autonomy, situated autonomy reflects what is truly valuable in the idea of self-governance: its instrumental contribution to the experience of meaningful life.

Conclusion

Meaningful life, defined as the pursuit of subjectively significant purposes, facilitates the development of mutually supportive conceptions of personal autonomy and identification with a community. Situated autonomy presumes identifications with communities-as-contexts-of-value. To be self-governing, one must have governing assumptions, and governing assumptions are derived from identifications with communities that embody traditions: no communities, no governing assumptions; no governing assumptions, no significant purposes. Further, since no self-identity, set of governing assumptions, or context of value is likely to be secure from dissonance, situated autonomy actually supports identifications because it is through exercising meta-agency that people shape and reshape their identifications and prevent their self-identities from losing meaning. Thus, when conceived on the basis of a conception of the person who has an essential interest in meaningful life, autonomy and identification work together to enable people to form and pursue significant purposes. Neither can do this on its own.

Chapters 3 and 4 pursue in further detail issues raised in this chapter. Chapter 3 demonstrates how the foundations of meaningful life can be used to justify special accommodations for communities, even where this requires imposing burdens on non-members. Unlike other approaches that justify such protection on the special nature of cultural communities, however, ours is based on a characteristic that cultural and other types of communities share – their status as communities that embody contexts of value that support meaning in their members' lives. Chapter 4 completes the consideration of foundational assumptions by discussing the relationship between situated autonomy and socialization and defending the association of situated autonomy with the life of open-minded conviction.

3
Justifying Cultural Accommodation: Identification, Communities, and Contexts of Value

Here I stand, I cannot do otherwise.

Martin Luther, Diet of Worms, 1521 (attributed)

In considering how the extension of cultural accommodations to sub-state communities might be justified, we must distinguish between accommodations that impose burdens on other members of the wider political community and accommodations that either do not impose burdens or that impose negligible burdens. The chapter begins by briefly discussing cultural accommodations that do not require imposing burdens on citizens who do not belong to the community in question (non-members). It then turns to the more complex topic of accommodations that require appreciable burdens. Any justification of this type of accommodation must address two questions: Can the extension of special treatment to particular communities be justified, and why should non-members accept the burdens this may require? I attempt to answer these questions by applying the conception of the person developed in Chapter 2. Of particular relevance is the description of self-identity as capable of being both fluid and fragile. The argument begins by explaining how the conception of the person can explain continuity in individual identity. The resulting "narrative account of selfhood" is used to explain why it may be unreasonable, in certain circumstances, to expect individuals to give up their identifications with particular communities. Finally, the burdens that may be imposed on non-members to help sustain valuable communities for others are justified by suggesting that the wider community should be understood as embodying a moral tradition that sustains the many purposive traditions on which all citizens rely. The chapter concludes by discussing how this compares with other approaches.

Accommodations That Impose Negligible Burdens

I do not have a lot to say about the justification of communal accommodations that impose negligible burdens. Only the imposition of appreciable burdens gives non-members a legitimate interest in the matter and so requires a strong justification: no burden, no interest; no interest, little need for justification. The main exception to this occurs where requested accommodations are offensive to justice for some reason other than that of imposing unreasonable burdens (see Chapters 6 and 7). In short, where people request accommodations that they believe are necessary to sustain valuable communities and satisfaction of these claims requires little or nothing from non-members, respect for the claimants' interest in meaningful life should be sufficient reason to provide the accommodations.

A brief example should suffice to illustrate what such a claim might look like. In an article in *The New Yorker,* Calvin Trillen describes a demand made by an Orthodox Jewish community in northwest London. The community requested planning permission to erect clusters of twenty-foot-high posts connected by fishing line to complete an eruv around a six-and-a-half-square-mile area. This eruv, the claimants said, would allow them to carry things within the neighbourhood on the Sabbath by enclosing it and making it part of their private domains, as their tradition requires. Assuming the Jewish community was willing to cover the cost of erecting the poles, their request strikes me as an undemanding accommodation. As Trillen reported, the claimants said that all that was required of non-members was to allow them "to connect the existing boundaries with wires stretched across eighty-five posts in an area that already had forty or fifty thousand posts of one sort or another."[1] The proposal did meet with opposition, but it was finally approved. This, I suggest, is the only just resolution of situations like this that could be consistent with respect for meaningful life.

Continuity and Change in Self-Identity

Things are much more complicated, however, where accommodations require imposing appreciable burdens. The burden in itself gives non-members an interest in the outcome, as it will impact their ability to pursue their own significant purposes. Why and when may such accommodations be justified?

First, consider the implications of the foundations of meaningful life for the processes by which traditions and individual self-identities change over time. It is common to speak of traditions and communities as having members. I wish to reverse this perspective and consider individuals as having communities and traditions. The exact way this is conceptualized is not important. We can imagine the individual to be like a crossroads at which traditions and communities intersect or a nodal point in a complex web of criss-crossing traditions and communities. The key point is that we reject the image suggested by cultural monism of each individual belonging to only one cultural community. As noted in Chapter 2, in such cases the exercise of situated autonomy resembles a struggle to maintain a meaningful equilibrium between one's various identifications, not an attempt to transcend one's situation or to create a coherent and unified self-identity.

The foundations of meaningful life can facilitate an exploration of the relationship between continuity and change in traditions and self-identity. This suggests that the vitality of traditions depends upon a reciprocal relationship between individuals and the traditions with which they identify: the individual is shaped in part by the dictates of his or her tradition(s), and traditions are shaped in part by the interpretations they are given by each of their members. Traditions evolve through their members' personal struggles to sustain meaning by trying to reconcile their various traditions with each other and with changing circumstances. Thus, each exercise of meta-agency by an individual has the potential to transform a tradition for present and future members. Martin Luther and Albert Einstein, for example, changed the meaning of Christian and scientific traditions for the generations that followed them. Situated autonomy, as expressed in meta-agency, then, should not be seen as a threat to traditions but as essential to their vitality.

Transformations in the French-Canadian identity provide a good example of this. Although many individuals who constituted the community defined by this identity continue to pursue the French-speaking lives that originally united them, changes in the Canadian political context have led them to express this underlying identification in new ways. As the struggle for the survival of their community has shifted from the federal to the provincial sphere, the French Canadian expression of this identity that had united those who resisted English Canadians, the British colonial administration, and the Durham Report, has transformed into Québécois, Franco-Manitoban, Franco-Ontarian, and Acadian identities. Despite these changes, the continuity between the French Canadian and the newer identities can be traced through the various transitions. This allows us to suggest, contrary to Kukathas (Chapter 1, p. 20), that changes in the expression of an identity do not necessarily reflect a change in the underlying nature of that identity. What is reflected are changes in the salience of identities, rather than in the identities themselves. In this regard, I like Iris Marion Young's suggestion that "a person's group identities may be for the most part only a background or horizon to his or her life, becoming salient only in specific interactive contexts."[2]

Similar processes explain the continuity of personal self-identity. Much as the continuity of a tradition persists, though some of its characteristics change, a person with self-identity$_{abc}$ (containing identifications or values a, b, and c) at time t_1 is the same person as a person with self-identity$_{def}$ at time t_4 if self-identities at times t_1 and t_4 can be linked by a narrative that explains how self-identity persists through these changes. Such explanation would present a series of transformations in which at least one identification was taken as "given" and therefore retained from one time point to the next.[3] This I call, borrowing from MacIntyre, a narrative account of selfhood:[4] I am the same person I was ten years ago if I can tell a story, without self-deception, that explains the sequence of changes in my self-identity as a linked series of additions to, deletions from, and reinterpretations of, my identifications.[5] No such account could link me to someone other than my own self at an earlier point in time or to some future person who might inhabit my body were I to suffer a loss of identity, from, for example, brain damage. More important, the reverse is also true: the content of one's present identifications may restrict the identifications that one can meaningfully make at any point in time. This insight forms the basis for the justification for communal accommodations.

Identifications with Particular Communities
To see how this narrative account of selfhood can justify the accommodation of particular communities, we must note two general ways in which people can be deprived of access to communities with which they identify. A person may be coercively prevented from associating with a community. This is clearly inconsistent with even the most basic conception of personal autonomy. Such denial of access cannot usually justify special accommodations, however, because it can usually be addressed through such negative liberties as toleration, freedom of association, and freedom of religion. A person can also lose access to a community when the community ceases to exist. Again, what it means for a community to cease to exist can vary. At the extreme, it may be the death or dispersion of so many of its members that it loses the ability to sustain or reproduce itself. According to Kymlicka, a cultural community is undermined if the majority of its members are dead, in jail, or on skid row.[6] It can also occur if some change in circumstances prevents community members from pursuing the shared purposes that defined them as a community. What this means in practice will vary with the nature of each community's traditions. Where such changes are the result of natural processes or are the unintended consequence of people pursuing private purposes, negative freedoms will often prove insufficient to sustain a community. For instance, the pursuit of private purposes by individuals in the economic market may undermine a community by pricing it out of existence, as when community members are outbid for land or other vital resources. In such cases, communities could be sustained only by recognizing positive rights to cultural accommodations.

The argument for such accommodation builds on the idea of fluid-yet-fragile self-identity. This conception of self-identity allows us to recognize that identities can be fluid, without obliging us to follow Kukathas in rejecting cultural rights, and to recognize that particular communities may have special signifi-cance for some individuals, without requiring us to accept the cultural monist assumption that people can rarely or never reject inherited identifications. In place of these assumptions, it allows us to claim that cultural accommodation may be warranted because, in the particular circumstances, certain identity transformations are contingently impossible.

The starting point of this argument is the claim that meaningful lives always depend on having access to *some* community and its context of value. There are at least two reasons for this. First, while a person may be aware that he treats an identification with a particular community as authoritative for making certain kinds of decisions, he may have incomplete knowledge of its context of value and so be unable to determine its implications by himself. In exercising normal agency, for instance, he may ask himself, "How should I, as a Welshman, act in this situation?" Having never considered the situa-tion before, he may find he lacks the cultural resources to respond to it and must consult other community members. Deprived of this resource, he may feel, as Taylor suggests, that he did not "know anymore, for an important range of questions, what the significance of things was for [him]."[7]

Second, people may need continuing access to particular communities because some significant purposes can be pursued only within the commu-nities that inspire them. As Raz suggests, for example, it would be impossible to be a lawyer in a community without a particular kind of legal system.[8] Similarly, certain purposes can be pursued only if they are integrated into and coordinated with those of others. An example is a person who finds meaning in what Benn calls a transcendent collective enterprise, such as an orchestra or a scientific research institute. The purpose of such enterprises is not the well-being of its members but either the activity the members perform or an ideal state of affairs the activity is intended to promote.[9] Clearly, someone whose purpose is not, say, simply to play the violin but to perform a concert as part of an orchestra cannot succeed without access to that enterprise. Thus, having access to communities can be vital to people's attempts to form and pursue significant purposes.

This explains why people need ongoing access to communities, but it does not explain why, if a particular community is endangered, its members can-not be expected to replace it by identifying with some other, more viable, community. A further argument is required. People need access to particular communities because, while self-identity can be fluid when the agent initi-ates changes, it can be fragile when changes are externally imposed. The reason, as we have seen, is that a person's ability to make new identifications is limited by the processes of normal and meta-agency as reflected in the narrative account of selfhood.

According to the narrative account of selfhood, a person's present gov-erning assumptions place limitations on the new identifications he or she can meaningfully make, at least over the short term. For instance, as David Archard suggests, a person's ability to critically appraise any community or society is limited by the "finite and determinate 'menu' of fundamental values" presently available to him or her.[10] It is also exemplified in Benn's suggestion that "someone reared in a tradition that took little account of some very general principle, such as respect for persons, or some value, such as the value of human life, could not be persuaded by reasoned argument into adopting it as a practical belief, because his culture (or language) lacked essential concepts for the formulation of such principles."[11] Without such prerequisites, this person could not meaningfully adopt this value.[12]

Another way such limitation might arise is reflected in Harry Frankfurt's idea of volitional necessity, which suggests that to treat an identification as authoritative (in his terms, to "care about it"), a person must avoid contradicting that identification in his actions. Frankfurt writes that a person "who is subject to volitional necessity finds that he *must* act as he does ... People are generally quite far from considering that volitional necessity renders them helpless bystanders to their own behaviour. Indeed many may even tend to regard it as actually enhancing their autonomy and their strength of will." Echoing Luther's, "Here I stand: I can do no other," Frankfurt says, "An encounter with necessity of this sort, characteristically affects a person ... by somehow making it apparent to him that every apparent alternative to [his present] course is unthinkable."[13]

The narrative account of selfhood explains how a person's present identifications can limit his ability to make new identifications. This is not to deny that a person can reject even his most fundamental or deepest values. Rather, it is to suggest that a person's ability to do so is limited both by the range of values that his present identifications allow him to draw on and by the nature of the alternative identifications presently available to him. This does not depend on whether his identification with the community resulted from birth or choice but on how strongly he identifies with it.

We can now see why people may need to be protected from being involuntarily deprived of access to particular communities. The voluntary loss of an identification – by deciding to reject it through an exercise of meta-agency – is not problematic precisely because people normally reject and replace identifications for reasons meaningful to them. Where the loss of an identification is involuntary, however, the ability to sustain meaning is not so easily assured. Once deprived of access to communities that sustain their governing assumptions, there can be no guarantee, contrary to Ronald Dworkin (Chapter 1, pp. 15-16), that people will "be able to reassemble their sense of identity."[14] This could occur for several reasons. For instance, deprived of access to their community, they may personally lack the cultural resources required to engage in deliberation that would allow them to make new identifications. Similarly, they may be prevented by volitional necessity from identifying with any of the alternative communities available to them. Where the loss of identifications is significant enough, people may be unable to reconstruct self-identities that can sustain meaning from what remains. Unable to cope, they may lose their capacity for situated autonomy and thus lead anomic or other similarly meaningless lives.

An example of how this might play out at the communal level is found in Ralph Linton's discussion of directed culture change. Where members of a community change their ways as a result of the persuasion or prestige of another community, "no element of culture will be eliminated until a satisfactory substitute has been found. In other words, there will be no point in the process of culture transfer where techniques for satisfying all the group's needs are not present." Where changes are involuntary (Linton considers only coerced changes, but his points apply also to changes that occur as unintended consequences), "the results for the subjects are often catastrophic": "Under culture change which is both directed and enforced, the normal process of retention of old elements until satisfactory substitutes have been found is inhibited. The result is a series of losses without adequate replacements. This leaves certain of the group's needs unsatisfied, produces derangements in all sorts of social and economic relationships and results in profound discomfort for the individuals involved."[15] The point, which is as true of individual self-identities as it is of whole cultures, is that involuntary changes can result in the loss of valuable identifications without securing adequate replacements.

This suggests two cases in which the extension of accommodations to communities-as-contexts-of-value can be justified. The remedial case occurs where there is an obvious connection between the loss or deterioration of specific communities, the inability of members to make the transition to other communities, and a loss of meaning in their lives. A literary example is that of the savage in Huxley's *Brave New World* who, removed from his community, eventually kills himself rather than continue to live in a utilitarian dystopia that makes no sense to him. A contemporary example is that of many Native people in North America who, being involuntarily deprived of access to their communities, are unable to make the transition to the wider society, and whose lives are characterized by high rates of poverty, alcoholism, and suicide.[16] Where this point is reached, the case for special accommodation is clear.

The second, preventative, case is more controversial. It concerns situations where accommodations are requested to sustain a valuable community. It is controversial because it involves two counterfactual claims: that the community requires the requested accommodation to survive, and that many community members would be unable to reconstruct meaningful lives were they to lose access to the community. Respect for meaningful life requires such claims to be taken seriously for two reasons. The first is predictive uncertainty. Given the fairly uncontroversial assumptions that people have different rudimentary characters (for example, temperament and natural talents)[17] and that they will have different experiences throughout their lives, it is reasonable to expect that each person's governing assumptions at any point in time will be, if not unique, at least virtually impossible for others to predict. Thus, one reason we must take claims for preventative protection seriously is that we can only *know* that a community needed protection after its members' lives have become meaningless. A second reason is that respect for meaningful lives suggests that, as a general rule, we respond to people in ways that make sense to them in terms of their own beliefs and values. Although outsiders may believe that they are able to understand the meaning of a culture or tradition as well as or even better than those inside it,[18] respect for meaningful life suggests that we generally resist imposing solutions that only make sense on the basis of assumptions that those affected do not accept.

As an example, consider John Kekes' discussion of the Dinka, an African tribe that traditionally practised the live burial of aged spear-masters on the belief that this was necessary to protect the life of the tribe.[19] Should special accommodation in the form of an exemption from laws on murder or assisted suicide be extended in such a case? Now, to be clear, I am not presenting this case as an example of individuals being sacrificed for the good of the community but on the assumptions that the spear-masters desire to engage in this unusual practice and that it forms an integral part of a way of life they value and from which they have benefited.[20] Kekes rejects a defence of this practice that would be compatible with my argument: that it should be tolerated if it were true that it sustained the tribe in a psychological, as opposed to a physiological, fashion. Kekes offers two reasons for rejecting this defence. The first is that since the Dinka tradition is complex and the burial tradition is only a small part of it, the tribe can sustain itself if the practice were banned. The argument for preventative protection suggests two problems with this. It ignores the problem of predictive uncertainty: Kekes' claim is just as speculative as the claim that the tribe could not survive; the complexity he attributes to the Dinka tradition serves only to make the consequences of intervention that much more uncertain. It also fails to respect the Dinka's own understanding of their situation and the meaningfulness of their lives. Kekes' second reason is that, as a matter of historical fact, when the practice was banned, the tribe survived. This is not much help since it relies on after-the-fact evidence that is never available when decisions need to be made. Respect for meaningful life can provide reasons for taking the Dinka spear-master's claim to engage in this practice more seriously than Kekes does.

This discussion of the conditions that must be met in order to justify special accommodations for particular communities illustrates our theory's

capacity to generate principles to guide the extension of cultural accommodation. In this case we have identified three: the community must connect
its members with a context of value that supports their capacity for situated
autonomy and thus meaningful life; members must be threatened with the
involuntary loss of access to the community; and members would be unable
to make alternative identifications with the communities presently available
to them.

Justifying Burdens on Non-Members

This brings us to the chapter's second question: Why should non-members
accept the burdens cultural accommodation may require? This question is
raised in the knowledge that the kind of accommodations being advocated
will likely result in a society characterized by Taylor's "deep" diversity, as
described in the epigraph to Chapter 1, in which some citizens connect with
the state directly as individuals while others connect through their membership in minority national communities. Such differentiated citizenship
faces many criticisms, including that it will undermine the shared identity
that binds the society together, that it will reduce citizens' willingness to
make "mutual sacrifices and accommodations,"[21] and that it will undermine
a country's sense of unity that can be achieved only with uniform citizenship.[22] These are important challenges; we must be able to provide answers.

Let us consider arguments found in David Miller's *On Nationality* and
Will Kymlicka's *Multicultural Citizenship*. My response to the challenges
posed above does not dispute Miller's and Kymlicka's arguments so much as
attempt to expand and build on them. Both theorists believe that the level
of commitment and sacrifice modern states require cannot be inspired by
appeals to justice alone; instead, the stability and unity of liberal democracies depend on citizens sharing an identity. For Kymlicka, "It is not enough
... to show that minority rights are consistent in principle with freedom
and justice" because liberal democracies rely on a "sense of shared civic
purpose and solidarity."[23] For Miller, "Schemes of social justice, particularly
schemes involving redistribution to those not able to provide for their needs
through market transactions," will be supported only where members trust
one another. Thus, he says, it is "virtually self-evident that ties of community
[and shared identity] are an important source of such trust between individuals."[24] I share this belief that the ability to appeal to such shared identity is
essential to legitimizing the kinds of accommodations advocated here.

When considering unity and special rights, both Kymlicka and Miller draw
a distinction between national minorities and multicultural or polyethnic
groups. Both argue that, contrary to popular wisdom, special rights for such
minorities bolster national unity. Multicultural rights, such as the general
right to working and shopping hours flexible enough to accommodate
competing Sabbaths and festivals, or the particular right of Sikhs in the

Royal Canadian Mounted Police to wear turbans, enable members of ethnic minorities to integrate into the wider community. Thus, both call for the reform of the wider national identity and its institutions to accommodate such differences.[25] This is certainly consistent with the requirements of meaningful life. My concern lies elsewhere.

Matters are more complicated with groups that refuse to acknowledge membership in, or the full authority of, the political community (for example, some indigenous groups and seclusionist religious groups). These groups differ from multicultural minorities because they do not want to integrate into the wider community; rather, they often challenge the authority that the state presumes to exercise over their communities and reject the wider civic identity that could provide a bond to justify mutual sacrifices across cultural communities.[26] Further, as Miller notes, when making claims for accommodations, these groups often forget that "much more rests on the majority's sense of fairness than [they] appreciate, and that sense of fairness is liable to be contracted if groups issuing demands reject the identity by virtue of which they belong in the same community as the majority."[27]

Miller believes these problems are so serious that, where possible, secession is the best solution.[28] Further, where secession is not practical and two national communities must share one state, he says that systems of distributive justice cannot be legitimated "in the eyes of the populace." This leaves the state only two options: "Either [the state] restricts the scope of its operations, providing only basic goods such as the protection of rights and national defence; or it embraces a form of federalism, making each constituent nationality responsible for promoting social justice within its own area."[29] Neither of these alternatives can support the kind of accommodations for which I have been arguing. If there are no others, then the present argument must fail, for it requires all citizens to be willing to participate in the very kinds of redistributions between communities that Miller thinks cannot be legitimized.

Fortunately, practical experience provides evidence that the trust and solidarity required to support cross-communal redistributions within wider political communities can be generated. Consider Miller's examples of situations where he suggests that the best outcome is "partial self-determination"; that is, a "constitutional settlement which creates a representative institution for the people in question and assigns to it legislative and policy-making powers over matters that are essential to their identity and material welfare." One of his examples is groups "where the nationality in question and/or the territory it aspires to control is very small, and so could not realistically function as an independent state." He refers, for instance, to the success of Native groups in North America that have negotiated "forms of self-government that give them control over land use, health and social services, etc." Although he notes that many of these groups "fall short of economic viability," he neglects to mention that the services they control often exist only because they receive the kinds of financial transfers from the majority community that Miller says cannot be legitimized. Miller also recommends partial self-determination for cases "where many inhabitants of the relevant territory have national identities that are somewhat ambivalent ... They see themselves as the bearers of both a wider and a narrower identity." For example, many Catalans feel both a Catalan and Spanish identity; many Scots feel both a Scottish and British identity.[30] What he does not explain, however, is why identification with this wider national identity cannot generate the mutual trust that socially just distributions require. Thus, these examples suggests that mutual trust and solidarity across national identities are possible to generate in practice. This, of course, cannot be decisive since it may be possible to generate in practice what cannot be explained in theory.

If such mutual trust is possible in practice, what can possibly act as its theoretical basis? Kymlicka points us in the right direction when he suggests that the basis of social unity in multinational states must be shared identity. He illustrates this by pointing out that Americans are highly unified around an American identity, despite disagreeing on important value issues, while Swedes and Norwegians have different national identities, despite sharing very similar values. Less encouragingly, although he believes shared identity is the key, he is not sure how it can be created where it is absent.[31]

We can begin to identify a basis for such an identity by noting that Kymlicka must certainly be right when he says that a "society founded on 'deep diversity' is unlikely to stay together unless people value deep diversity itself."[32] My aim here is not to explain why people would want to create from scratch a society characterized by deep diversity, but why, given that they live in such a society, it would be reasonable for people to try to create the level of solidarity necessary to sustain it, even when secession is a viable option. This is possible, I believe, if they recognize that the wider political community fulfils an important function for them. This function is not that the wider political community acts as a context of choice or provides standards to choose by for any or all of its citizens – although, of course, it might. Rather, applying our theory, the valuable function the wider political community performs is the providing of a context that sustains the particular communities-as-contexts-of-value that contribute directly to meaning in its citizens' lives; that is, it embodies a moral tradition. As such, all citizens have at least an indirect interest in its survival. Further, as a community embodying a moral tradition, the wider political community is capable of generating a shared identity.

Consider the Canadian case. The threat of Quebec separation has made this point clear to many Canadians who once felt that the problems of French-speaking Canadians were not their concern. English-speaking Canadians have had to face the possibility of living in a Canada that no longer stretches from sea to sea to sea and that is much less culturally distinct from the United States. Mohawk and Inuit communities have had to face the possibility of their people being further divided by a new international border. The Cree of northern Quebec have faced the possibility of being separated from the federal government, which they believe owes them fiduciary obligations. Many Québécois who value their dual identity as Québécois and Canadian have had to consider what it might mean to live without it. In this case, for most members of a political community, most of the time, the political community itself embodies a valuable moral tradition with its own context of value: some, including many English Canadians, rely on it directly, as a community with which they identify and which informs some of their governing assumptions; others rely on it indirectly as a precondition of the particular communities that directly inform their governing assumptions.

In recognizing the wider political community as embodying a moral tradition, we identify a basis for generating a shared identity without denying the importance of other valuable communities. This in itself, of course, cannot justify the kinds of redistributions I advocate. That would require the moral tradition to promote the principle of equal respect for individuals with an essential interest in pursuing meaningful lives. To achieve this, the political community would have to be conceived as a social union of individuals united to facilitate the pursuit of meaningful lives.

How could such a conception of the wider political community be justified? We can begin by rejecting a few possibilities. One is strict reciprocity. In many states, circumstances are such that vulnerable communities will never be able to reciprocate the benefits they receive from more secure communities. Another possibility, suggested by Parekh, is that to justify multiculturalism we must "make a positive case for cultural diversity, showing how and why it is worth cherishing, and that it benefits not just minorities but society as a whole."[33] Our approach could never do this. From our perspective, what is important is the individual's interest in leading a subjectively meaningful life, not any benefits that others may derive from this. If this results in a political community characterized by cultural diversity, that's fine; if it doesn't, that's also fine. Cultural diversity is accorded no independent value.

Fortunately, other justifications, both moral and prudential, are available. The moral justification is most direct. Since all, or at least most, members of the political community can recognize that they rely on the political community to sustain the communities and purposive traditions that inform their own pursuit of significant purposes, it follows that equal respect requires the state to ensure that it perform this function for all its citizens, not just members of the majority. This, I argue more thoroughly in Chapter 5, suggests that justice may require extending special treatment to some citizens. Focus on communities-as-contexts-of-value suggests multiple bases for generating support for this moral claim by creating sympathy between members of communities. Consider, for example, a community within Canada that embodies a moral tradition that may perceive itself to be threatened: the Oka Mohawks. It makes sense for other Canadians, in considering claims for special treatment, to sympathize by drawing comparisons not just between the Mohawk community and their own English- or French-Canadian societal culture but also between the Mohawk community and any of the various, often less secure, communities that support meaning in their lives – for example, religious communities, ethnic communities, and local communities. It is often such communities and not the wider Canadian community that perform an analogous role in the lives of English and French Canadians.

The prudential justification, although not as universal in application, could probably be shown to apply in most cases. While some citizens will likely always carry the burden of supporting accommodations for other citizens who will never be able to reciprocate, the prudential claim is that members of all communities benefit from the overall arrangement. The reason is that such sacrifices ensure the survival of the political community that sustains the particular communities each values. This is consistent with Kymlicka's insight that "people from different national groups will only share an allegiance to the larger polity if they see it as the context within which their national identity is nurtured, rather than subordinated."[34] In making sacrifices to sustain the overall arrangement, then, one helps secure the communities one personally values. Thus, citizens may view the burdens this involves as both a moral obligation to provide all members of the polity an equal chance to pursue meaningful lives and an investment in the conditions sustaining the communities that support meaning in their own lives.

A further advantage of recognizing the bases of social unity in the wider political community as a moral tradition is that it presents the purpose of intercultural dialogue as discovering, articulating, and improving a basis for social unity that already exists, rather than as creating such a basis. Kymlicka and Tully have presented interesting examples of what this might look like from cultural monist and anti-monist perspectives. From our perspective, Kymlicka's example presents the wider Canadian political community as providing the context for an ongoing and constitutive "conversation" between distinct communities. It appears when he notes approvingly that "Jeremy Webber argues that Canadians are ... united by their participation in what he calls 'the Canadian conversation'. He argues that English, French, and Aboriginal people grow up listening to this conversation, and that it becomes a part of all our identities."[35] I call this a cultural monist perspective because the conversation contributes to most individuals' identities by their listening to it as it is conducted (presumably) by the elites of their various groups, not by their participating in it themselves.

Tully presents a striking image of the constitutive role of intercultural dialogue from an anti-monist perspective in his discussion of Bill Reid's sculpture *The Spirit of Haida Gwaii*. The sculpture depicts thirteen spirit creatures representing different cultures and identities engaged in dialogue while paddling a boat. Tully, too, describes their relationship as a "conversation," which, like our "wider society as moral tradition," is partly constitutive of their identities: "They exist as they are, in all their distinctiveness, not in spite of, but in virtue of, their interdependency over time and history. These aspects are embodied in the endless ways in which they overlap and crisscross without losing their identities."[36] I suspect Tully likes this image precisely because it challenges the cultural monist's conception of the problem of social unity as that of justifying the coexistence of separate and distinct cultures. Viewed from Tully's *Haida Gwaii* perspective, the basis for unity exists not in the conversation between cultures but in the relationships between the individual members of the various groups within the political community. I expect that in reality, the alternatives are not nearly so stark; some individuals connect with the state-level moral tradition directly through complex relationships with other groups and their members, while others connect as passive observers of these conversations. In either case, the moral tradition forms a pre-existing and constitutive basis of social unity.

This approach has many promising features. First, by associating the basis of social unity with an existing moral tradition, it presents the bases of shared political identity as independent of any attempts to foster it. Second, it suggests a reason for maintaining the borders of existing states, even where secession is a viable option: borders often sustain the context for these constitutive conversations – "That specific debate is ours, one we know and care about."[37] Finally, it reinforces the prudential argument for dominant or majority groups to engage in serious dialogue with minorities: to the extent that the conversation is constitutive of their own identities, they may "find the prospect of stopping the conversation unacceptable."[38]

That said, we must consider the nature of the moral tradition that supports this shared identity. Here our intuitions are likely to pull in opposite directions. On the one hand, realizing that national majorities have as much right as any minority to expect the state to sustain their valued communities and traditions, we accept that state-level moral traditions will likely reflect their history and values. On the other hand, we realize that the existing moral tradition is the result of a historical conversation between majority and minorities. As with any relation where power is shared unevenly, we recognize that these moral traditions may embody what Carens called, in discussing the situation of African-Americans, "relations of domination and subordination."[39] These concerns are best addressed by following the earlier recommendation: treat the political community as a social union of individuals united to facilitate the pursuit of meaningful lives. Equal respect for the interests of all individuals in pursuing meaningful lives will require the reform of moral traditions that reflect relations of domination and subordination. (As I suggest in Chapter 7, pp. 141-44, the use of international adjudication may also encourage this process.) The result will be that limitations are placed on the majority's ability to use the wider political community to promote its purposes.[40] In practice it will likely mean, as others have suggested, that the account of this moral tradition will be fairly thin. For example, as values Canadians share at the national level, Taylor suggests: "law and order, collective provision, regional equality, and mutual self-help."[41] As for more substantive goods that members of the majority may wish to sustain, these would have to be pursued as members of particular communities-as-contexts-of-value within the wider political community.

Conclusion

Special accommodations for particular communities, as well as any burdens this may place on non-members, can be justified. I will conclude by emphasizing the important roles the concepts that constitute the foundations of meaningful life play in this argument.

The conception of a fluid-yet-fragile self-identity is important because it helps explain why there may be circumstances in which the threatened loss of a particular community may justify cultural accommodations, even though it is true in general that individuals can reject and replace identifications with communities. This allows us to reject the cultural communitarian's claim that people should be treated as if they were permanently constituted by communities of birth, without accepting Kukathas' conclusion that identity is so fluid that cultural rights are never justified.

Focus on communities as embodying traditions allows us to disaggregate such entities as Kymlicka's societal cultures and Raz's encompassing groups into the communities-as-contexts-of-value that exist within and across them. This has two effects. First, it allows us to focus on the actual communities that support meaning in people's lives – those that connect them with contexts of value – whether they constitute national communities or not. Another effect of disaggregating such communities is that it enables us to recognize that many people sustain valuable identifications with several communities at the same time. In particular, it allows us to recognize that people can simultaneously identify with moral traditions embodied in national communities and the wider political community, as well as with purposive traditions embodied in communities existing within and across such communities. This compares well with cultural monist approaches that have difficulty identifying a basis for a shared state-level identity because they associate cultural interests with particular types of groups or communities. The present approach does not face this problem because it associates cultural interests with individuals and so can suggest that social unity may find a basis in people's identifications with the wider political community without having to deny that they may also identify with other communities. Finally, when the wider political community is recognized as embodying a moral tradition requiring a commitment to equal respect for all individuals' interests in pursuing meaningful lives, accommodation for particular communities no longer appears anomalous or unprincipled.

4
Situated Autonomy and Socialization

It is not an easy life. If they fall sick, they must wait for a helicopter that can take days or weeks to arrive. Sometimes an entire camp of several families will die of starvation because they are too sick to feed themselves. The average Nenets man has a life expectancy of about 45, the average woman 55. They are always vulnerable to a disastrous change in the weather, which could devastate their reindeer herds.

But when they glimpse the Russian towns at the southern end of their migration routes, the reindeer-herders feel no temptation to leave their nomadic life. "We live well," says Volodya, a young Nenets man. "In the city it's boring."

Geoffrey York, "Where Reindeer Are a Way of Life,"
Globe and Mail, 1997

Most readers will have noticed that, contrary to Socrates, by defining situated autonomy in terms of the life of open-minded conviction, I have implicitly suggested that the unexamined life may be worth living. Some may consider this is a controversial claim.

My defence of this claim can be placed within the context of a question: How can a person make the identifications he or she developed through socialization his or her own? To address this question, I make two basic moves. First, I argue *against* holding autonomy to the standard of the examined life. This involves considering and rejecting two arguments: that autonomy should be treated as the idealization of a conception of agency in terms of choice or critical reflection, and that the examined life is the good life. The second move involves arguing *for* holding autonomy to the standard of the life of open-minded conviction by suggesting that it can be distinguished from the dogmatic or unreflective life.

Making Second-Order Preferences One's Own

Consider Gerald Dworkin's definition of personal autonomy and criticism to which it has been subjected. Dworkin defines autonomy as "a second-order capacity of persons to reflect critically upon their first-order preferences, desires, wishes, and so forth and the capacity to accept or attempt to change these in light of higher-order preferences and values."[1] This conception is relevant because it shares many similarities with situated autonomy. First, like situated autonomy, it is "compatible with the recognition of a notion of (limited) authority, and can accept the relevance (if not the conclusiveness) of tradition in moral life."[2] Second, both conceptions suggest that autonomy does not need to transcend or overcome socialization but rather needs to be reconciled with it. This is reflected in Dworkin's work when he acknowledges the impact of various unchosen influences on our lives, including "parents, siblings, peers, culture, class, climate, schools, accidents, genes, and the accumulated history of the species" and suggests that "it makes no more sense to suppose we invent the moral law for ourselves than to suppose we invent the language we speak for ourselves."[3] In other words, both conceptions of autonomy accept that the identifications that inform governing assumptions and second-order preferences "are not themselves the products of our choices" but are acquired, at least partly, through socialization.[4]

As a result, both conceptions are subject to the criticism that they fall short of true autonomy because they rely on second-order preferences that have been absorbed uncritically through socialization. Marilyn Friedman, for instance, suggests that by emphasizing the act of identification, such "top-down" approaches threaten to collapse into an infinite regress. This can occur, she suggests, if second-order preferences must be held autonomously in the same way as first-order preferences – that is, if one must identify with them according to even higher-order preferences.[5]

It is in Dworkin's response to this criticism that his definition and situated autonomy part ways. He says that "if a person's reflections have not been manipulated, coerced, and so forth and if the person does have the requisite identification then they are, on my view, autonomous. There is no conceptual necessity for raising the question of whether the values, or preferences at the second order would themselves be valued or preferred at a higher level."[6] Situated autonomy cannot accept this for two reasons. First, Dworkin's response appears to reduce autonomy to normal agency, thus excluding meta-agency. Second, it provides no way of distinguishing the life of open-minded conviction from the dogmatic life: it can distinguish only people who have second-order preferences (whatever their origin) that they refer to when deliberating from wantons who do not. Thus, in John Christman's words, Dworkin's account is flawed from the outset because "it involves the claim that desires can be autonomous without foundations."[7] Situated autonomy, then, needs an alternative response.

To address the problem of the autonomy of second-order preferences and avoid infinite regress, we must explain how second-order preferences may become one's own "in some way *other* than that of critical assessment in accord with a higher principle."[8] Before developing my own response, I must consider and reject two possible solutions: the existentialist life and the examined life.

While the existentialist claim that the autonomous agent must "invent the law for himself"[9] would certainly establish the autonomy of second-order preferences, it is inconsistent with the value of meaningful life as expressed in the narrative account of selfhood. As Benn notes, practical rationality requires "criteria, rules of inference, and a conceptual scheme for grasping options" that are developed, in the first instance, through socialization. To deny this would result in such a "desocializing independence of mind that the autonomous person [would be] endowed with a capacity to live according to a law he prescribes to himself but bereft of any resources with which to fabricate such a law."[10] The existentialist position is unacceptable precisely because situated autonomy requires the person to have reasons for acting – "it is not," to quote Benn, "to have a capacity for conjuring criteria out of nowhere."[11]

Autonomy as the Idealization of a Conception of Agency

Unlike the radically free choice of the existentialist, proponents of autonomy as the examined life suggest that people make their second-order preferences their own by considering and critically reflecting on alternative preferences.

Agency as Choice and Critical Reflection

The first of two versions of this position treats personal autonomy as the ideal realization of a conception of agency as choice and critical reflection. Here the person is conceived as "an initiator of events which will go differently, sometimes at least, if [he decides] to do this rather than that."[12] Such autonomy, Thomas Hurka suggests, is an ideal of agency as "causal efficacy, of making a causal impact on the world and determining facts about it."[13]

My concern with this conception is not that it emphasizes the person as an initiator of events. It is that choice and critical reflection, which certainly can play a role in the autonomous life, are misrepresented as its essence. This can be demonstrated by comparing situated autonomy with the approaches of Hurka, who emphasizes choice, and Benn, who emphasizes critical reflection.

Choice

On Hurka's account, autonomy is intrinsically linked to choice: "Many of us think that autonomy is intrinsically good. When we imagine an ideal human life we think that its leading features must be chosen by the agent herself, and chosen from many options all fully understood." The importance Hurka places on choice is revealed when he says that it is "better to choose autonomously among ten options than to have only the best among them." The association of causal efficacy with choice appears when he writes: "We want a person to direct her life, and to do so meaningfully. To be autonomous, on at least one understanding, is to direct oneself where different directions are possible."[14]

Yet making choices among options is not the same as directing one's life meaningfully. In our approach, to direct oneself meaningfully, one needs a set of beliefs and commitments that can be treated as authoritative. Such governing assumptions, I suggested in Chapter 3, limit, through volitional necessity, the options one can meaningfully exercise in the future. Situated autonomy, then, can distinguish among the options a person faces in a way that Hurka's account cannot. Consider a person who has one option, which, given the nature of her governing assumptions, is open to her. On Hurka's account she would be more autonomous if presented with nine more options, even if none of them were meaningful to her and she would never choose them. For Hurka, this entirely predictable response makes her more efficacious. Although there is a sense in which this is true – there are more possible states of the world that she has chosen not to create – her ability to pursue significant purposes has not been enhanced.[15]

While Hurka's conception recognizes the importance of choice, it overemphasizes its value. Autonomy, contrary to Hurka, lies not in the number of options one has to choose from but in being free to pursue purposes one finds significant. A more compelling account of options and autonomy is suggested by Jon Elster when he writes: "Freedom is a function of the number and importance of the things that one (i) *wants to do*, (ii) is free to do and (iii) is free not to do."[16] Choice contributes to the individual's autonomy to the extent that the options in question might conceivably be exercised. Of course, the availability of a wide array of options may contribute to the autonomy of all citizens because different people (and the same people at different times) may find different options meaningful. Conversely, the problem with traditional societies that provide their members with extremely limited choices is not so much that people cannot choose their options but that if they find their unchosen way of life meaningless, they have no alternatives with which to replace it.

Critical Reflection

Benn's "natural person" provides an example of a conception of personal autonomy that emphasizes critical reflection. A natural person understands himself as a chooser and attaches "a kind of higher-level importance to ... arranging his conduct according to the importance he attaches to states of affairs." Autonomy, for Benn, is the apogee of natural personhood: being "a chooser is not enough for autonomy"; the autonomous chooser must also choose his standards of choice. He appraises "not only his performance, but also the very standards he uses for the appraisal." His standards become his own through "a still-continuing process of criticism and re-evaluation." He "emerges as the author of his own personality, ... his own cause, his own handiwork."[17]

Benn's suggestion that government policy require the development of citizens' capacity for such autonomy faces two major problems.[18] The first is that, where compelled, critical reflection can undermine otherwise meaningful lives. The second is that treating critical reflection as a necessary component of autonomous lives takes a valuable insight too far. To see this second point, consider how Benn conceives people making their standards their own. He rejects existential choice, but he says the autonomous agent, while socialized into traditions like other people, searches for coherence and "does not rest on the unexamined if fashionable conventions of his sub-culture when they lead to palpable inconsistencies."[19] It is in working through such inconsistencies, he suggests, that the agent makes his standards his own. This is troubling because it suggests that people can become autonomous only by choosing their own standards, which, it seems, requires that they experience the kind of "palpable inconsistencies" we have called dissonance.[20] It is unclear why anyone would want to become autonomous if it *requires* them to experience dissonance.

This might seem a tragic but unavoidable aspect of the human condition, were alternative conceptions of autonomy not available. As it is, however, situated autonomy, by relying on the life of open-minded conviction, suggests that people can make their standards their own without leading lives of critical reflection. By focusing on meaningful lives, situated autonomy recognizes the pain and angst that often accompany "palpable inconsistencies" as an unqualified tragedy that autonomy should redress, not require. As with choice, then, critical reflection is best treated as an important component of autonomous and meaningful lives, but not as its essence.

The Examined Life as the Best Possible Life

An alternative way of defining autonomy in terms of the examined life links the examined life to the best possible life. This is reflected in John Stuart Mill's famous claim that "it is better to be a human being dissatisfied than a pig satisfied; better to be Socrates dissatisfied than a fool satisfied."[21] This approach differs from that advocated by situated autonomy in two key ways.

First, although situated autonomy treats choice and critical reflection as only contingently and instrumentally valuable, this approach treats them as a necessary condition of the good life. This takes two forms. For Mill, the exercise of critical reflection to evaluate one's conception of the good life is an element of the good life itself. Choice and critical reflection enter his account through his idea of man as a "progressive being" who pursues the "higher pleasures," which are experienced through the exercise of such "higher faculties" as "perception, judgment, discriminative feeling, mental activity, and even moral preference, [which] are exercised only in making a choice."[22] For Mill, people who exercise the higher faculties to examine their lives exhibit character: "A person whose desires and impulses are his own – are the expression of his own nature, as it has been developed and modified by his own culture – is said to have a character. One whose desires and impulses are not his own, has no character, no more than a steam-engine has a character." Mill's equation of the examined life of critical reflection with the good life is also reflected when he writes: "Where, not the person's own character, but the traditions or customs of other people are the rule of conduct, there is wanting one of the principle ingredients of human happiness."[23] The idea of character is important, as E.G. West argues, because it provides the fundamental justification for Mill's advocacy of negative liberty: liberty is valuable only to the extent that it enables people to express their nature as progressive beings. If negative liberty did not promote this, it "could be dispensed with."[24] Such strong endorsement of the examined life is clearly incompatible with situated autonomy and the life of open-minded conviction, which does not require people to critically evaluate their governing assumptions.

The approach of treating the examined life as the good life also differs from the approach situated autonomy suggests when its proponents advocate state action to develop citizens' capacity for choice and critical reflection. For example, Mill, clearly unhappy with the person who is never troubled "that mere accident has decided which of these numerous worlds is the object of his reliance, and that the causes which make him a Churchman in London, would have made him a Buddhist or a Confucian in Pekin,"[25] considers the failure to educate a child's mind and to train it in the skills required to use its liberty properly a moral crime that can justify state intervention. The form of education he advocates is clearly designed to have people lead examined lives. Mill says of the effects of the education he advocates: "The rising generation would be no worse off in regard to all disputed truths than they are at present; they would be brought up either churchmen or dissenters as they are now, the State merely taking care that they should be *instructed* churchmen, or *instructed* dissenters." The emphasis on examined lives is made clear when Mill describes what he means by "instructed." While he says that schools may teach religion, he also says the state "may very properly offer to ascertain and certify that a person possesses the knowledge requisite to make his conclusions." Such requisite knowledge includes learning the views of those who oppose one's beliefs (for instance, an atheist must study the "evidences of Christianity").[26]

This willingness to use the state to advance a capacity for critical reflection as an essential element of the good life is shared by contemporary authors.

Kymlicka suggests that our "highest-order" interest in leading a good life requires that we develop the capacity to "assess and potentially revise" our conception of the good and that the state require "children to learn about other ways of life (through mandatory education)."[27] Kenneth Henley, in considering the preparation of children to exercise religious liberty, suggests standards that are more concerned with children's capacity to choose among religious beliefs than their ability to live by any one of them — for example, children must not be isolated among their co-religionists or co-atheists, they must learn of the variety of religious and non-religious ways of life, and they must learn that their parents' way of life is not socially obligatory.[28] Amy Gutmann laments that in the United States, "some citizens still hold religious beliefs that reject teaching children the democratic [value of] ... rational deliberation (among differing ways of life)." She suggests that democratic states should act on the belief that the examined life is superior to the unexamined life and use education to prepare people to engage in rational deliberation by exposing them to different ways of life and by fostering "the ability to defend their personal and political commitments, and revise those that are indefensible."[29]

This examined-life-as-means-to-best-life conception of personal autonomy is both powerful and popular, demanding a response. Richard Arneson and Ian Shapiro have issued a strong defence of state promotion of the examined life, which I use as a foil to my position: "To deny the moral appropriateness of requiring all guardians to promote in their charges the disposition to critical reasoning and the skills needed to practice it, it would seem that one must deny that an individual of normal potential competence is likely to benefit from such exercise of critical reasoning skills. One must hold that the epistemic strategy of uncritical acceptance of the values that the individual was taught is a superior strategy for maximizing the goodness of the life the individual will have."[30] This statement has two key components. One is the assumption that the only alternative to the life of critical reflection is the life of uncritical acceptance. The other is the claim that the development of critical reasoning skills is universally beneficial.

My concern with the assumption that there is only one alternative to the life of critical reasoning is that it gains much of its force from reliance on a false dichotomy. If Arneson and Shapiro are right to assume that the only alternatives are the life of "uncritical acceptance" and the life of "critical reasoning," I share their conclusion. I believe, however, that this dichotomy is false because it excludes an intermediate and more desirable orientation towards one's inherited values, which I have called the life of open-minded conviction. While I will leave the defence of the possibility of this alternative for later in the chapter, let me indicate here a subtle distinction that it reflects. The distinction concerns the implications of the claim that people *may* want to re-examine their fundamental values and ends. Unlike Arneson and Shapiro, who treat the following descriptions of lives as synonymous, I believe they represent two distinct alternatives: the life that places "a positive value on engagement in critical thinking about one's fundamental values" and the life in which one is willing "to step back from those of our current beliefs *that have been rendered problematic in some way* and to think critically about them."[31] While the first alternative is consistent with defining and promoting autonomy in terms of the examined life, the latter supports only the more modest claim that people should not be prevented from engaging in critical reflection if they so choose. If my defence of this second alternative as reflected in the life of open-minded conviction succeeds, then the move from not prohibiting re-examination of one's values to enhancing the capacity to do so requires justification, and, I will suggest below, there are good reasons to resist this.

As for the second claim, that most people are "likely to benefit from such exercise of critical reasoning skills," I believe it is wrong. By forcing all people – not just those experiencing dissonance – to develop the capacity to critically reflect on their way of life, the promotion of autonomy as the examined life may actually undermine otherwise autonomous and meaningful lives. The danger is that this may undermine situated autonomy by frustrating or even preventing the formation of identifications situated autonomy requires. Proponents of "liberal education" may think this overstates the problem. For example, Kymlicka writes: "There must always be some ends given with the self when we engage in such reasoning, but it doesn't follow that any *particular* ends must always be taken as given with the self."[32] This, however, ignores two points: the difference between voluntarily and involuntarily initiated critical reflection, and the process by which people initially develop secure identifications.

Consider the difference between critical reflection undertaken voluntarily in response to dissonance and that undertaken involuntarily because others impose it. When people engage in critical reflection in response to dissonance, they usually reflect only on a limited number of governing assumptions. Since most of their identifications remain unquestioned, there is little doubt about what to take as given. Such critical reflection is normal and desirable and is recognized in situated autonomy as meta-agency. When critical reflection is imposed, however, the agent may find herself without any secure identifications to take as given. As Galston suggests, the greatest threat to children who receive such liberal education is not that they will believe anything too deeply but that they will not believe anything deeply at all: "Even to achieve the kind of free self-reflection that many liberals prize, it is better to begin by believing something."[33] Rather than leading to more meaningful lives, then, the requirement that people develop the capacity for examined lives may actually cause dissonance – not something most would consider part of the best possible life.

Another danger with the coerced development of a capacity for critical reflection through liberal education is that it may actually prevent children from developing secure identifications that can inform autonomous choice. It is difficult to develop such identifications where the values, beliefs, and conceptions of the good life of one's community are presented in a neutral fashion along with the contradictory beliefs of others.[34] For people so educated, the identifications that situated autonomy presupposes may be undermined or may never develop in the first place.[35] For example, in the *Wisconsin v. Yoder* decision, Chief Justice Burger wrote: "Compulsory school attendance to the age of sixteen for Amish children carries with it a very real threat of undermining Amish community and religious practices as they exist today."[36] For some, especially those who begin with no clear givens, the strain of such comparison, reflection, and choice may prove overwhelming: "Preferring even a negatively valued identity to a bundle of contradictions, they become delinquents and dropouts ... [or they may] prefer to submerge themselves totally in a single role commitment ... For these people, the alternative to heteronomy that they fear is not autonomy, which they lack the strength and confidence to aspire to, but an intolerable anomie – a moral lawlessness, in which there is no freedom, but only a total lack of orientation."[37] This appears likely to have been the case with the residential schools to which many Native children were removed in Canada during the nineteenth and twentieth centuries. The Royal Commission on Aboriginal Peoples reported: "At almost every hearing intervenors raised the issue of residential schools and spoke of their impact on Aboriginal language and culture, and of the chain of abuse, violence, suicide and problems with the law that the experience of these schools had generated in Aboriginal communities."[38] Thus, there are good reasons to believe that using the state to require people to develop a capacity for critical reflection is not likely to benefit everyone.

Even if the examined life were defended by the lesser claim that it offered the only chance of leading the best possible life, it could not justify the use of state power to educate people against their will or the will of their parents and communities. The refusal to exercise this power can be grounded in the desire to show equal respect for meaningful life. This requires us to show maximal (although not unlimited) respect for the lives they have actually created. Thus, we should refrain from imposing our conceptions of the good life on them, including conceptions that valorize critical reflection and the examined life. As Galston suggests, to implement proposals such as Gutmann's, a state would have to throw "its weight behind a conception of the human good ... at odds with the deep beliefs of many of its loyal citizens."[39]

Further, equal respect for individuals requires that we let people decide for themselves if they want to risk undermining otherwise meaningful lives on the chance that they might develop better ones. To suffer anomie is terrible when unavoidable. It is much more so where it could have been avoided but for the actions of the state. If proponents of the examined life could guarantee its success, this argument would lose much of its force. As it stands, those who define the autonomous life as the examined life should refrain from imposing their views on others and restrict themselves to proselytizing on the basis of their arguments about its desirability.[40]

Scientific Principles and True Selves

This last criticism – that defining the good or autonomous life as the examined life is dangerous because its proponents cannot guarantee that people will be able to replace any sources of givens they might lose in the process – would lose much of its strength if it could be demonstrated that people will always be able replace secure identifications. Some who define autonomy as the examined life appear to attempt this by assuming that people *will* always have sources of givens — such as scientific principles and the person's "true self" – available to them. Reliance on such givens, I argue, is flawed and only reinforces the criticism that critical reflection in and of itself is incapable of generating the secure identifications on which autonomy depends.

Scientific Principles

Richard Lindley explicitly treats scientific assumptions as a reasonable source of givens. He defines autonomy such that its perfect achievement is beyond normal human intelligence: autonomy "in regard to a particular set of beliefs, desires, or actions does require an agent's relevant beliefs to be true, and that she be able to give a justification for them." On this basis he suggests that people can be autonomous only in limited areas of their lives. People do not need to be autonomous in their theoretical scientific beliefs since, he writes, such beliefs "are unlikely to have wide ramifications throughout our life projects." Rather, people should be concerned about autonomy in "matters of opinion" (religious, moral, and political beliefs) since there is no guarantee of truth in such matters. Indeed, there is "a danger that people will adopt life styles not because they represent truly their best options, but because they have not properly considered alternatives, and are carried along by the force of public opinion, or at least the opinions of influential individuals or groups."[41] The irony is that, contrary to Lindley, the same could be said about scientific beliefs – there is no guarantee of truth in these matters either, and most people *are* carried by the force of public opinion.[42] Thus, paradoxically, following Lindley's approach, a person may appear autonomous in a "matter of opinion" even though in determining her position she relied on a scientific belief that she accepted entirely on the authority of others.[43]

Examples of such contradictions are not hard to find. Consider liberal attacks on a favourite target: conservative Christians. Diana Meyers says the mother who "is a fundamentalist preacher's poorly educated daughter who has never been exposed to less benighted theological doctrines and who has never questioned her faith" acts heteronomously (that is, not autonomously) when she protests a teacher's dismissal of creationism.[44] As Katherine Addelson notes, Meyers does not apply the term "heteronomous" consistently: "The fundamentalist mother is faulted for accepting creationism uncritically, but we do not ask about the schoolteacher's acceptance of Darwin – evolutionary theory is true, is it not?"[45] Similarly, Henley says of religious teaching in private education: "Surely no school could be licensed which refuses to teach scientific theories on the grounds that they contradict religious revelation. It is a difficult question whether religious objections to scientific theories should be discussed in schools; such discussions would tend to be partisan and would encourage a view that science and religion are competitors."[46] But why this inconsistency? Why are proponents of the examined life so shy about examining scientific beliefs? A possible reason is that, consciously or not, they realize that without some ground on which to stand, without some givens to base deliberation (such as scientific truths), it would be impossible for people to act autonomously at all. This reliance on scientific beliefs may be interpreted, then, as an unintended acknowledgment that autonomous deliberation presupposes second-order preferences that critical reflection alone cannot generate.

Autonomy conceived in terms of the life of open-minded conviction avoids these problems by not requiring people to critically reflect unless they encounter dissonance. This does not commit it to accept relativism of truth, or to reject the idea of progress. So long as there is no perfect paradigm, we must accept that traditions (including scientific traditions) are all we have and that people can begin only where they are, starting their search for truth or the best life from within traditions. Rather than rejecting the idea of progress towards truth, this approach claims that progress can be made only within or across traditions. Even Mill, a defender of progress, acknowledged that "it would be absurd to pretend that people ought to live as if nothing whatever had been known in the world before they came into it."[47] Progress is not impeded by people who identify with traditions but by those who refuse to allow their traditions to evolve. Rather than promoting progress, training in neutral facts and exposure to various ways of life may simply undermine people's identifications and leave them without access to the traditions on which real progress depends.

True Selves
Besides scientific principles, another source of givens that has been defended by proponents of autonomy as the examined life is the idea of a true self – that a person has a true self that can be distinguished from those aspects of his or her character that society has imposed. For example, Lindley writes:

"Autonomy requires a person to reflect on the influences of her culture, to sort out those of her felt impulses which are really expressions of her unique nature, from those which are merely the product of external influences."[48] The idea of a unique nature is useful in two ways. It suggests a firm and enduring ground from which people may conduct deliberations, and it suggests a reason why the examined life and critical reflection might lead to the best possible life: one's best possible life is the one that reflects one's true self.

What, it seems reasonable to ask, is this true self or unique nature? Joel Feinberg provides a reasonable account in his idea of "rudimentary character" – a person's "temperamental proclivities and genetically fixed potential for the acquisition of various talents and skills."[49] I have no doubt that people possess such rudimentary characters, but I believe they are insufficient to build a life on. As Lindley acknowledges, the idea of unique natures "is consistent with the view that it would be impossible for a human being to develop a character except within a culture."[50] The true self, it seems to me, lacks sufficient substance to guide deliberations and support autonomous lives.

A different problem with the idea of a true self is this: since one does not choose one's true self, all the issues of how one makes one's guiding principles one's own are reintroduced. Consider how Feinberg resolves the following paradox (described by Henley) of how a child may be socialized without undermining his or her self-determination: "Whether a certain sort of life would please a child often depends on *how* he has been socialized, and so we cannot decide whether to socialize him for that life by asking whether that kind of life would please him."[51] To resolve this, Feinberg appeals to the right of children to an "open future," a right-in-trust that is violated "if certain crucial and irrevocable decisions determining the course of [the child's] life are made by anyone else before he has the *capacity of self-determination* himself." Feinberg says the paradox is resolved if the parents make decisions for the child consistent with the child's rudimentary character. He says this "is the most sense that we can make of the ideal of the 'self-made person.'" If achieved, "the child's future is left open as much as possible for his own finished self to determine."[52]

I think much is true in Feinberg's account of the true self, but it does not eliminate the issues we have been discussing. First, although a person's pre-social or natural preferences may clearly be his, this approach offers no account of how the agent might make them his own. In fact, it seems to treat one's true self as being just as constitutive as the communities of communitarians. Second, true selves, at least as Feinberg describes them, do not seem to provide the critical perspective that accounts of autonomy as the examined life require. While critical reflection may reveal that my true self is patient and dextrous, this offers little insight into whether I should choose to be a spear-master in the Sudan or a pool shark in Chicago. In answering such questions, Feinberg's account still relies on socialization.

Diana Meyers develops an account of a true self that seems to address the problem of how one's true self might become one's own. This account also suggests how a person's true self might contribute to her autonomy without either denying the reality of socialization or abandoning people to it. To achieve this, Meyer suggests that we accept that all socialization involves some degree of coercion, stop trying to overcome socialization, and, instead, socialize people for autonomy.[53]

Meyers sees the autonomous life as squeezed on two sides. On one, socialization threatens to displace a person's internal desires: "If people are products of socialization, they have no true selves, and they cannot control their own lives." On the other side, she recognizes, autonomy can be undermined by too much reliance on one's true self. Even if a person's true self were coherent and harmonious (which she doubts), autonomy requires more than simply following its dictates – that would mean being determined by one's pre-social true self.[54]

Given these pressures, Meyers says autonomy depends on the exercise of three "autonomy competencies": self-discovery, self-definition, and self-direction.[55] Through self-discovery a person uncovers her true self; through self-definition she develops an authentic self out of her true self; and through self-direction she governs herself in accordance with this authentic self. Critical reflection enters Meyers' account by way of the ideas of autonomy competency and the authentic self. The authentic self "is the repertory of skills that make up autonomy competency along with the collocation of attributes that emerges as a person successfully exercises autonomy competency."[56] Those with autonomy competency possess and exercise two types of skills: self-referential responses (the ability to consider what it would feel like – shame, pride, and so on[57] – to be a certain way or do a certain thing), and critical rationality (the ability to consider values independent of one's feelings or inclinations –forbearance, loyalty, and so on).[58] The autonomous person poses the question "'What do I really want, need, care about, believe, value, etcetera?" and then acts on her answer, correcting herself when she gets it wrong.[59] Autonomous people "choose" the constitutive qualities of their authentic selves by placing themselves in situations and acting in ways "designed to bring about such changes."[60] Despite its reliance on the idea of a true self, and much like situated autonomy, this account of autonomy is fairly flexible, and compatible with many types of lives. It also recognizes that self-identity is always open to evolution and transition.[61]

Meyers thinks the lives she advocates are valuable, despite the potential for complexity and stress, because those who lead them support their self-respect and avoid future disillusionment by setting their life plans on secure psychological foundations. This ensures that their "personal ideals and life plans befit their individual strengths and needs and that their lives match their personal ideals and life plans."[62]

Although I have much sympathy for Meyers' approach, I believe its reliance on true selves leaves it unable, like all approaches emphasizing critical reflection, to account for the kinds of secure identifications that support people's ability to conduct complex deliberations, or what Meyers calls exercising autonomy competency. Consider Meyers' response to the suggestion that children be exposed "to a wide variety of options in a nonprejudicial fashion through public education." Meyers recognizes that "bombarding children with sundry options will only confuse them," but she thinks the problem could be remedied by having this policy "dovetail" "with a method of nurturing the competency of autonomy ... [by developing children's] ability to select [options] that match one's authentic self."[63]

The problems with this, as I see it, are that true selves, and the authentic selves derived from them, lack sufficient substance to inform such deliberations and that while methods for developing such substance can be imagined, the self that emerges may not necessarily be the person's own. One method by which people might develop sophisticated governing assumptions from their true selves would be to have them construct successively more complex self-identities by being presented with choices between simple options, which would then be increased in complexity. It would be unreasonable, however, to describe such a process as being determined by the person's true self. Instead, it would be at least as much the product of those who determined the nature and order of the choices the person was presented with. This does not pose problems for situated autonomy, which accepts the unchosen nature of moral starting points, but it is a problem for accounts of autonomy that justify the examined life and critical reflection on the ground that it allows people to choose lives that reflect their true selves. As Christman notes, such "integration can be achieved by the fiercest manipulations emanating from outside their person."[64]

Approaches that define personal autonomy as the examined life cannot ensure that the requisite capacity for critical reflection can be developed without jeopardizing the development of the secure identifications on which situated autonomy and meaningful lives depend. Further, appeals to enduring bases of givens in scientific principles or true selves are also unconvincing. This leaves one last justification for defining autonomy as the examined life: that it is intrinsically valuable. This, however, requires demonstrating the rather implausible claim, which, to their credit, none of its proponents makes: that the exercise of critical reflection is valuable even if it undermines people's governing assumptions and leaves them with meaningless lives.

Why Autonomy as the Examined Life?
Those who define personal autonomy as the examined life extend the reasonable insight that people *may* need to question, revise, and transcend received beliefs (in our words, to exercise meta-agency) to the unreasonable

conclusion that autonomy *requires* critical reflection and choice. The danger, I have argued, is that requiring people to develop this capacity may undermine the secure identifications on which autonomous deliberation and meaningful lives depend.

If my argument is correct, then it might be asked why anyone would ever have defined autonomy in terms of the examined life? I believe that at least part of the explanation lies in the almost exclusive focus that advocates of this approach often place on modern plural societies. People in such societies often find themselves *thrown* into many varied, often conflicting and irreconcilable, communities and traditions. This creates a potential for dissonance unknown in well-functioning traditional societies. In such circumstances, critical reflection and meta-agency will often need to be exercised. The danger in focusing on such societies is that one may assume that this is true for all.

Stanley Benn seems to recognize this danger when he writes that his conception of autonomy as "a critical, creative, and conscious search for coherence within [one's] system of beliefs" presupposes "a system of beliefs in which it is possible to appraise one sector by canons drawn from another."[65] Where such systems of beliefs prevail, critical reflection is often necessary to avoid loss of self-respect, disillusionment, and the conclusion that one's life is not good. Thus, he describes autonomy as critical reflection as "an ideal for troubled times."[66] This, however, is just the point. While some may choose to pursue the examined life as their personal conception of the good life, critical reflection is universally valuable only for living in troubled times and through personal crises. It is not valuable for all people in all circumstances. This is what proponents of autonomy as the examined life fail to recognize.

This observation is compatible with two ways of dealing with critical reflection in definitions of personal autonomy. One is to define autonomy as the examined life but to limit its application to modern plural societies. This is Benn's approach (and Raz's, see Chapter 1, pp. 30-31). The other approach, the one advocated here, is to treat autonomy as universally valuable – that is, valuable in all societies, be they modern or traditional – but to define autonomy in terms of the life of open-minded conviction. This allows us to recognize the valuable contribution that choice and critical reflection can make to meaningful lives, without assuming that they are equally valuable to all people living in every kind of society.

Distinguishing Open-Minded Conviction from the Dogmatic Life

The question that motivated this discussion of situated autonomy and socialization is this: How can a person make the identifications he or she developed through socialization his or her own? This question reflects the conviction that if people's purposes, or first-order preferences, are to be autonomous, we must be able to characterize the governing assumptions or higher-order preferences that lead them to adopt these purposes as their own. If it cannot be shown that this is the case, then it is unclear that there really is a significant difference between agents who exercise situated autonomy and dogmatic agents. I have argued against basing this distinction on the requirement that autonomous people live examined lives. I will now complete the case by arguing that the life of open-minded conviction should be the standard for situated autonomy because people can make governing assumptions developed through socialization their own, without leading examined lives. People can do this by having "good reasons" for continuing to adhere to them. If this succeeds, we can reject the ideal of the examined life while continuing to distinguish personal autonomy from dogmatic or unreflective lives.

While normal agency, which involves people regulating their lives by reference to governing assumptions, distinguishes those who exercise situated autonomy from wantons who act capriciously, it does not distinguish them nearly so clearly from people who lead dogmatic or unreflective lives, for the dogmatic may also derive significant purposes from governing assumptions. A key difference is that when those who lead lives of open-minded conviction experience dissonance, they respond by exercising meta-agency, while those who lead dogmatic lives refuse to re-evaluate their beliefs, acting like Stanley Benn's heteronomous agent who "looks in his uncertainty to others for cues, to point a way to resolve his dilemma, or ... suppresses the intrusive ideas, denying to himself that they are or ever were his."[67]

This distinction may become apparent when people experience dissonance, but it will not help distinguish the autonomous from the dogmatic in their exercise of normal agency. A critic may take this to mean that the distinction between the dogmatic life and the life of open-minded conviction is not real, and thus situated autonomy fails as a conception of personal autonomy. For example, Benn, a proponent of the examined life, would probably describe situated autonomy as autarchy, not autonomy. The autarchic agent "knows what he will (or would) choose because he knows his own preferences, character, and beliefs, and expects to act on his decision." For the autarchic agent to be autonomous (on Benn's account), his values and principles must be "*his*, because [they are] the outcome of a still-continuing process of criticism and re-evaluation."[68] For the present argument to succeed, this possibility must be ruled out.

First it must be conceded that, given the accounts of these types of lives, it would be difficult, if not impossible, to make this distinction by simply observing people's behaviour. The dogmatic and the open-minded would appear very similar when exercising normal agency.[69] The difference, I will argue, is only likely to appear if we consider how these people might explain why they continue to adhere to their traditions: people who lead lives of open-minded conviction can give accounts of the validity of their governing assumptions and the traditions that inspire them, while those who lead dogmatic lives cannot.[70] The ability to articulate such accounts gives those who lead lives of open-minded conviction "good reasons" for continuing to adhere to their identifications and, in their capacity to articulate these good reasons, they make their governing assumptions their own.

Now, this raises a further question: What can it mean to have good reasons for continuing to adhere to a tradition or an identification? At a minimum, it means that an identification must do what we value it for: it must connect the person with a context of value that informs and supports the pursuit of subjectively significant purposes. What counts as evidence in this case is that the context of value exhibits consistency, both internally and externally, with objective reality. An example of this is David O. Brink's moral coherentism, which suggests that continued adherence to "one's moral belief p is justified insofar as p is part of a coherent system of beliefs, both moral and non-moral, and p's coherence at least partly explains why one holds p."[71] Thus, one's reasons for continuing to adhere to a tradition are better the more consistent the tradition is with one's other beliefs, both moral and non-moral. When such consistency is present, those who adhere to a tradition find it provides a useful map for navigating what they see as objective reality and so does not lead them into inescapable contradictions.

Now, some may suspect that I am merely reintroducing the requirements of the examined life through the back door. This is not the case. To offer such an account of good reasons, a person neither needs to have experienced dissonance nor, especially, to have stood back from one's values and way of life and critically evaluated them in comparison with other ways of life, as the examined life requires. Just as in arithmetic, it is reasonable to have faith in the validity of a tradition if, in following its dictates, a person experiences "no disturbing conflict, either between results already obtained or between a result already obtained and one he might reasonably expect to obtain if the sequence were to continue."[72] As for evidence of the absence of inescapable contradictions, MacIntyre points us in the right direction when he says that no tradition is either self-sufficient or self-justifying: "The standpoint of a tradition cannot be presented except in a way which takes account of the history and the historical situatedness, both of traditions themselves and of those individuals who engage in dialogue with them."[73] Thus, evidence of the absence of contradictions may be drawn from the tradition's own history, which may show that it has survived sporadic dissonance-generating experiences without proving self-defeating.[74] This need not require any comparative evaluation of other traditions or contexts of value.

A key advantage of conceiving the relationship between autonomy and socialization in terms of the life of open-minded conviction is that it allows us to avoid the problem of infinite regress associated with other conceptions of autonomy that rely on higher-order preferences. In appealing to good reasons, we set a standard by which people make their governing assumptions their own and so put an end to the "potentially endless sequence of evaluations" involved in justifying principles by appeal to increasingly higher orders of principles. Such decisive identification, however, is not arbitrary and escapes the charge of dogmatism, precisely because we have reasons.[75] As Harry Frankfurt says of volitional necessity, identifications, despite elements of historical contingency, "may be both self-imposed in virtue of being imposed by the person's own will and, at the same time, imposed involuntarily in virtue of the fact that it is not by his own voluntary act that his will is what it is."[76] Decisive identification is important because there is more to autonomy than meta-agency: while we need our governing assumptions to be our own and to have some confidence in their validity, achieving the kind of assurance that the examined life demands is inconsistent with other needs essential to the experience of a meaningful life, such as exercising normal agency and pursuing significant purposes.

The distinctiveness of lives of open-minded conviction can be illustrated through examples that contrast them with dogmatic lives. The dogmatic can offer no evidence that she has made her governing assumptions her own. For instance, she may say of her decision to engage in a practice: "My people do this, and so I must do like they do."[77] The explanation of someone leading a life of open-minded conviction, however, would attempt to account for the validity of the assumptions on which she decided to act. For instance, she might say something that amounts to: "This practice is part of the way of life that has proven satisfactory for me and past generations of my people. It provides me with practical guidance for ordering my life, and has, so far, yielded no inescapable contradictions."

It may be useful to consider more specific examples. Compare the behaviour of Jehovah's Witnesses in the Nazi concentration camps who, according to Bruno Bettelheim, refused to use their positions of authority to "feather their own nests" or abuse and mistreat fellow prisoners[78] with that of the character of Stepan Arkadyevitch in Tolstoy's *Anna Karenina,* who absorbed his principles from his favourite newspaper, neither reflecting on them nor being aware that they changed with those of the paper.[79] While neither Arkadyevitch nor the Witnesses (from what we are told) ever stood back from their values and ways of life and critically evaluated them in comparison with other ways of life, the Witnesses appear to be in a position to defend their continued adherence to their tradition in a way Arkadyevitch is not. For instance, they might explain that they have confidence in their beliefs and have never seriously considered other ways of life because their tradition has never failed as a source of meaning and motivation, and by following these beliefs they have always, more or less, attained the results they expected. Arkadyevitch, not even aware of the source of his principles, could offer no such account. To the extent that the Witnesses are able to offer one, their principles are their own, while to the extent that Arkadyevitch cannot, his principles are merely his. This example illustrates how situated autonomy can apply the standard of open-minded conviction to distinguish autonomous from non-autonomous lives, by providing an account of how people may or may not make their governing assumptions their own that does not require the kind of critical reflection associated with the examined life.

What are the potential criticisms of the relationship that has been suggested between situated autonomy and identifications resulting from socialization? One likely criticism is that this account relies on a radical relativism that cannot support the kind of intercultural judgment and evaluation a liberal account of justice requires. For instance, it may be asked, does this account require us to tolerate the racist who finds her purposes worthwhile and can successfully execute them? The suspicion of radical relativism results from the ultimately subjective nature of the test of whether someone has good reasons for continued adherence to a tradition: the test turns on whether the tradition actually sustains meaningful lives for its members, not whether it should according to an objective standard. This follows from the rejection of the Cartesian scepticism associated with intrinsic meaning: even if a tradition could be invalidated on the basis of facts or beliefs of which its adherents are not aware or do not understand or accept, this cannot determine whether their reasons for continued adherence are good, as reasonable evaluations must, as a general rule, carry weight within the tradition.

While the test of meaningfulness is ultimately subjective, we are not thereby compelled to accept a radical relativism that would leave us with nothing to say to the racist. The idea of meaningful life, respect for which is the very reason we extend such deference to the judgments of others, has other requirements that can justify not extending tolerance to the racist. Respect for meaningful life also requires respect for situated autonomy, for communities that embody contexts of value, and for meaningful life itself. As I argue in Chapter 7, these values support a very thin account of universal values that can justify state interference with the internal practices of communities. Thus, for example, we do not need to tolerate the person who finds meaning in racist values, because such values are irreconcilable with equal respect for meaningful life.

Another criticism of the position that good reasons need to carry weight within a tradition is that this does not allow us to protect people from oppression that has been accepted through false consciousness. For instance, Susan Moller Okin writes that "oppressed people have often internalized their oppression so well that they *have* no sense of what they are justly entitled to as human beings."[80] The concern here is not so much with cases such as the Dinka, where the spear-masters who allow themselves to be killed appear to be in a position of privilege within their community, but with cases where those who act against their interests do so in a way that clearly serves the interests of others within the society. A good example is that of women in African cultures that condone polygamous marriage. It seems clear, at least to many who do not belong to these cultures, that this really serves the interests of men, although of course there is diversity in opinion among the women involved. For example, a husband is quoted as saying, "one wife on her own is trouble. When there are several, they are forced to be polite and well behaved. If they misbehave, you threaten that you'll take another wife."[81] The criticism, then, is that any account of autonomy that would include people who seem so clearly to be acting from false consciousness must be wrong. Carens illustrates this concern when he asks whether people's acceptance of the "legitimacy of 'traditional' authorities ... is not just the product of a manipulative system of socialization?"[82] In answering this criticism, I do not seek to deny that false consciousness captures some truth about reality, for I think it probably does, but to indicate how we should address it in light of concern for meaningful life.

In general we should refrain from using coercion or the law to enforce our judgments about the goodness of other people's reasons for accepting the authority of their traditions, even where we believe our evaluations are right in an objective sense. To do otherwise is inconsistent with respect for meaningful life. This is true in at least two ways. First, even where false consciousness is at play, it is in the nature of false consciousness that its victims consider their practices to form their own significant purposes. To prevent them from pursuing them is to interfere with their pursuit of meaningful lives. Second, it may be that we and those whom we observe simply do not share the same understanding of interests. For example, while the feminist may consider the Christian housewife to have been deceived into denying her interest in pursuing a career, the Christian housewife may consider the feminist to have mistakenly rejected her interest in motherhood and eternal salvation. Who is right? From our perspective, it does not matter. Again, to be clear, I am not adopting a radical relativist position here; in refusing to enforce our evaluations of the goodness of others' reasons, we do not have to abandon them to what we consider false beliefs. Rather, we limit ourselves to trying to persuade them to see things our way by engaging them on their own terms, or on terms that we can convince them to share with us. In this way, if they come to accept our position, it is for reasons that make sense to them, not because we happened to be in a position of power that enabled us to impose our evaluations. The reverse is also true: we insist that they behave in the same way with respect to their evaluations of our reasons.

Another possible criticism is that the life of open-minded conviction involves self-deception. This may appear to be so because situated autonomy, recognizing that no tradition comprehends objective reality in its totality, does not require people to be able to defend every last detail of their traditions. The criticism, I suggest, confuses this fact with self-deception. Real self-deception is inconsistent with situated autonomy because, by its very nature, self-deception disregards the requirement that our beliefs sustain meaningful lives by bridging the gap between the world of values and the world of blind causes. A behaviour that may seem like self-deception is a person's deliberate avoidance of influences she believes may lead her to reject her present commitments. Some religious sects, for instance, may avoid higher education or television because they believe that if exposed to these for too long, they would reject their present way of life. Many people avoid participation in cults and experimentation with cigarettes or drugs for similar reasons. Unlike self-deception, however, this is self-governance. As Frankfurt says of "volitional necessity," "not only does [a person] care about following the particular course of action which he is constrained to follow. He also cares about caring about it. Therefore, he guides himself away from being critically affected by anything – in the outside world or within himself – which might divert him or dissuade him either from following that course or from caring as much as he does about following it."[83] Such behaviour is self-deceptive only if what is avoided are not undesirable influences but dissonance-generating evidence based in objective reality.

Conclusion

By treating meaningful life as an essential interest, we have developed a reconfigured conception of personal autonomy. The key insight of situated autonomy is that lives do not have to be characterized by critical reflection to avoid being dogmatic. Appeal to the life of open-minded conviction and reliance on "good reasons" provide an alternative both to the claim that one only really makes her preferences her own through choice and critical reflection and to the insistence that one's preferences are simply one's own.

Having considered the foundations of meaningful life, we are ready to turn to Part 3, where advocacy positions are developed on the basis of these foundational assumptions.

Part 3:
A Politics of Liberal Multiculturalism

5
Defining Communities and Justifying Accommodation

The things you value, that which makes life meaningful to you are not the same with us in many respects. But we respect your beliefs. We expect nothing more in return.

Benny Atencio, Santo Domingo Pueblo, in *Amendments to the Indian Bill of Rights*, US Senate, 1969

Part 3 explores the practical implications of the foundations of meaningful life. This is achieved against the background of two propositions suggested in Part 2. First, the wider political community should be treated as a social union of individuals united to facilitate the equal opportunity to pursue meaningful lives. Second, while, other things being equal, the uniform distribution of political rights and economic resources to individuals is sufficient to satisfy people's autonomy interests, and freedom of association, as advocated by Kukathas, is sufficient to sustain interests in identification with communities, other things are not always equal. If we accept these propositions we must also accept that equal respect for individuals may require asymmetrical distributions of rights and resources and that universal individual rights and particular cultural accommodations represent equally legitimate tools the state may employ to achieve the single goal of equal respect for meaningful life. The aim of Part 3, then, is to develop a principled politics of liberal multiculturalism and provide the grounds to reject the characterization of communal accommodations as anomalous and illegitimate.

This chapter is divided into two main sections. The first section acts as a thematic introduction to Part 3 by drawing attention to an issue that is implicated in one way or another in all of the policy questions it raises: communal definition. I then begin to develop a politics of liberal multiculturalism in the second section by applying the foundational assumptions laid out in Part 2 to consider the conditions under which claims for cultural accommodations can be justified. Since accommodations for members of one group often limit the resources and opportunities available for non-members to pursue their purposes, equal respect for meaningful lives requires that only those claims for accommodations which are necessary to sustain meaningful lives succeed. This second section introduces the case studies explored further in Chapters 6 and 7.

Communal Definition

Communities may contribute to the meaningfulness of their members' lives in three ways. First, and primarily, they connect individuals to contexts of value that inform significant purposes. Communities that embody moral or purposive traditions perform this function. Second, communities that embody moral traditions can contribute to meaningful lives by providing a context that sustains other communities whose contexts of value directly inform people's purposes. Finally, communities may provide a context that facilitates people's ability to pursue significant purposes.

In the normal course of events, valuable communities exist unnoticed and do not require special protection. This is generally a good thing. As Amelie Oksenberg Rorty notes, "Cultural cohesion and continuity are sometimes best served by allowing ends and norms to remain vague and ambiguous so that contending groups can interpret them in their own ways without pressing for a consensus on their specification."[1] This cannot remain the case once special accommodations are extended to a community. The community must be defined: first, to evaluate whether it warrants protection; second, where protection is warranted, to determine the extent of legitimate protection; and third, to define membership – that is, who has a right to enjoy the accommodations. The very process of definition, however, is fraught with difficulties.

Problems with Communal Definition

The problem of communal definition has implications that permeate all major aspects of policy involving communal accommodation. To extend protection to a community, we need to have some idea of its nature and its membership. The problem, as I noted in Chapter 1 (p. 22), is that these two aspects – the community's nature and its membership – are so inter-related that it is unclear where to begin. On the one hand, if we begin with the community's nature, a likely strategy to discover it is to see what the community's members have in common; this, of course, presumes we know who its members are. On the other hand, if we begin by studying the members, we need to know the nature of the community in order to identify them. Hence the circularity.

I point out this circularity not to suggest that it is impossible to define communities and their membership but to begin the process of mapping out the complexity and potential sources of conflict to which it is susceptible. As Parekh writes of "Asian values," the "fact that some [citizens of Asian countries] do not share these is immaterial. After all, the racists, sexists and many conservative members of western societies do not share the value of equality, yet these societies rightly consider it central to their self-understanding and impose it on them without the slightest hesitation."[2] Thus, awareness of the potential negative effects of defining communities requires that we attempt to minimize such effects, not that we abandon the project altogether.

Communal definition matters because how a community is defined has important implications for liberal multiculturalism. One is that it will affect who is recognized as a member of the community. Another is that it will affect which measures, if any, are required to sustain the community. Combined with the problem of circularity, the implication is that communal definition is always likely to be contentious because people's stakes in the outcome can be high and because there will rarely be clear and uncontested principles available for resolving the issues.

Now, who has a stake in the outcome? The answer is everyone in the political community, but, of course, to varying degrees. We can best discuss the stakeholders by dividing citizens of the wider political community into two groups: those who claim membership in the community requesting accommodation, and those who do not – that is, non-members. Those who claim membership have several interests in how the community is defined, including that the community be defined in such a way that they qualify as members. If a person actually depends on access to the community to secure meaning in his life, it is vital from his perspective that he gain the recognition necessary to participate in the community. The potentially undesirable effects of this are noted by Rorty: "A liberal state attempting to preserve a culture must, of course, specify the identity of the culture. But cultural descriptions are politically and ideologically laden ... The implicit cultural essentialism of a good deal of celebratory multiculturalism disguises the powerful intracultural politics of determining the right of authoritative description."[3] Thus, communal definition can affect people's ability to sustain meaningful lives since it can result in people being excluded from the community.

Such problems can arise if a community is defined so narrowly that its membership criteria are too exclusive. This can reflect a conflict between the members' collective need to protect the community and individual members' need to exercise normal and meta-agency. This usually pits those who impose exclusive or essentialist definitions of membership that threaten the "more complex understanding of multiple identities that change both over time and according to the context"[4] against those who identify with the community and rely on it, but who, often through the exercise of situated autonomy, have come to challenge such essentialist definitions. Serious harm can result if the membership criteria exclude not just those whose beliefs or purposes are inconsistent with the community's survival but also those who pose no such threat and rely on their identification with the community for meaning.

Typically, definitions are too narrow where those who are excluded are committed to the community's goods and values but disagree about how the values have been interpreted or put into practice. A newspaper account of a dispute in a Sikh community in British Columbia provides an example of such conflict.[5] Equality, a basic tenet of Sikhism, is said to be expressed in *langar,* the after-service meal in which "everyone prepares the food together, sits together and eats together." The newspaper story relates a controversy over whether equality requires all to eat on the floor or whether it is consistent with the use of tables and chairs. While no perfect definition of this community is probably forthcoming, it seems clear that any definition excluding people who identify with the community and accept the value of equality (while taking one or the other position on the *langar* issue) would be too exclusive to be consistent with respect for meaningful life. Conversely, the exclusion of those who reject the value of equality altogether would seem to be consistent. Thus, communal definition can be problematic when it leads to membership criteria that are too exclusive.

While overly narrow definitions of membership can give rise to conflict, problems also arise when criteria are too broad. One concerns free riders – people who try to benefit from a community without contributing to its survival. Not all free riders seek the same benefits. For instance, some may wish to access a community without doing anything to sustain it. Coulombe provides the example of "French-Canadian parents [in Quebec] who wish to send their children to English schools as long as nobody else does the same. This way their own children might have better chances at upward mobility and Quebec would remain French!"[6] In other cases, free riders are simply interested in the privileges associated with membership. This is an undesirable manifestation of the phenomenon Kukathas described as group boundaries shifting with political contexts (Chapter 1, p. 20). For example, it has been said of returnees to Pueblo communities: "Now that tribal lands have shown great economic potential, those Indians are looking back to the reservation, not so they can identify with those who stayed and hold on to vestiges of tribal entity and thus far preserved it, but so they may claim property rights."[7]

A problem with membership criteria that do not exclude free riders is that the actions of these free riders may undermine the context of value that makes the community valuable for its more committed members. For example, Coulombe writes, in discussing Quebec's language laws, that "with community membership come certain duties to respect the good of the community, especially if non-respect leads to the disruption of the community's values that are central to its identity."[8] Similarly, Harrison Bull warned of the effect of returnees to Canadian Indian reservations under Bill C-31 (which returned legal Indian status to women who had married non-Indians): "Bill C-31 will accelerate the loss of the Cree language and culture because of the permitting of non-Cree-speaking persons into [the reserve] ... Many of the reinstatees and their children no longer speak Cree, and many have little appreciation of Cree culture. Bill C-31 undermines the customs and values of traditional Indian families and communities."[9] Emory Sekaquaptecco Jr. described Pueblo returnees as "Indians who have experienced life away from the reservation for extended periods and have become habitual [sic] in the individual rights concepts of their economic and social surroundings."[10]

A second interest of those who claim membership is that the nature of the community be defined such that it receives the protection it needs to survive in a form that will allow it to perform the functions for which they rely on it. For example, if an ethnic community is defined and preserved purely in its linguistic characteristics but religious aspects that many of its members actually valued were thereby allowed to be undermined, this interest would not have been satisfied. Third, and finally, those who claim membership in a community have an interest in the community being defined so as to exclude those whose beliefs and purposes are inconsistent with the community's survival.

Non-members have reciprocal stakes in the definition of communities that receive protection where such protection imposes burdens on them. Such burdens may be monetary (for example, taxes to finance subsidies) or may involve lost liberties or opportunities (for example, denial of the right to use certain parcels of land or to post signs in one's language). Also, as the definition of a community affects the size of its membership, non-members have an interest in it being less inclusive rather than more inclusive. Similarly, as the definition of the community affects the type of protection it needs, non-members have an interest in it being defined so that the protection is least burdensome.

Another concern for non-members is that overly broad membership criteria may lead to their being treated as members of communities with which they do not identify. People can be involuntarily included in a community's membership in two ways: community members who reject their membership in a community may be denied freedom of exit, and communities may impose membership duties and obligations on people who do not identify with the community. The danger in both cases is that involuntary members may be forced to fulfil obligations or participate in practices they either find meaningless or that frustrate the purposes they have set for themselves.

So far I have suggested that the definition of the nature of a community has implications for who can belong to the community, the nature of the protection it receives, and the weight of the burden this will place on non-members. I have also suggested that arriving at such definition is likely to be difficult. Let's now turn briefly to a case that made its way to the Canadian Supreme Court, to illustrate how complicated this can be in practice.

Complexities of Communal Definition in Practice: *R. v. Powley*

R. v. Powley concerned two hunters from northern Ontario who claimed their rights as Métis were violated when they were charged for hunting moose without a licence.[11] The Supreme Court of Canada held that this did in fact constitute a violation of the "right to hunt for food in the environs of Sault Ste. Marie" (19). My concern is not with the question of whether the Métis should have been entitled to this right. Instead, I wish to discuss it because it illustrates how communal definition affects communal membership, the nature of protection, and the burdens placed on non-members, as well as how even fairly precise definitions will always be open to contestation.

We can begin by noting how the court defined the community: "Aboriginal rights are communal rights: They must be grounded in the existence of a historic and present community" (24). The specific "historic and present" community was described as the Métis community "in and around Sault Ste. Marie," which predated the signing of the Robinson-Huron Treaty in 1850 (24). This specification of the community had important implications. First, while it does not unambiguously determine which individuals will be found to belong to the community, it does set clear parameters for who can and who cannot be recognized as members. The court suggested three factors for making this determination. The first was self-identification (31). The second, ancestral connection, followed from the definition of the community as historic and present: "We would require some proof that the claimant's ancestors belonged to the historic Métis community by birth, adoption, or other means" (32). Finally, of the third factor, community acceptance, the court wrote: "The core of community acceptance is past and ongoing participation in a shared culture, in the customs and traditions that constitute a Métis community's identity and distinguish it from other groups" (33). The significance of the court's definition of the community in terms of historic continuity was driven home, however, when it wrote: "No matter how a contemporary community defines membership, only those members with a demonstrable ancestral connection to the historic community can claim [this] right" (34). Clearly, then, the court defined the nature of the community such that membership for the purpose of accessing hunting rights can never be available to those who satisfy only the self-identification and community acceptance criteria. Had the court not included this historical element in its definition of the community, membership could have been much more inclusive.

R. v. Powley also illustrates how the definition of the nature of a community can affect the types of protection that can be claimed. Having defined the community by its continuity with the historic community, the court indicated that only those aspects of the present community that reflect this historical continuity qualify for protection. The right to hunt was deemed suitable because the "Métis continued to live in much the same manner as they had in the past – fishing, hunting, trapping and harvesting other resources for their livelihood" (25). The implication is that elements of the present community for which no similar continuity could be demonstrated could not justify protection. Had the community been defined purely in terms of its present nature, this would not have placed such limitations on the kinds of protection that could be justified.

The implications of this case for burdens on non-members are clear enough. Assuming that the amount of moose and other wildlife to be harvested is limited, as the number of people who are recognized as members of this community – and therefore as having privileged access to hunt and fish – increases, the resources available to others decreases. Had the community been defined so as to create a larger membership, this burden would have been heavier; had the community been defined to create a smaller membership, it would have been smaller.

Finally, further consideration of the factors the court suggested for determining membership illustrates how even fairly precise definitions can be open to contestation. The best example concerns community acceptance. All the examples the court gives of how we might determine if an individual is a member turn on the presumption that we can identify at least some of the community's members. How else are we to know if the customs, traditions, and activities in which the person petitioning for membership says she participated were those of that community and not some other? What is the use of testimony of witnesses unless we can verify that the witnesses are themselves members of the community (33)? I suspect this problem is generalizable beyond this case.

R. v. Powley indicates the importance and complexity of defining principles for determining the nature of communities that receive protection. How communities are defined affects who is recognized as a member and so allowed to participate in the community; what protection the community will receive and thus which purposes will be protected and promoted and which discouraged or prohibited; and the extent of the burdens that will be placed on non-members. It also illustrates why any approach for recognizing communities must reflect the fact that definitions will always be open to contestation.

Meaningful Life, Contexts of Value, and Communal Definition

The foundations of meaningful life developed in Part 2 can inform a practicable and defensible approach to defining the nature of communities for the purposes of extending cultural accommodations. The line of reasoning is fairly straightforward.

The argument begins from the foundational value of meaningful life. Chapter 2 suggests that meaningful lives involve the pursuit of significant purposes. These purposes, in turn, depend on the person being able to exercise situated autonomy. Situated autonomy requires having access to communities that support the governing assumptions informing autonomous decision making. Finally, communities support governing assumptions by allowing people to access contexts of value embodied in their traditions. Thus, it is argued, communities are valuable only to the extent that they embody contexts of value, provide a forum for pursuing significant purposes, or both. The implication, then, is that if accommodations are to be extended to communities out of respect for meaningful life, communities must be defined in terms of their context of value for this purpose.

It should not be surprising that this insight is reflected in the three conditions identified in Chapter 3 for justifying the extension of cultural accommodations that impose appreciable burdens on non-members. These were that accommodations are justified only where it can be demonstrated that the community contributes to the meaningfulness of its members' lives, where it can reasonably be established that people are threatened with the involuntary loss of access to the community, and where it is likely that they would be unable to replace their community with new meaning-sustaining identifications. The practical applicability of these conditions are explored in the next section of this chapter. Principles to guide the design of cultural accommodation are developed in Chapter 6.

In sum, in defining a community we must aim to strike a balance between several interests: those of people who rely on the community as a context of value, those of individual members' in preserving the fluid and multiple nature of their self-identities and identifications, and those of non-members in retaining the ability to pursue their own purposes.

Justifying Cultural Accommodation

In Chapter 3, I explore the three conditions under which claims for cultural accommodation can be justified. Here I illustrate what they might mean in practice by considering six cases: two representing national communities, Welsh speakers of Wales and francophones of Quebec; two representing indigenous communities, the Pueblo of New Mexico and the Coast Salish of British Columbia; one representing a non-indigenous traditional community, the Amish of Wisconsin; and finally, an ethnic immigrant group, Muslims in Ontario. Two points will become clear: that the problems associated with identifying and describing communities as contexts of value are not insurmountable, and that the approach developed here is applicable to all types of community covered by the liberal culturalist consensus.

Communities as Contexts of Value

The first criterion for justifying special protection is that the community contributes to the meaningfulness of its members' lives. An interesting feature of the first case, the national community of Welsh speakers in Wales, is that there appears to be no one Welsh-speaking purposive tradition. Borland, Fevre, and Denney have suggested that Welsh-speaking Wales contains four communities, each of which fits our description of communities embodying purposive traditions. Membership in the open community is available to anyone willing to share the community's purposes and embrace and promote the Welsh language and culture, "peace, ecology, freedom from nuclear contamination, and ... [the defence of] Welsh *communities* in both north and south Wales."[12] The culturally closed, religiously based community is described as "the Congregation before God, those who speak Welsh and those who share the Christian values of tolerance, freedom, democracy and family life." Membership in this community is open only to those ethnic Welsh who will share obligations to follow God's will in their lives, "to support family life, to be tolerant and respectful of others, to give everyone in Wales the opportunity to reclaim their heritage and to seek political change."[13] Membership in the culturally closed, secularly based community, which is characterized by a commitment to language and community, is restricted to "those who speak Welsh and will promote the language" and obliges people "to speak the language, promote its development, defend houses, jobs and the community's resources."[14] Finally, the racially closed community is only open to ethnic Welsh in whom *eneidfaeth*, the "Spirit of the People," flows. Obligations of membership include guarding and defending Welsh civilization, drawing nearer to the true Welsh of the countryside, and rejecting outside, especially English, influences.[15]

While these competing definitions of the Welsh-speaking community may appear to unsettle our project, this complexity at the level of purposive traditions actually suggests a shared identification with the wider Welsh-speaking community as a moral tradition. This moral tradition aims to preserve the linguistic environment that sustains all of these sub-communities. A shared value of the community so-conceived is the maintenance of a Welsh-speaking linguistic community. By focusing on the linguistic community, we are able to describe the community in a way that both includes everyone who relies on it and enables it to be protected.

The francophone national community in Quebec poses another interesting problem. Here one might question whether the community's declared shared value of promoting the French language – as "a means by which a people may express its cultural identity" and "by which the individual expresses his or her personal identity and sense of individuality"[16] – is substantive enough to contribute meaning to lives. This concern is reflected in Rorty's claim that "multicultural though they may be, the citizens of most European and

American states ... are significantly motivated by similar economic practices ... Typically, their shared identity-defining motives – and the vast range of interpretive habits they carry with them – permeate and often outweigh their cultural differences."[17] This criticism needs to be addressed because it reflects a strength of our conception of the person. Rorty's claim is directed at defences of cultural rights that rely on the cultural monist assumption that cultural communities have a special or exclusive relationship to people's identities. This is not our position. Rather, we say cultural communities are important because people's identifications with them support meaning in their lives. We make no claims about exclusivity. In the case of the francophone community in Quebec, while there can be no doubt that there is much similarity between living as an entrepreneur or a union leader in Quebec, Ontario, and upstate New York, that one fills these roles as a francophone Québécois adds a layer of meaning and purpose that would be undermined if this community ceased to exist. Thus, one may also identify with communities whose boundaries overlap these political jurisdictions without undermining one's claims about the importance of the Québécois identity.

A more troubling question about the Québécois case is whether it should be defined on a purely linguistic basis or on a linguistic *and* ethnic basis. The problem with the latter is that it risks both the inclusion of people who qualify ethnically but who do not subjectively identify with the community and the exclusion of people who do not satisfy the ethnic criterion but lead their lives in French and identify with the community. In this case, definition of the community's context of values as a moral tradition based on a life lived in the French language is apt. It provides a common denominator to both conceptions of the community while ensuring that everyone who does subjectively identify with the linguistic account of the community is able to participate.

The Pueblo of New Mexico, the first of the two indigenous cases, present a good example of a community whose description has been contested. The controversy, in our terms, turns on the question of whether the community's context of value should be recognized as requiring a commitment to a "semi-theocratic" form of government or whether some other definition is possible. This was manifested in a conflict about whether individuals who considered themselves Pueblo but who had converted to Protestantism should be excluded from membership. This conflict is addressed in Chapter 6.

What can be said about a Pueblo context of value? Having been in almost continuous contact with Europeans in one form or another (Spanish, Mexicans, Americans) since first encountering the Spanish in 1540,[18] the Pueblo have developed a culture that, although infused with many European values and ideals, remains recognizable. In terms of contexts of value, I believe the wider Pueblo community can be viewed as embodying a broad Pueblo moral tradition that sustains a context within which co-exist several communities defined by purposive traditions: Native spiritual, Spanish Catholic, and American or Anglo.[19]

The Pueblo moral tradition appears to be at odds with the values of Western individualism. The traditional Pueblo spiritualism of the pre-contact community encouraged the values of harmony, unanimity, and duty while downplaying individual freedom. These aspects were further engrained by innovations that evolved in the face of Spanish attempts to impose Catholicism and Spanish civil government. The origin of these values appears to lie in the Pueblos' being a sedentary people in an arid part of the world whose survival depended on complex irrigation systems and the whims of nature. In such circumstances it is not surprising that they developed a markedly non-personal communal religion that focused on the reciprocal relationship between the community and nature in which "man performs rites and ceremonies and nature responds with the essentials of life, withholding the bad."[20] When this is combined with the "conviction that it is the responsibility of all to work together in secular and religious activities to keep the universe functioning smoothly," it is understandable that the Pueblo would develop conceptions of virtue and vice such as those traditionally held by the Tewa Pueblos, according to whom "negative attributes such as unco-operativeness, moodiness, aggressiveness, and uncontrolled anger are considered violations of the ideal of unanimity concept, whereas generosity, hospitality, deference to the old, and a mild and conforming demeanor are accorded high value."[21]

The emphasis the Pueblo place on unanimity and harmony appears to have been reinforced by their experience of the Spanish. Many Pueblo found no inherent contradiction in sincere adherence to Catholicism while continuing to practice their Native religion. Each religion addressed different concerns: Pueblo religion dealt with the here and now (rainfall, illness, warfare, communal relations); Catholicism dealt with life after death. Thus, both the church and the kiva (the Pueblo religious building) are important religious structures "where the worship of two sets of deities are conducted separately."[22]

However, the refusal of the Spanish authorities to accept dual religious loyalties necessitated a collective response that could not have succeeded without rigid communal compliance. In particular, it required a strict compartmentalizing of religious life: "Those dances and rites that aroused no opposition or displeasure from the non-Indian population were given openly and frequently, indeed as if these activities were all that remained of their indigenous culture. But behind closed doors, in heavily guarded areas, there was the performance of another set of complex rites shorn of all borrowed elements from the intruding culture. These were the ceremonies that in all their pagan glory offended Spanish civil and church authorities."[23] Survival of the Pueblo religion required that compartmentalization be extended to

Spanish civil institutions. The traditional Pueblo social organization, which required civil institutions to control religious as well as civil functions, had been sustained by the practice of having secular officers of the civil government mask "the identities and activities of the native officers who are additionally concerned with ceremonial matters." In effect, they carried out the decisions of a "de facto governing group" of ceremonial leaders constituted by "a hierarchy of native 'priests.'"[24] This has been described as "theocracy" or "quasi-theocracies."[25] Maintaining such a compartmentalized existence could only have reinforced the traditional values of harmony and unanimity and would have left little room for the tolerance and individualism characteristic of the wider American community.

This experience has resulted in the development of a distinctive Pueblo community with its own way of life and its own context of value. Despite internal diversity – the Pueblo community "encompasses some forty thousand people speaking six mutually unintelligible languages and occupying thirty-odd villages stretched along a rough crescent of more than four hundred miles"[26] – a reasonable account of the values that characterize this moral tradition would need to include a sense of communal duty, a desire for harmony, identification with the land, and a keen sense of Puebloness. These values are embedded in the social forms constituting the Pueblo community.

The sense of duty and preference for communal harmony over individual achievement and aggrandizement are reflected in Pueblo practices, institutions, and ways of thinking. The traditional Pueblo special events calendar, for instance, contains no days to commemorate individuals' accomplishments since, as Suina and Smolkin explain, in this "group-oriented society ... individual status has been of minimal importance."[27] Institutionally, this is expressed in the requirement that in lieu of taxation, all tribal members "perform certain community functions which will benefit the whole tribe."[28] It is also expressed in ways of thinking: the belief that making oneself useful to "the people that I care about and to my community," and making "a commitment to your group of people" is "what Zuni is all about";[29] in the rhetorical question "What is the goal of every society or government? Is it not harmony?"; and in the fear that "one man, one vote" majority rule is incompatible with the practice of consensus seeking.[30]

Regarding identification with the land, Ortiz suggests that the fact that the Pueblo have never been displaced from their homelands has contributed to their cultural survival because "the Pueblos only believe in what they see and experience, and in their homeland they can see what they believe."[31] For example, for the Tewa Pueblo, this means having a religious shrine located two miles north of town.[32] For the Taos, it means the return of Blue Lake (the "sacred place in which life began") to Native control after a seventy-year struggle.[33]

Finally, the Pueblos' keen sense of identity is expressed, reinforced, and constantly reinterpreted through the complex ceremonial-festival networks that Ortiz says "may well constitute the single most important mechanism of cultural survival and revitalization that the Pueblos have."[34] Dance, especially the communal burlesquing of non-Pueblo groups such as the Comanche and Navajo, and the individual burlesquing by "clowns" of Others such as tourists, Catholic priests, Bureau of Indian Affairs school teachers, politicians, and village members who have "behaved in an unacceptable manner" performs two significant functions. It serves a function of boundary maintenance; dance "simultaneously expresses what is Pueblo and what is not Pueblo ... [and] reminds the Pueblo people of community obligations, their beliefs, their values, and their vision of the world." It also appears to perform what we could call collective meta-agency by helping the Pueblo, who "have strong notions of world order and boundaries," make sense of and adapt to their ever changing world.[35] Through ritual dance they "take important events of the past that intruded upon them and freeze them into place ... lock[ing] those events comfortably onto their own cultural landscape. This renders what may have begun as a disturbing and disruptive historical intrusion into a permanent, ... unvarying and therefore, unharmful, part of their communal experience."[36]

Thus three purposive traditions can be identified within this broad Pueblo moral tradition: Native spiritual, Catholic, and American or Anglo. Suina and Smolkin argue that despite much mutual interpenetration, the Catholic and Native religious communities "remain very separate and distinct in overall philosophy and forms of expression."[37] In fact, Catholicism has gained such importance for "a small segment of the Pueblo population ... [that they] have chosen not to participate in native religious ceremonies."[38] The American or Anglo context of value is reflected in both communal practices and individual values. For instance, American cultural celebrations such as Christmas, President's days, and Thanksgiving are integrated into the Pueblo ceremonial calendar; Halloween is a tri-cultural event – it is an American cultural celebration whose Christian roots, All Souls' Day, have special resonance with Natives who believe in ancestral spirits.[39] Those who identify with this community might be characterized as sharing convictions like these: "The reservation, regardless of what may be said, is part of the United States of America and should abide by the same laws, rules, and regulations as anyone else"; and "[the United States] includes the Indian reservation. We are not a different nation."[40] These purposive traditions are nested within the broader Pueblo moral tradition, and individuals may consistently identify with more than one.

In the case of the Pueblo, we are able to provide a fairly substantive account of the core values of its moral tradition. This, we shall see in Chapter 6, is essential to discussing the kind of protection it should be afforded *and* to considering the question of how to deal with internal minorities, in this case, the Pueblo Protestants.

Unlike the communities discussed to this point, where relevant contexts of value have been associated with moral traditions, the indigenous community of the Coast Salish of British Columbia is defined by a purposive tradition – the practice of the Spirit Dance. While not all Salish are dancers, the dance and the social gatherings called big dances, to which spirit dance are integral, appear to embody and express a context of value that defines the community and helps sustain meaning in members' lives. The functions of spirit dancing are evident from two perspectives: the dancers' and the observers'.

The practice of the spirit dance has changed from pre-contact times. Then it was believed that to "produce either food or wealth, a man had to have one of a number of special skills which ... were acquired and practised with the aid of the supernatural." Such aid was believed to usually arrive in the form of a vision during which "the seeker encountered some animal – real or mythical – which conferred upon him a particular skill and became, in anthropological language, his 'guardian spirit.' The seeker also usually received a ... 'spirit song,' which came to him some winter later in life and made him sick. A shaman or ritualist recognized the sick person as ... a 'new dancer' and helped him to control his song and ... to dance with it in a state of possession."[41] Today, spirit dancers' songs are rarely associated with specific skills or professions: they no longer suggest "I am a great hunter, or a great canoe maker, or warrior."[42] Although the Salish themselves have explained the continuing functions of spirit dancing in many ways – as therapeutic ("If we can't sing, we'll get sick!"), as an expression of the Indian Way, as an instrument of social control[43] – Suttles and Amoss believe it performs several latent functions. For Suttles, it acts as an expression of identity: to spirit dance is to proclaim, "I am an Indian."[44] He says the "big dances" have "become the vehicle for the survival of a good deal of potlatch behavior," which has declined with the integration of the Salish into the modern economy.[45] In addition to spirit dancing, big dances involve "the work," a remnant of the potlatch in which people engage in complex naming and gift-giving traditions that affect their status within the community.[46] Amoss believes these rituals perform the latent functions of keeping people from assimilating into the dominant society by preventing them from fully participating in its economic system,[47] and of promoting in-group solidarity by giving "people a chance to affirm their worth as individuals and as Indians in a milieu from which whites are excluded."[48] Big dances seem to provide members of the many Salish peoples with a "common pilgrimage" – to use Benedict Anderson's term – by "getting people from different parts of the Salish area together."[49]

As Amoss suggests, the community defined in relation to the Spirit Dance provides its members with a system of meaning. The Spirit Dance grounds, in our terms, a purposive tradition that expresses and validates central communal values for both dancer and observer: personal autonomy ("The dancer's relations with the supernatural are direct, singular, and immediate. There can be no interference between a person and 'what he has'"); kin solidarity ("A person's vision is his alone, but he cannot really develop a full relationship with his vision unless his kin support him during the initiation process"); and differential social rank (to attain prestige, one must do things right, which "includes knowing how to behave, knowing how to reply when called as a witness, knowing what to do in the event of an accidental fall or loss of part of a costume, as well as being able to pay for things.")[50]

The inclusion of kinship in the definition of the Coast Salish community draws attention to a controversial issue. Some will not be comfortable with the inclusion of ascriptive elements such as kinship, race, and ethnicity in definitions of membership. For example, Kymlicka rejects race and descent as bases for membership in societal cultures because they "have obvious racist overtones." Instead, he recommends defining "national membership in terms of integration into a cultural community," which he specifies as a willingness "to learn the language and history of the society and participate in its social and political institutions."[51] A second concern is that such criteria might exclude people who identify with a community's context of value but fail to satisfy such ascriptive criteria. A third and final concern is that community members may fail to respect individuals' autonomy and self-identification by treating everyone who fits an ascriptive description as members, including those who do not subjectively identify with the community.

A case involving the initiation of a British Columbia Salish spirit dancer is a good example of this last concern. Two of the traditional processes by which one can become a spirit dancer are consistent with voluntary membership (seeking one's vision on a solitary journey and having one's dream come unsought while suffering grief), but the third, inducing a person's spirit song "by means of a ritual abduction and isolation," is not.[52] In the British Columbia case, a man was grabbed and initiated into the spirit dance tradition even though he clearly did not identify with the community: "He never authorized anyone to have him initiated into the society, and he did not want to be a member of it. He knew very little about the religion of the Coast Somenos people. He was not, and is not, really interested in learning about their culture. He was not brought up in it and lived off the Reserve most of the time."[53] Imposing this process on a person who did not identify with the community demonstrated a lack of respect for the self-identity he had constructed for himself.

Although these concerns are serious, the suggestion that membership in communities be open to anyone willing to learn and participate in its culture also has considerable problems. One is that a key element in the self-understanding of many ethnic and cultural communities is the belief that members of the community share a common ancestry. Another is that one of the core values uniting members of some communities is a commitment to the project of sustaining and perpetuating the community so-defined. For example, Tim Schouls suggests that the source of Aboriginal identity in Canada lies "within ancestry, history, location, and the abiding ties of loyalty and affinity that these connections generate."[54] This is certainly true of many indigenous communities, but it is also true of non-indigenous communities. Further, such understandings of communities are not inherently racist; one doesn't have to believe all other communities inferior to sustain a commitment to one's own community. If we are concerned about the role communities play in sustaining meaningful lives, we cannot declare all such communities unjust simply because some of them might be racist and intolerant.

Another reason for resisting such open membership is that if minorities were required to admit anyone who professed and could demonstrate a commitment to participate in their communities, this could ultimately lead to their demise. No matter how committed outsiders might be to a minority's way of life, it is unlikely that those who were not raised in the culture will ever understand it in much depth. If enough of these wannabes were permitted to join a community, they might, by their numbers, misunderstandings, and the foreign values and practices they bring with them, undermine the ability of the original members to sustain the community among themselves and, more important, to reproduce it in their young.

An especially complex issue is raised by one significant way by which outsiders enter communities: marriage. This is a hard case. On the one hand, respect for situated autonomy leads us to desire to respect the individual's wishes in one of life's most important choices – the selection of a marriage partner. On the other hand, where members of minority communities marry non-members, allowing those members to remain in the community necessarily involves admitting the non-member spouse. In such cases, I think it is best to insist on respect for community members' situated autonomy by prohibiting the placement of arbitrary barriers such as race and ethnicity on who one can marry and who can remain in the community. Any threats the spouse may pose to the community's survival should be addressed like any other threats, by applying the non-ascriptive elements of formal membership codes, as discussed in Chapter 6, pp. 130-31.

And so, definitions of communities that include ascriptive elements can be justified under three conditions: where community members are unable to disentangle the ascriptive elements from the community's context of value; where inclusion of the ascriptive elements does not inherently entail denial of respect for other people's interest in leading meaningful lives (for example, where it is not inherently based on theories of racial superiority);[55] and where these ascriptive elements are not used as a prima facie basis to expel members based on their selection of marriage partner.

Returning to the discussion of cases, the Amish who were involved in the much-discussed case of *Wisconsin v. Yoder* provide an example of a non-indigenous traditional community. Amish communities provide another example of a context of value embodied in a narrow purposive tradition. Their tradition emphasizes rejection of institutionalized churches, a "return to the early, simple, Christian life de-emphasizing material success, rejecting the competitive spirit, and seeking to insulate themselves from the modern world ... a fundamental belief that salvation requires life in a church community separate and apart from the world and worldly influence ... [and] devotion to a life in harmony with nature and the soil."[56] Given the narrow focus of the community's shared purposes, there appears to be no way to define it such that those who did not share these convictions could be included in its definition of membership. This is not especially problematic, though, since anyone excluded on this basis would not seem to be harmed in their pursuit of a meaningful life. I return to the discussion of the Amish, and *Wisconsin v. Yoder,* in Chapter 7.

The final case involves an ethnic immigrant group, Muslims in Ontario. A subgroup, the Islamic Institute of Civil Justice (IICJ), wanted to establish arbitration panels under Ontario's then Arbitration Act to adjudicate disputes according to Sharia (Islamic law).[57] The Arbitration Act allowed parties to sign an agreement to authorize a third person to adjudicate their disputes about some matters of family and inheritance law according to an agreed-on set of principles or legal system. Such agreements could cover division of property upon dissolution of marriage, spousal support, and matters concerning children, such as custody, access, support, and moral and religious education.[58]

Here the context of value is clear enough: it is broadly embedded in Islam as a purposive tradition. The particular community that would be formed around the IICJ's demand, however, would be more narrowly based, constituted by those who shared IICJ head Syed Mumtaz Ali's understanding of the Sharia of minorities. Natasha Bakht summarizes Ali's position:

> Muslims in non-Muslim countries are expected to follow the Sharia to the extent that it is practical. According to Ali, until recent changes to the Arbitration Act, Canadian Muslims have been excused from applying Sharia in their legal disputes. Now that arbitration agreements are considered final and binding, "the concession given by Sharia is no longer available to us because the impracticality has been removed. In settling civil disputes, there is no choice indeed but to have an arbitration board.[59]

I think it is clear that for those who share Ali's interpretation of their obligations under Islam, the creation and use of such an arbitration board would constitute a case of volitional necessity.

Further benefits of making such accommodation have been noted by Marion Boyd in her report to the provincial government on the matter. One is that "arbitrated decisions may be more acceptable to the parties, and more reflective of some elements of the parties' shared values." Other personal benefits include conducting the arbitration in one's own language and respect for privacy. Allowing groups to apply their own personal law may also promote people's interests in their community by enabling groups to "maintain their cultural identity, by allowing them to continue to control their definitions of family and community."[60]

Together, these cases demonstrate the practicality of the first criterion for justifying cultural accommodation by showing that it is possible to identify communities' contexts of value. In the process it has also demonstrated an important strength of this approach. Unlike many of the approaches discussed in Chapter 1, a foundational approach is able to discuss the nature of all of the types of cultural community represented in the liberal cultural consensus (national, indigenous and traditional, and immigrant and ethnic) without straying from its core normative language of meaningful life, communities-as-contexts-of-value, and situated autonomy.

Threats to Communal Viability

The second criterion for justifying cultural protection is that the community reasonably demonstrates that its viability will be threatened without it. In Chapter 3, several distinctions were drawn that are relevant here. One was between measures that impose burdens on non-members and those that do not. Accommodations that do not impose burdens do not need to meet this test. For instance, the Sharia arbitration panels some Muslims in Ontario attempted to establish under the province's Arbitration Act would not have to meet this test because, if anything, they would reduce burdens on non-members by relieving pressure on the court system.[61] A second distinction was drawn between remedial cases where communities are clearly being undermined and preventative cases where cultural accommodations are requested on the assumption that the community will become unviable without them. Remedial cases are fairly straightforward. An example is the Innu community in Labrador that recently gained national notoriety for its high rates of drug abuse, alcohol abuse, and suicide.[62] Preventative cases, the focus of this section, are more challenging, because they necessarily rely on counterfactual assumptions. Yet, despite this hypothetical aspect, reasonable and plausible conclusions are possible.

In *Ford v. Quebec*, the evidence presented was sufficient to convince the Supreme Court of Canada that legislation designed to preserve and promote the place of the French language in Quebec represented "a response to a substantial and pressing need." Evidence included the declining franco-phone birth rate, the assimilation of francophones outside Quebec, the pref-erence of immigrants to assimilate into the anglophone community, and the "dominance of English at the higher levels of the economic sector."[63]

Similar evidence can be marshalled to demonstrate the precarious status of Welsh-speaking Wales. The population of Welsh speakers has steadily declined in both absolute and relative terms over the last century.[64] The inability to create suitable employment has resulted in significant out-migration. Deindustrialization has undermined the "coalfield communities ... where the largest numbers of Welsh speakers in Wales were to be found."[65] And the immigration of non-Welsh speakers, especially English retirees, has compounded the effects of emigration by reducing available housing stock and forcing prices up.[66] The cumulative effect has been a dilution of concentrations of Welsh speakers to the point where it is increasingly difficult for them to pursue their purposes in Welsh. As Gareth Elwyn Jones notes, "The health of the language lies not only in the actual number of speakers but also in the contexts in which it is spoken ... The numbers of communities in which Welsh is the normal language of communication, so recently contiguous over the whole length of west Wales, continued to contract in the last decade [to 1994]."[67]

The Pueblo and Coast Salish already receive accommodation in the form of communal ownership of land and limited self-government. If we ask counterfactually whether the perpetuation of such protection is necessary to preserve their communities, the lamentable experience of American Indian tribes that lost protection through allotment and termination policies suggests that it is.[68] Specific to the Coast Salish practice of spirit dancing, a threat seems to have come from a judicial ruling that the practice of "grabbing" is unlawful because it involves the illegal use of "force, assault, injury and confinement."[69] While I have argued that spirit dancing is of central importance to the community's context of value, this does not appear to be true of the practice of grabbing initiates. That there exist alternative non-coercive and voluntary ways to initiate dancers appears to make grabbing indefensible.[70] If somehow it could be shown that grabbing was so integral to the community that its prohibition would make the community unviable, provisions would to be needed to ensure only those who subjectively identified as community members could be grabbed and that all community members agree on the possibility of being grabbed as an obligation of membership.

Finally, as Chapter 7 discusses, it seems a reasonable supposition that the ability of the Amish to socialize their children into their way of life would be endangered if they were not provided accommodations such as the ability to keep their children out of urban high schools.

A corollary to this second criterion reflects concern about the burdens that such accommodations may place on non-members. In addition to demonstrating that they will be threatened with destruction if they do not receive the requested accommodation, communities must also demonstrate that such protection can reasonably be expected to make the community viable. As Raz suggests, in determining whether to satisfy a community's request, we must consider that the requested protection is likely to change "the prospects of survival for cultures it supports."[71] M. Estellie Smith's description of a successful sociocultural system provides a nice model for what I mean by viability: "There is a sufficiently viable population for the reproduction of new members who mature committed to the continuity of the socioculture's identity writ large (i.e., details may vary, but basic principles remain)." She includes as possible evidence: "that members state a preference for the life-style of their own natal society; that the majority, despite other available options, prefer living within their natal community to leaving and adopting a 'foreign' life-style; and that members explicitly strive to make whatever adjustments are considered necessary to ensure the continuity of the socioculture."[72] Where long-term viability is not assured, protection may be extended in a way that recognizes the burdens it imposes on non-members by limiting it to a period sufficient to allow members to reorient their identifications and integrate into new communities.[73]

As with identifying a community's context of value, the condition that communities demonstrate that they face threats to their viability appears to be achievable in practice.

Inability to Make New Identifications

The final criterion is that the community provide evidence that its members would be unable to make new meaning-sustaining identifications from among the available alternatives. Given the need to rely on counterfactual arguments to assess such claims, it is too much to expect precision in these matters. This said, a few examples illustrate the kinds of claims that might satisfy and fail to satisfy this criterion.

An example of what a successful argument might look like can be constructed from Amoss' explanation of why the many Nooksak (a subgroup of the Coast Salish) found it difficult to replace their identification with the spirit dancing community. The short answer is that none of the alternative religious communities available to the Nooksak was capable of allowing them to express such values, which were central to their identities, as a personal and immediate relationship with the supernatural, being Indian, and social hierarchy. A slightly longer answer involves assessing the alternatives. Amoss tells us that while the Nooksak found Pentecostalism appealing because, "like spirit dancing, [it] offer[ed] opportunities for affirming personal worth in a supernatural context," it provided no basis for affirming their worth as Indians. Conversely, while the Indian Shaker Church shared Pentecostalism and spirit dancing's encouragement of "spontaneous emotional expression," it was not as successful as the practices that accompany big dances at expressing the value of social hierarchy or inequality.[74] Thus, there appeared to be no viable alternative communities that would permit the Nooksak to express the key values they cared about.

Similarly, the Pueblo spiritual community and the wider Pueblo community require specific communal forms of political, social, and economic organization that would be difficult, if not impossible, to sustain and express in the main available alternative – the wider American society. Meaning in lives whose purposes presuppose the importance of values such as harmony and communal obligation would be difficult to sustain if communal land ownership were abandoned and the Pueblo were to integrate into the competitive political and economic systems of the Anglo community. The case is clearer with linguistic communities such as the francophones in Quebec and Welsh speakers in Wales. To the extent that their members have constructed lives in the context of these linguistic communities, the surrounding anglophone communities do not constitute reasonable alternatives.

Of course, the members of many communities could not establish similar claims. A fairly straightforward case might involve congregants of a shrinking church community or parents of a linguistic minority community whose church or school was facing closure in a city in which there were other viable churches or schools of the same denomination or language for them to join. This case, however, would be made more ambiguous if their institution was the only one of that particular nature within a reasonable driving distance. Another case difficult to justify is that of an isolated, resource-based community in which the sole industry was closing. While it is likely that people would have constructed identities based on the way of life the town provided, the strength of any claim they might make would be weakened by the existence of other communities sharing the same national culture in which they might employ their skills and pursue their purposes, and it being well known that resource towns don't last forever.

Conclusion

This chapter began the process of developing a politics of liberal multiculturalism by translating the underlying assumptions that constitute the foundations of meaningful life into principles to guide practical policy decisions. As we have seen, creating cultural accommodations necessitates defining the nature of communities and their membership, and the interests various groups have in the outcome are such that the process will almost always be complex and conflictual. The best way to address this is to adopt the principle of defining communities in terms of the contexts of value they embody that support meaning in their members' lives. Corollary principles may help determine when membership criteria might legitimately include ascriptive characteristics. While practical application of the general principles for identifying legitimate claims will vary with contexts, the principles provide sufficient guidance to ensure that the room for variation is highly constrained.

6
Designing Cultural Accommodation

> In our tradition, there is the principle that when one party benefits and the other party loses little or nothing, the first party shall be permitted to proceed ... Sure it's absurd to and irrational to believe that your life is going to be changed by the presence of a wire, but it's even more absurd and irrational to oppose it.
>
> Emeritus Chief Rabbi Lord Jakobovits, quoted in Calvin Trillen, "Drawing the Line," *The New Yorker*, 1994

If it is determined that a community warrants cultural accommodation, how should such accommodation be designed? Given our conception of the person, any principles must respect three key insights: first, individual members of a cultural community share an interest in the preservation of the community as a context of value; second, individuals also have private interests in maintaining freedom to define their self-identities and pursue their purposes by exercising situated autonomy; and third, both the nature of the communal context of value and the self-identities of individuals are open to change over time. Given such competing interests, any discussion must be sensitive to the possibility of conflict. On the one hand, the invocation of both shared and private interests creates the possibility of intracommunal conflict; where this gives rise to conflicts between interests in identification and autonomy, neither interest should be allowed to trump the other. On the other hand, the existence of different communities creates the possibility of intercommunal conflict; in such cases, equal concern must be shown for the interests of the members of both communities. In both cases, resolution should be sought by reconciling interests in ways that show equal respect for the universal interest in leading meaningful lives that underlies and ultimately justifies both autonomy and identification interests.

In developing principles to guide the design of special protection, the focus on community-as-context-of-value really demonstrates its usefulness. As contexts of value, communities cannot be protected directly because they have no independent existence of their own: they exist in the minds of those who share them, and they are reflected in the projects, practices, and institutions they inspire. Since they cannot be protected directly, contexts of value must be protected indirectly by preserving the underlying conditions that sustain them. This focus on underlying conditions is crucial because it encourages the development of general principles to govern communal accommodation that can generate creative tensions that, I believe, offer the best hope for reconciling shared and personal interests within communities.

This chapter addresses the topic of designing accommodations by discussing four areas of concern. Two involve the design of communal accommodation itself: the extent of protection and the duration of protection. The other two concern the definition of communal membership: the cost of protection and limitations on protection.

Principles Governing the Design of Communal Accommodations

Chapter 5 identified two potential sources of conflict that may arise from accommodations: the definition of community membership and the burdens imposed on non-members. While some might conceive such conflicts as occurring between incommensurable collective rights of communities and the autonomy rights of individuals, the present approach suggests that these conflicts be treated as occurring between claims derived from a common underlying value: meaningful life. This perspective cannot guarantee the resolution of all conflicts, but it does suggest a way to proceed: we should aim to ensure that all citizens have an equal opportunity to pursue meaningful lives. A corollary to this, however, is that where one or both parties refuse to recognize the right of others to pursue meaningful lives, no balancing is required: their claims are illegitimate.

In thinking about such conflicts, we should begin with this observation: the more extensive the accommodation, the greater the potential sources of conflict associated with the definition of membership and the burdens placed on non-members. There are several reasons for this: factions within the community face greater temptations to exclude people for illegitimate reasons; people who are involuntarily included in the community experience greater harm; membership becomes more attractive to potential free riders; and the burdens imposed on non-members are more likely to generate resentment. All these sources of conflict can be moderated by applying the principle that protection must always be minimal. Protection is minimal when it is no more extensive than necessary to sustain the community as a context of value and to exclude people whose beliefs or purposes are so at odds with the community's values that to include them would pose a threat to its survival. Let us consider two principles intended to ensure that protection remains minimal: that protection be extended only to the minimal bases of communities, and that it be impermanent.

Minimal protection sustains a space within which the traditions of a community can be carried on without predetermining which particular interpretations or purposes will be favoured over the long run. Demands inspired by a context of value, but which do not relate directly to its survival, do not figure in determining minimal protection and must be left to fend for themselves. Minimal protection is intended to strike a balance between individuals' shared interest in protecting the community as a context of value on which all rely and each individual's personal interest in safeguarding his or her capacity for fluid self-identity and multiple identifications.

The emphasis placed on maximizing space for individuals to exercise situated autonomy may appear similar to Kymlicka's approach, but there are significant differences. One is that community as context of value applies to a much wider range of communities than does societal culture. Another is that, unlike Kymlicka, for whom attempts to protect elements of a community's character are always suspect, our focus on protecting communities as contexts of value will often justify accommodations designed to protect particular aspects of a community's character. In short, while our theory of liberal multiculturalism shares Kymlicka's desire to promote individuals' interests in autonomy, it differs in that it promotes a much more substantive conception of community and applies it to a wider range of communities.

Protection of Minimal Bases

The exact nature of appropriate measures of protection will vary with context and circumstances. In the ideal case, protection need be extended only to the minimal bases of communities. The idea of minimal bases can be understood by comparing the relationship between a community's minimal bases and its context of value to the relationship Iris Marion Young describes, borrowing from Jean-Paul Sartre, between series and group. A series is "a social collective whose members are unified passively by the objects around which their actions are oriented or by the objectified results of the material effects of the actions of others." The classic example is that of people waiting for a bus. They constitute a series in their "relation to a material object, the bus, and the social practices of public transportation."[1] The bus, and the social practices associated with it, result from human action but each particular individual experiences them as something he or she cannot change, at least not over the short term.

Unlike members of a series, who have no common goals, only a similar relationship to particular material objects and practices, Sartre's group "is a collection of persons who recognize themselves and one another as in a unified relation with one another. Members of the group mutually acknowledge that together they undertake a common project." The relationship between group and series is illustrated in the bus example: "The latent potential of this series to organize itself as a group will become manifest ... if the bus fails to come; [the riders] will complain to one another about the lousy bus service, share horror stories of lateness and breakdowns, perhaps assign one of their number to go call the company, or discuss sharing a taxi."[2]

To work the metaphor, if communities embodying contexts of value are like series, and those who share particular interpretations of the meaning and substance of the community's context of value are like groups, then the minimal bases of communities are like the material objects and practices that define the series (that is, the bus and the social practices of public transportation). The value of limiting protection to minimal bases is that it allows us to protect a community's context of values while showing maximal respect for the fluidity of individual members' self-identities and the multiplicity of their identifications. This allows communities to be preserved while minimizing opportunities for communal factions to define membership in ways that marginalize those who do not share their understanding of the community or its traditions. The same point can be put another way by considering Parekh's claim of cultures that "it is rare, even impossible, for the entire system of meaning to become a subject of contestation and dispute. The contestation is limited to some areas, and is only possible because of a broad consensus on others."[3] We might think of protecting minimal bases as trying to preserve the basis of this broad consensus while trying to avoid privileging the competing positions to the contestations.

To return to the bus metaphor, this suggests two ways of protecting the groups that arise out of the series of bus riders: we can tailor special protection to the specific characteristics of one particular group of bus riders, or we can make sure the bus keeps running and shore up the social practices of public transportation. While the first approach privileges one particular group of bus riders and likely excludes or marginalizes other members of the series, the second approach sustains the conditions for the survival of groups with many different interpretations of the meaning of the series without necessarily privileging any one of them. Applying this approach to identifying the minimal bases of communities suggests the possibility of protecting substantive communities while maintaining maximal space for expression of situated autonomy. A necessary corollary is that once such space has been provided, individuals will have to find a way to live in the community so-constituted or leave. To provide further flexibility for them would require jeopardizing the viability of the community for others.

The examples of the francophone Québécois and Welsh speakers illustrate the context-dependent nature of minimal protection. Although both communities treat the ability to conduct life in their communal language as a central value, and thus have similar minimal bases (the ability to live, work, and raise children in the communal language), the Welsh speakers' position is much more precarious than the Québécois'. The Welsh constitute a minority in their own homeland, their communities are being undermined by the immigration of anglophones, and, unlike the Québécois, who speak an international language, there is a very limited market for their cultural products. Such contextual differences can justify different types of protection to achieve similar outcomes.

The main form of protection that has been employed in Quebec is language legislation. The history of this legislation suggests the importance of ensuring that protection is minimal. Some provisions of Quebec's language law, Bill 101, have never been controversial from our perspective. The requirement that large workplaces operate in French is reasonable given the predominance of English in the North American corporate sector. So too is the requirement that newcomers to Quebec have their children educated in French: those who have chosen to immigrate presumably have purposes consistent with moving to a French-speaking community.[4] To the extent that this legislation simply ensures the ability of francophone Québécois to live, work, and raise children in French, it protects only the community's minimal bases: individuals are free to form whatever other identifications they wish within this linguistic environment.

Conflicts have arisen, however, when this legislation has exceeded what is minimal. The best-known instances are provisions that threatened the equal right of members of the long-standing anglophone community to pursue their purposes. For example, at one point, English lost status as an official language in the legislature and courts, all public signs were required to be in French only, and all school boards, municipalities, and hospitals, including those in predominantly anglophone communities, were required to use French for internal communication.[5] These provisions, as the Supreme Court ruled on the sign provisions, were neither necessary to protect the French language nor proportionate to the threats it faced.[6] Subsequent court challenges and legislative amendments have resulted in protection more in line with our position: English is an official language, local institutions may communicate internally in English, and signs need only give *predominance* to French.[7] These revised provisions do a better job of reconciling the interest of all citizens of Quebec in leading meaningful lives.

Yet this legislation may have the effect of requiring people who are ethnic Québécois by descent, but not by subjective identification (and thus are not trying to free-ride on the communal good), to have their children educated in French. This fails to respect the capacity of individuals to reject inherited identifications by exercising meta-agency. It creates a dilemma because, as a practical matter, it is difficult to distinguish free riders from people who have truly stopped identifying with the community. Such cases require us to consider the relative effect of the alternatives on the equal opportunity of all citizens to pursue meaningful lives. We must compare the harm done to community members by allowing some to free-ride with the harm done to those who no longer identify with the community by forcing them to fulfil obligations they have renounced. I believe the present situation, where francophone parents do not have a right to send their children to publicly funded English-language schools but are free to send them to private schools at their own cost, strikes a reasonable balance between respect for communal survival and situated autonomy.[8]

The Welsh-speaking community has required more extensive protection. It has received subsidies to the communications media, provision of bilingual and Welsh-medium education, official bilingualism in the public service, and linguistic provisions in housing and planning regulations. The focus on minimal bases is especially important in the Welsh case because the Welsh community has been given such a wide range of competing interpretations by its members: the open community; the culturally closed, religiously based community; the culturally closed, secularly based community; and the racially closed community (see Chapter 5, p. 103). The provision of such extensive protection always creates the danger that communal factions will attempt to control it in order to define the community on their own terms and exclude all other interpretations. By focusing protection on the minimal bases of the community, some of these sources of conflict may be pre-empted, both by retaining maximal room for competing interpretations of the meaning of the Welsh community and by reducing the burden that must be imposed on anglophones in Wales and the United Kingdom.

Communications media, especially television, are crucial to the ability to live in one's own language in the modern world. As Michelle Ryan notes, they influence "the way we see ourselves and understand the rest of the world."[9] Unlike in Quebec, the private sector in Wales has done a poor job of providing Welsh-language media. Thus, the use of public subsidy to support Welsh media could be justified on the basis that it helps ensure equal opportunity to pursue meaningful lives by supporting this minimal basis of the Welsh community. The British policy of public provision or subsidy of Welsh-language books and magazines, public radio (Radio Cymru) and television (Sianel Pedwar Cymru [S4C]), while perhaps slightly excessive in practice, is justifiable in principle.[10] Still, an ever present danger is that control of such subsidized media will be captured by those who advance an exclusive interpretation of the community. Imposing an obligation on those who access these subsidized media, perhaps by making provision of the services dependent on the collection of a user fee, might minimize this. Provision of such services would then be dependent on fairly broad-based support in the Welsh-speaking community, which would discourage factions from trying to use the media to promote an exclusive conception of the community – the effect being reduced burdens on non-members.

Another aspect of the minimal bases of the Welsh-speaking community is the ability to educate children in Welsh. A minimal approach has been taken in the most straightforward situation where linguistic communities are spatially separated. The national curriculum is consistent with equal respect for meaningful life by making Welsh a "core subject" in Welsh-speaking areas and a "foundation subject" in non-Welsh-speaking areas.[11] A harder case occurs where community size makes it practical to provide only one school with one curriculum. In 1975, the county of Gwynedd developed a policy consistent with our approach. It seeks to reconcile the interests of members of anglophone and Welsh-speaking communities by identifying areas as traditionally Welsh or non-Welsh. Welsh-medium primary education is provided in the former and bilingual education in the latter. Anglophone children who move into traditionally Welsh areas are given intensive Welsh instruction to help them adjust quickly.[12] This shows respect for all interests since the threat posed to the ability of Welsh speakers to pursue meaningful lives by the deterioration of their communities much outweighs the threat posed to anglophones who could choose to locate elsewhere and who have easy access to English-language culture outside of school.

Many aspects of bilingualism, such as printing documents, notices, and advertisements in both English and Welsh as required by the Welsh Language Act 1993, are uncontroversial from our perspective. Bilingualism policies would exceed what is minimal and place an unreasonable burden on anglophones, however, if they resulted in Welsh speakers having privileged access to public employment. This would occur, for instance, if all officials, rather than institutions, were required to be bilingual.[13] Official bilingualism could be advanced in a minimalist fashion by insisting only that institutions be bilingual and, perhaps, by instituting a policy of linguistic proportionality in public employment similar to a system of ethnic proportionality used in Italy's South Tyrol.[14]

Finally, the threat posed to Welsh-speaking communities by the inflow of anglophones and the conversion of housing to holiday homes could justify the use of special planning restrictions. Policies such as Dyfed Region's Policy CS1, which states, among other things, that "development proposals likely to be prejudicial to the needs and interests of the language will not be permitted," satisfy the minimal principle since they aim only to preserve Welsh-speaking communities. The county of Ceredigion's 1993 plan, however, appears to be excessive. It proposed "to limit occupation of new and converted dwellings in five community council areas where 70 per cent or more of the population spoke Welsh, to persons whose origins are or who have previously lived for 5 years in the district or within 25 miles of the district" and "to allocate land for employment generating purposes in the same five communities."[15] This appears to impose an unreasonable burden on newcomers by requiring them to finance economic development from which they would be excluded.

It was suggested in Chapter 5 that the Pueblo community embodies a moral tradition that sustains several purposive traditions (Native spiritual, Catholic, and American.) This case highlights the very real danger that protection extended to specific communities will be used by a faction to exclude those with whom it disagrees. This has been reflected in the past in attempts by Pueblo officials to define membership to exclude converts to Protestantism. The approach advocated here encourages us to recast our interpretation of this case from a zero-sum conflict between the community's right to enforce what it considers its standards and the individual's right to practise his or her religion of choice to a disagreement about the nature of the community's minimal bases.

The typical pattern of conflicts involving Protestant dissidents was documented by Florence Hawley in a case study published in 1947.[16] It involved several Pueblo individuals who, having converted to Pentecostalism, felt obliged by their new beliefs to proselytize non-believers and to refrain from dancing, drinking, smoking, and taking medicines of any kind. This brought them into conflict with communal authorities who considered participation in communal religious dances and deference to the decisions of the chief priest to be basic duties. The deviants were reprimanded and then, after repeatedly breaking promises to refrain from the offending activities and to participate in communal dances, were banished from the village and their access to communal lands revoked.

This case represents an excellent opportunity to demonstrate what is special about our approach, by comparing how Will Kymlicka and Frances Svensson each deal with the case. Such comparison is valuable because the contrast shows the importance of defining communities in terms of contexts of value.

The central question the case raises differs subtly yet significantly when viewed from each perspective. Kymlicka is concerned with the legitimate claims a community can make on an individual: Should village authorities have the right to expel dissidents who refuse to accept communal practices? Svensson is concerned with the amount of deviance a community should be expected to tolerate: At what point should dissidents lose their privilege to participate in the life of the community? These different perspectives inform conflicting proposals for resolution.

For Kymlicka, the Protestants raise questions of religious freedom. Having justified cultural rights instrumentally as a precondition for a conception of personal autonomy that places great emphasis on individual choice, his approach provides little ground on which to justify limitation on religious freedom.[17] As we saw in Chapter 1, Kymlicka says that once a cultural community has been protected, it should become a "cultural marketplace" within which the survival of particular practices and traditions is determined by decisions of individuals.[18] Thus, he suggests that allowing religious freedom within the Pueblo community – in effect, denying that semi-theocracy is essential to the community's description – would not undermine it as a context of choice since it "wouldn't make the Pueblo vulnerable to being outbid or outvoted on crucial issues by the non-Pueblo population ... ; nor would it create internal disintegration." This allows him to conclude that the decision by the community to expel dissidents represents an unjustifiable restriction on religious freedom: "If the goal is to ensure that each person is equally able to lead their chosen life within their own cultural community, then restricting religion in no way promotes that. Were the theocracy ended, each majority member of the Pueblo would have as much ability to use and interpret their own cultural experiences as the dissident minority, or, indeed, as members of the non-Indian community."[19] From our perspective, however, this raises two questions. First, how can we determine whether granting religious freedom will cause the Pueblo to be outvoted on crucial issues without first determining whether the Protestants are still members of the Pueblo community? Second, how can we know that the Pueblos' ability to "use and interpret their cultural experiences" has been preserved if we refuse to define those experiences? To answer either question we need a definition of the Pueblo community and its minimal bases.

Svensson proposes a different solution, one reflecting her presumption that cultural communities have intrinsic value as a natural and enduring aspect of every human's experience. She describes the cultural community as a multidimensional group that has "many interlocking dimensions or facets shared by its members – in an ideal case, for example, language, religion, ethnicity, race, *and* historical experience. It is comprehensive, in that members express virtually all of their social identities through the group."[20] Given the cultural monist assumptions underlying multidimensional groups, Svensson views the Protestants not so much as individual deviants but as bearers of the values of a foreign culture. In other words, the conflict they create is not viewed as occurring within the Pueblo community but between representatives of the American cultural community and the Pueblo cultural community. From this perspective, the degree of difference the dissidents represent could be accommodated within the community only by undermining the characteristics that define it. Thus, for Svensson, this case concerns whether the values of the minority community or the dominant community will prevail. Having decided that the Protestant converts have assumed the values of the dominant society, she says that

> there remains an "appeal" of last resort, an outlet for them – merger with the dominant society. If the rules of the dominant society are imposed upon the minority community across the board, the minority community has no place left to go, no refuge in which its values and priorities can be recognized. Of two possible injustices, the former appears to be more acceptable than the

latter, since it preserves the maximum openness of opportunity to members of both dominant and dependent communities.[21]

From our perspective, this is problematic because it presumes that individuals either identify with the dominant community or with the minority community. Although this makes the idea of the Protestants simply merging into the dominant society seem reasonable, it is inconsistent with our conception of the person as capable of constructing self-identities based on identifications with multiple communities. This conception of the person problematizes Svensson's solution by recognizing the possibility that people have constructed self-identities that rely on both their Protestant and Pueblo identifications. Again, a satisfactory solution requires a definition of the Pueblo community and its minimal bases such that we can decide whether the Protestants are members or not.

The approach based on the underlying value of meaningful life suggests a different, and I believe more satisfactory, way of understanding this situation. By assuming a conception of the person as capable of identifying with multiple communities and of having a fluid self-identity, we resist prejudging whether the Protestants remain members of the Pueblo community; instead, we view this as a question that needs to be answered. Further, our conception of communities-as-contexts-of-value enables us to answer this question by defining the Pueblo community in terms of its values and asking whether the Protestant Pueblos share them and whether their presence poses a threat to the community's continued existence.

To answer the questions posed by the case of the Pueblo Protestants, and thus to determine the extent of protection that should be provided to the Pueblo community, we must first identify the community's minimal bases. Two would seem to be communal control of traditional homelands and village self-government. Preservation of the integrity and communal ownership of traditional homelands support the Pueblo context of value in several ways: it could enable the community to maintain a concentration of members sufficient to sustain its languages and other traditional practices, such as the ceremonial-festival network; it could guarantee members access to sacred sites that express and affirm their beliefs; it could permit the expression of the value of "communal obligation" in duties such as working communal dikes and pastures; and, perhaps most important, it could sustain a separate space within which children could be socialized to become Pueblo.

Village self-government is also an expression of communal values. Many Pueblo have argued that their traditions of self-government express and embody distinctive values that would be undermined by rights accepted in the wider American community. For instance, it has been suggested that "one man, one vote" elections could undermine the legitimacy of those Pueblo governments whose authority is derived from traditional religious beliefs and, as well, that the behaviour required to succeed in competitive elections is inconsistent with the value of "harmony between the individual and his social institutions."[22] As minimal bases of a Pueblo context of value, communal control of homelands and self-government would no doubt privilege values embodied in the Native spiritual purposive tradition. By keeping protection minimal, however, the Catholic and American purposive traditions, which have managed to survive within the broader moral tradition for many years, are less likely to be marginalized in the future. I address specific questions raised by the Pueblo Protestants below (pp. 131-35).

As for Muslim Ontarians and Sharia arbitration, the existing Arbitration Act is an example of extending protection to minimal bases. The protection afforded by facilitating culturally tailored arbitration is minimal to the extent that it applies only to those who avail themselves of it; one must consent to it for it to apply. It is also minimal to the extent that it is up to the parties themselves to decide which principles they wish an adjudicator to apply. Thus, while there are several Islamic schools of thought and versions of Sharia, this form of arbitration avoids privileging any one of them by allowing the parties to choose the one meaningful to them.

This rather limited degree of protection is consistent with the status of Ontarian Muslims as an ethnic minority. As immigrants, or the descendants of immigrants, who voluntarily chose to immigrate to Canada, they are presumed to participate in the moral tradition of the wider political community. While the Islamic tradition that unites them provides a context of value rich enough to inform a self-governing community, in the Canadian context it must be treated as a purposive tradition that can justify important claims but not extensive claims such as that to self-government.

The cases discussed so far suggest that by restricting protection to minimal bases we may reconcile individuals' shared interests in communities with their personal interests in preserving situated autonomy, but we must consider the possibility of circumstances in which protection may need to be more extensive. Of course, the more extensive protection is, the more limited the ability of individual members to exercise situated autonomy. The difference, to employ Sartre's example, is like that between protecting the series of bus riders by preserving the particular bus schedule, leaving them free to form or not form whichever groups they choose in relation to it, and protecting a specific group of bus riders that has formed out of the series at one point in time. Although protecting communities at the level of minimal bases is always to be preferred, there may be circumstances where we must be willing to protect particular communities.

One such instance occurs where members understand their community as including only people identified by ascriptive characteristics such as race, ethnicity, or kinship. I am thinking here of communities, such as Aboriginal communities like the Coast Salish and possibly the Pueblo, in which the significance of the community's context of value for its members rests in no small part on the fact that they are the values of a particular kinship group. This is in contrast, say, to membership in the francophone Québécois community, which is, at least theoretically, open to anyone willing to live a French-speaking life and have his or her children educated in French-language schools. In addition to the reasons discussed in Chapter 5 (pp. 109-10), such cases pose a challenge because the more narrowly the community is conceived, the greater the danger that factions may use membership criteria to illegitimately exclude people who identify with its context of value. Consider, for example, the Sawridge band in Alberta. In 1998 it was reported in the *Globe and Mail* that while 220 people claimed membership in this band, only 27 (all but one of whom were members of the same family) lived on the reserve and so were entitled to vote in band affairs and control the membership code. This situation came about, it was alleged, because members of this faction used their majority position to force others to leave the reserve.[23]

The possibility that communities conceived in ascriptive terms may warrant protection should not be understood as an endorsement of essentialist accounts of identity. Instead, it reflects simple acceptance that, in the world as it is, some members conceive of their communities such that it is impossible for them to disentangle the community's context of value from these features. The risk that prohibiting such communal definition might pose to the members' pursuit of meaningful lives, combined with the improbability of non-members coming to identify with communities so conceived, can justify the extension of protection in such cases. Thus, it seems that ascriptive elements should be included in the minimal bases of communities under the same conditions as suggested in Chapter 5 for including them in definitions of communities: where community members are unable to disentangle the ascriptive elements from the context of value; where inclusion of the ascriptive elements does not inherently entail denial of respect for other people's interest in leading meaningful lives (for example, where it is not based on theories of racial superiority); and where these ascriptive elements are not used as a prima facie basis to expel members based on their choice of marriage partner.

Respect for meaningful life requires that protection be kept as minimal as possible. This is advantageous because by limiting protection to a community's minimal bases we pre-empt many potential sources of conflicts among members and between members and non-members. Where conflict cannot be avoided, the principle of equal respect for meaningful life provides a commensurable standard for reconciling competing claims.

Protection Must Be Impermanent
As for the duration of accommodations, respect for meaningful life requires that it be impermanent. Since it is warranted only where it is required to

preserve the community as a context of value and where the community's members rely on it to sustain meaning, accommodation can be justified only for so long as these conditions apply. This will surely disappoint those who believe communal accommodations should ensure the survival of communities "through indefinite future generations."[24] The impermanence principle simply reflects the assumption that in exercising meta-agency to sustain meaning in their lives, people may reject their inherited identifications. Respect for this capacity requires that the ability of individuals to ensure their community's survival be limited to their efforts to reproduce this desire in their young. Thus, for instance, if, as recent books have suggested, "North America's Jews, as a whole, simply don't care enough to imbibe Judaism themselves and convey it to their children," the state should not empower the community to prevent this.[25]

How impermanence is incorporated into protection will depend on circumstances. It might be made explicit by requiring community members to express periodic support for the protection. For example, the continuation of communal land ownership or village self-government for the Pueblo or language laws in Quebec could be made subject to approval through elections or through referenda taken periodically or perhaps on the signing of enough names on an initiative. This would allow a majority of community members to choose not to renew the protection if they found it unnecessary or too burdensome. In other cases, impermanence may be only implicit; in the Welsh case, were people simply to stop purchasing subsidized cultural products, or to fail to qualify as competent Welsh speakers for public employment, these protections would simply fade away. Similarly, in the case of Sharia civil arbitration, while the Arbitration Act may remain in force, private civil arbitration as a form of cultural maintenance would last only so long as individuals chose to invoke it by signing private agreements.

Principles Related to the Definition of Membership
Chapter 5 noted that to extend protection to a community we must be able to define its nature so that we can determine who belongs (p. 96). Without some definition of membership it would be impossible to know, for instance, who should have access to the accommodations or who has a right to participate in decisions about retaining them. Such definition, it was suggested, can be achieved consistent with our conception of the person by defining communities in terms of their context of value. Two principles – freedom of exit and obligations and rights of membership – are suggested for governing the definition of membership criteria consistent with the foundations of meaningful life.

Freedom of Exit
The first principle related to membership definition is that individual members

must be free to exit the community. Like the impermanence principle that makes communal membership collectively impermanent, the freedom to exit makes membership impermanent for individuals. Unlike the impermanence principle, though, freedom of exit must be respected by communities that do not receive special accommodations as well as by those that do.

Freedom of exit is valuable for several reasons. (Its nature is considered further in Chapter 7.) First, it reflects the potential fluidity of self-identity – respect for meaningful life requires that people be free to leave communities with which they no longer identify. A practical example of this is provided in Marion Boyd's recommendation that the Ontario Arbitration Act be amended "so that if a co-habitation agreement or marriage contract contains an arbitration agreement, that arbitration agreement is not binding unless it is reconfirmed in writing at the time of the dispute and before the arbitration occurs."[26] If a person's identifications have changed since he or she entered the relationship such that religious arbitration is no longer meaningful for them, this rule would allow them to reflect this change. Second, freedom of exit allows respect for fluidity without undermining the ability of the community to sustain a context of value for others who continue to identify with it. This reflects that the decision by one individual to leave a community does not in itself prove that the community is no longer valuable. Thus, the possibility of exit need not undermine the community's ability to survive as a context of value. A third reason for valuing freedom of exit is that, when taken together with the impermanence principle, it provides a measure of community members' preference for their way of life – if they really didn't like it, they were free, both individually or collectively, to renounce it.[27]

The case of Miriam Wilngal, as reported in the Toronto *Globe and Mail*, illustrates the significance of this freedom.[28] Ms Wilngal chose to leave her tribe in Papua New Guinea for the capital of Port Moresby after she had been offered to another tribe as compensation for a killing, in accordance with tribal tradition. Ms Wilngal, it turned out, wanted to finish high school, become a typist, and have her own money so she would not have to depend on a man. Several things are notable about this case. First, having the freedom to exit allowed Ms Wilngal to leave a community that could no longer support her significant purposes. Second, it allowed her to do so without undermining a community that continued to provide a context of value for those members who remained. Third, while the possibility that more women may choose to exercise this freedom may have a transformative effect on the community,[29] if the community is not subjected to involuntary culture change from outside, it should be able to respond to this pressure in ways meaningful to its members. This is reflected in the comments of Dr. John Muke, a professor of archaeology and a member of Ms Wilngal's clan: "There are certain changes that we have no choice but to accept, like women's rights and notions of equality. But there are certain things that we have to hold on to."[30]

Obligations and Rights of Membership

The fourth principle requires that the definition of membership place some obligation on members that demonstrates their reliance on, and commitment to, the community as a context of value. These obligations and rights of membership should be formalized and made public in a membership code. Such obligations could take different forms. They could be monetary. For instance, for subsidized Welsh cultural products, a funding formula might be worked out that required Welsh speakers to pay an amount roughly equivalent to what anglophones pay for similar products in English. Obligations also could be non-monetary. For example, membership in the francophone Québécois community might include an obligation to have one's children educated in French.

Such obligations could be effected by requiring communities to create membership criteria that include definitions of rights and obligations. Foremost among such rights of membership would be the right to access and participate in the community. Other specific rights would vary with circumstances. An example is provided in Sandel's discussion of the case of *Thornton v. Caldor, Inc.* The case involved a Connecticut statute that guaranteed all workers one day off per week but granted only Sabbath observers the right to choose their day.[31] This law is consistent with our approach since it extends a special right in the form of the right to people who, for reasons of volitional necessity, are unable to work on a particular day. Sandel provides a defence of such provisions that is consistent with our endorsement of the idea of volitional necessity: "The role that religion plays in the lives of those for whom the observance of religious duties is a constitutive end, essential to their good and indispensable to their identity."[32] The obligation Sandel's description implies, and which our model would require, is that, to enjoy this privilege, a person observe his or her Sabbath.

Respect for the community may also require the attachment of obligations to the right of exit. In the Pueblo case, communal ownership of land was identified as one of the community's minimal bases. If individuals were permitted to retain private ownership of their share of this communal land after exiting the community, this minimal basis would soon be destroyed. In cases like this, a reasonable obligation might require members to accept that their right to enjoy benefits associated with membership lasts only for so long as they remain members and fulfil communal obligations. The custom law of Zia Pueblo provides an example of what this might look like. It holds that "all rights in land are in the pueblo, and are under the pueblo, and all rights of use of land by allotment, inheritance, gift, sale, or lease, depend on proper performance of his duties in the pueblo ... everything moveable can rightly be taken away by a person who is thrown out of the pueblo, except sacred things which do not belong to any single person as a person, but are held in trust for all."[33] Such an obligation is consistent with respect for situated autonomy: while it may make the decision to leave the community expensive, it does not make it impossible.

The attachment of obligations to membership in communities that provide their members access to special privileges or exempts them from the application of laws would pre-empt many potential sources of conflict: it would reduce burdens placed on non-members by ensuring that only those who really rely on the community seek membership; it would reduce intracommunal conflict by reducing the attractiveness of membership to free riders; and it would ensure that only those who self-identify and understand and accept the obligations of membership are subject to its obligations.

Together, the four principles for the design of cultural accommodations consistent with the foundations of meaningful life – protection of minimal bases, impermanence, freedom of exit, and the definition of obligations and rights of membership – create competing tensions that will put pressure on individual members and community leaders to respect individuals' shared interest in preserving their communities and their personal interest in retaining flexibility to exercise situated autonomy.

Protestant Pueblos and Competing Tensions

The case of the Pueblo Protestants illustrates how the four principles can work together to create these tensions. The general points that emerge are applicable to all the cases, especially those concerning Sharia arbitration and the Amish.

By emphasizing contexts of value, we are able to treat the Pueblo Protestant case with more subtlety than Kymlicka or Svensson. In particular, by rejecting cultural monism, we are able to acknowledge communities that exist within and across cultural communities (for example, familial, religious, ethnic, linguistic), which, like cultural communities, may contribute to meaningful lives in ways that deserve recognition. And so, unlike Svensson, we can acknowledge that the Protestants may have constructed meaningful lives that depend on having access to both Pueblo and Protestant contexts of value; unlike Kymlicka, we can recognize that the Protestants' attempts to live in accordance with their new values may actually pose a threat to the survival of the Pueblo community.

To see why this subtlety is important, consider Melissa Williams' comment regarding Kymlicka's discussion of the Pueblo: "It strikes me as a tricky bit of surgery so neatly to separate religion from culture."[34] Unlike Kymlicka's societal culture, the language we have developed allows us to parse the various communities more finely. First, we are able to distinguish the wider Pueblo community as a moral tradition from the Native spiritual community as a purposive tradition. This distinction allows us to discuss the Native spiritual and Pentecostal purposive traditions, without equating either with the wider Pueblo or wider American communities. We can also recognize that the survival of the Native spiritual community is bound up with the survival of the wider Pueblo moral tradition in a way that is not true of the Pentecostal tradition. Conceptualizing the situation in this way complicates the contested terrain, but in a way that rings true; rather than viewing this case as a matter of dissident members opposing "the" community, or as conflict between members of different societal cultures, we can see it as a matter of people who identify with different religious communities contesting the definition of the wider Pueblo community with which they all identify.

From this perspective, we are presented with a genuine dilemma involving meaningful lives on both sides. The dissidents appear to be forced to decide between identifications with two communities that sustain meaning in the lives they have constructed; both embody contexts of value that inform governing assumptions and sustain forums within which significant purposes are pursued. Choice will involve significant loss whether they stay in the Pueblo community and conform, abandoning their Pentecostal identification, or leave, abandoning their Pueblo identification. The decision to leave the community must be particularly difficult, as it represents their home, their linguistic community, and access to kith and kin.[35] Meanwhile, the dominant group appears forced to choose between retaining its traditional interpretation of the community, thus imposing the difficult choice on the dissidents, and allowing the dissidents to stay without renouncing their new commitments, and in so doing altering the character of the wider Pueblo community in a way the dominant group believes will endanger it and the Native spiritual community it supports. Rather than accepting this either-or characterization, our approach suggests a different question: Can protection be extended to the wider Pueblo community in a way that shows equal respect to all individuals' interests in leading meaningful lives? Or, more practically, how can the community be preserved as a moral tradition while maximizing the space for individuals to exercise situated autonomy?

The answer to these questions, I suggest, has already been given in the four principles for the design of special accommodation. Together these work to create tensions that place pressure on both the majority and the dissidents to moderate their understandings of the nature of the wider Pueblo community in the interest of sustaining it as a context of value. Let me explain.

The principles of impermanent protection and freedom of exit place pressure on community leaders and the dominant group they represent to respect individuals' interests in maintaining the freedom to define their self-identities. Since any benefits the leaders may hope to derive from the wider Pueblo community depend on its survival, the possibility that people may reject their membership and exit should encourage communal leaders to refrain from imposing overly narrow or restrictive definitions of the community. Most relevantly, this should be the case in the definition of the rights and obligations of membership. This is made more likely by the requirement of formalized membership codes that make official conceptions of the community transparent – and open to criticism and debate. Criticism is especially likely to be generated where community members see friends and family being treated unfairly, or worse, being forced to leave the community because they cannot comply with its obligations. From what I understand of the Pueblo case, the obligations that might result could include a duty to respect the form of government presently in place (this obligation, of course, cannot be unlimited – see pp. 150-55), as well as duties directly related to sustaining the wider community, such as the duty to contribute to the maintenance of communal pastures and dikes. Minimal rights of membership might include the right to participate in the observance of communal practices; the right to participate in the use of communal property such as pastures and equipment; the right to use one's share of communal lands and resources in ways that do not threaten the wider community; and, of necessity, the right to participate in public discussions about the rights and obligations of membership.

Similarly, the principles of minimal and impermanent protection should place pressures on the dissidents to moderate their demands. If the accommodations that have been made to protect the community are truly minimal – and thus the space created for them to exercise situated autonomy by developing new identifications and pursuing new purposes is truly maximal – then the Protestants' interest in having continuing access to the community, if it is sincere, should motivate them to avoid taking actions that would put those minimal bases at risk. As well, the impermanence of protection should encourage them not to attempt to change the community so rapidly or so radically that the majority finds the community's continued existence to have lost any value for them.

I believe these and similar pressures, and the principles that generate them, provide the best hope for an optimal practical solution. Pressure from non-members in the wider state-level community – those who will also be expected to shoulder burdens associated with accommodations – should ensure that accommodations are minimal but, one hopes, not insufficient. The need to win support from the membership of the Pueblo community at large and the fear of driving too many members away will put pressure on community leaders to create membership obligations that are not excessive. With such obligations of membership in place, the actions of both the majority and dissidents will be constrained in highly beneficial ways. The establishment of clearly defined membership criteria shows respect for the meaningfulness of the dissidents' lives by providing the maximum room for them to exercise situated autonomy consistent with equal respect for other members of the community; so long as the dissidents comply with these obligations, tribal officials would be unable to expel them. If this space proved insufficient for the dissidents to pursue the purposes they had established for themselves, respect for the meaningful-ness of the other members' lives requires them to exercise meta-agency to resolve any resulting dissonance. They would face a choice that would be theirs alone to make: remain in the community, comply with obligations believed necessary to sustain it, exercise situated autonomy to the extent consistent with the survival of the community, and work to change the membership obligations over time; or leave the community, enjoy less constraints on the pursuit of their purposes, and, perhaps, enjoy limited privileges to participate in the community.

This strikes me as more satisfactory than Svensson's approach of simply allowing the community to expel dissidents or Kymlicka's position that the community should accommodate almost any new-found identification. The key advantages are that it forces both dissidents and mainstream commu-nity members to recognize that the real choice they all face is not between their ideal conception of the community and one they think is flawed but between having access to a community that meets most, if not all, of their needs and having access to no community at all. This reflects the idea that a community, at least one composed of human beings, will always be a work in progress and a product of compromise. It is a willingness to participate, and a commitment to do what is required to keep the community/conversa-tion/dialogue going, that ultimately separates members from non-members.[36] It is my contention that cultural accommodation designed according to the four principles outlined here are the most likely to foster and encourage this spirit of compromise, and that it is this spirit that is most likely to result in arrangements that show equal respect for meaningful life.

Dozier's discussion of the Santa Clara pueblo provides an example, albeit an imperfect one, of competing factions in a community moderating their understandings of the community in the interest of sustaining it as a context of value. In 1894 the Indian Agency in Santa Fe recognized a conservative faction as the de facto government. This was opposed by a progressive fac-tion that, among other things, was against involuntary participation in com-munal dances, refused to participate in the repair of dikes where it benefited only a few, and judged some Native customs by Catholic moral standards. Despite their differences, however, the dissidents continued to act in ways consistent with the preservation of the community. In particular, they showed respect for the Pueblo "values of unanimity and the need to express such values through ceremonial activity." Rather than exit, the dissidents chose, as Dozier quotes B. Aitken, to "be in the pueblo but not of it." In practice, this meant that they participated in public works when they found them acceptable and openly defied the governing faction when they did not. Overall, while their actions disrupted the functioning of the community, they were careful not to completely undermine it. The schism was repaired in 1935, when the factions agreed with an Indian Agency proposal to adopt a written constitution and an elective form of government. The result was a de facto separation of church and state.[37]

Even though the village ended up in a situation similar to that advocated by liberals such as Kymlicka, the route by which the community arrived at it allowed for the exercise of situated autonomy. Instead of moving immediately to a liberal compromise, a period (forty-one years) elapsed during which individuals could reorient their self-identities and reinterpret their identifications, and as well, a fair amount of generational replacement could occur. This enabled the villagers to make radical changes to their community without destroying it or themselves. Despite its imperfections, this example draws our attention to the importance of letting people develop their lives and communities in ways meaningful to them, as suggested by the discussion of Linton's idea of coerced cultural change in Chapter 3. As well, this example suggests that while communal survival may ultimately require the expulsion of dissidents, attempts to respect dissidents' autonomy are not futile. The dissidents at Santa Clara provide an example of how to express disagreements, even fundamental ones, while continuing to co-operate for the survival of a community and its core values.

A corollary to note is that the tensions these principles create will not always prove sufficient to create the results we desire. The conflict in the Sawridge Indian band case, for example, appears to be driven primarily by the band control of valuable oil assets.[38] When membership includes a right to share in such wealth, the tensions I have discussed are likely to be overridden: few obligations attached to membership are likely to discourage potential free riders, while the desire to control such wealth can overcome most leaders' concerns about reducing the community below a sustainable size. In cases like these where the tensions created by the four principles cannot be relied on, formalized membership codes may prove valuable by providing a basis on which disputes about membership can be settled through litigation. More long-term solutions may require the development of a political economy of liberal multiculturalism.

Conclusion

This chapter has continued the process of translating the foundations of meaningful life into the principles of a politics of liberal multiculturalism. Four principles have been suggested to govern the design of communal accommodations: protection of minimal bases, impermanence, freedom of exit, and the definition of obligations and rights of membership. Discussion of these principles shed two key insights. By encouraging us to think in terms of protecting the minimal bases of communities, we have seen how accommodations for communities can be sensitive to the complexity of self-identity and thus able to reduce the risks of marginalization by maximizing space for the exercise of situated autonomy. We have also seen that the space that can be provided for individuals to exercise situated autonomy is not unlimited. At some point, concern for the survival of the community may necessitate dissidents to choose between constraining their behaviour out of respect for communal survival or leaving the community to maximize personal freedom.

7
State-Community Relations

[When some pueblos adopted majority-rule elections,] they did so of their own free will ... [When they] felt prepared for the change, they freely adopted their own constitutions, designed to meet their own needs ... But if the changes are forced upon us without our consent – and before our people are ready for them – they will drastically undermine our ability to govern ourselves.

Domingo Montoya, chairman, All Indian Pueblo Council, in *Amendments to the Indian Bill of Rights*, 1969

To complete the development of the politics of liberal multiculturalism, two questions about state-community relations must be considered: How are claims for accommodations to be initiated and evaluated, and on what grounds may the state intervene in the internal practices of communities?

The chapter opens with a discussion of the initiation of claims and the possibility of introducing an element of international adjudication, highlighted by a case study of the recent struggles of the Mi'kmaq people of Atlantic Canada for recognition of logging and fishing rights. Principles to govern state intervention in the internal practices of communities are then suggested, with the cases of *Wisconsin v. Yoder* and Sharia arbitration in Ontario illustrating how they might work in practice.

Initiating Claims for Communal Accommodations
One key aspect of state-community relations involves communities' appeal to the state for accommodations. Chapter 5 establishes the feasibility of the three conditions under which the extension of special accommodation is consistent with respect for meaningful life. But who should make the claims? To whom should they be made? How should they be dealt with? Is there a role for international adjudication?

Who Should Make Claims for Accommodation?

In considering who should make claims for accommodation, two points arise. One is that any provisions for making claims must allow groups to represent themselves. The other is that the permanent representation of specific groups is inconsistent with the foundations of meaningful life.

I take seriously suggestions that people must be allowed to speak for themselves or their communities in any claim-making process. I accept Anne Phillips' point that while it is important *which* ideas receive political representation, it is equally important *who* represents them, since "no amount of thought or sympathy, no matter how careful or honest, can jump the barriers of experience."[1] Likewise, I accept Iris Marion Young's claim that "unless confronted with different perspectives on social relations and events, different values and language, most people tend to assert their own perspectives as universal."[2] These problems are particularly acute when the interests being represented originate in different cultures.

While it is important that groups represent themselves, we can find in the foundations of meaningful life good reasons to resist any approaches that require the predetermination of eligible groups. The problem is that such mechanisms do not reflect the multiple and fluid nature of identifications. Consider the idea of guaranteed group representation within legislative assemblies. Two of the most obvious methods for achieving this – affirmative gerrymandering (redrawing electoral boundaries to increase the voting power of a territorially concentrated minority) and reserved representation (setting aside seats to represent self-identified members of minorities) – rely on the assumption "that a single identification ... is the most important identification for the voter and that it remains so across time."[3] This does not fit well with our conception of the person. It is inconsistent with the belief that people can identify with more than one community at a time and will want their interests in each represented. It also fails to respect the belief that few communities are monolithic in their interests. Mechanisms such as the single transferable vote electoral system can address part of the problem by allowing people to choose which identification they want represented at each election, but such systems do no better at enabling people to represent more than one identification at a time.

Besides failing to reflect the multiplicity of individual identifications, such mechanisms are inconsistent with the fluidity of self-identities. Some forms – affirmative gerrymandering among them – can force people to continue to represent one of their identifications, whether it remains central to their identity or not. Even where people are not assigned such designations, their ability to reflect changes in the salience of their identifications is usually limited since elections occur only periodically. This is problematic because communities given protection today may not need it tomorrow, and communities that did not need it today may have difficulty attaining it tomorrow.

Another problem is that such mechanisms tend to create a hierarchy of in-groups and out-groups. This can create incentives for groups to engage in zero-sum conflicts over the distribution of privileged status.[4] This will ensure neither that groups really needing protection will receive it nor that group leadership will take a favourable attitude towards their members' participation in cross-cutting groups. Instead, by permanently institutionalizing identity groups, we risk granting excessive power to group leaders over their members. This increases the possibility of group closure, which could block development and change within communities. Thus, I agree with Phillips' dismissal of arguments "for the extreme reversal of current liberal democratic practice that would substitute group representation for the more general representation by political parties."[5]

If groups are not to receive special representation within the state, how are they to be identified? This, to quote Iris Marion Young, "pose[s] a paradox of political origins."[6] While we are fairly comfortable dealing with membership issues in communities that have already been organized, it is another question altogether how communities not presently recognized should become so. The answer, I suggest, is that communities that make claims for special accommodations should find their origins in self-generation. People who believe they belong to a valuable community that is in need of accommodation should exercise their freedom of association to organize their members and enter the political arena to make their case. This may require creating entirely new groups from scratch, or it may involve reorienting existing groups to pursue this goal.

In sum, claims for accommodation should be initiated by groups that find their origins in the shared perception of a threat to the viability of a valuable community. This principle will not be popular with communities presently enjoying a special role in policy processes. It does, however, promise to ensure that communities receive the protection they require, while reducing incentives to engage in the zero-sum games often associated with schemes of permanent group representation.

To Whom Should Claims for Accommodation Be Made?

The question "To whom should claims for accommodation be made?" has a short answer and a slightly longer answer. The short answer is implicit in many of the cases discussed. Claims for accommodation should be made to the state institutions that have the constitutional jurisdiction to enact the accommodations the group seeks. Thus, the answer varies with the nature of a group's claims and the constitutional distribution of jurisdiction of its state: for the Orthodox Jewish community in Barnet, it was the local council; for Muslims in Ontario, it was the provincial legislature; for indigenous communities in Canada, it is usually the federal government; and, of course, for group seeking to promote rights through litigation, it is the courts.

The slightly longer answer is that none of this will matter unless the people who staff these institutions are motivated by a concern for justice, defined here to mean showing equal respect for all individuals' interests in leading meaningful lives. Nothing I have said or will say in Part 3 is intended to explain how this concern might be developed among people who do not care about justice. Rather, my intent is to suggest principles and provide examples to help us think about how a conception of justice based on the essential interest in meaningful life might be put into practice. If the discussion itself serves to motivate people to be concerned about this conception of justice by illustrating its desirability and practicality, so much the better.

In more practical terms, this concern for justice can be operationalized as a guiding ethic or commitment to "adopt special measures that respond to the legitimate claims" as they arise.[7] This ethic could simply be left to political culture, but if rights that might conflict with it were constitutionally enumerated, it should probably be given formal constitutional recognition as well.[8] For example, such a clause might state: "Citizens shall be granted special measures to protect their meaningful communities, when, and only for so long as, the viability of those communities is immanently and remediably imperilled." Such a non-group-specific right is particularly promising since it may create valuable tensions that may serve to generate compromise. The opportunity to launch, or to threaten to launch, legal challenges could provide minority communities with leverage to gain decision makers' attention and to get them to take demands seriously. Yet, the risk of losing everything if their case fails provides an incentive for community members to negotiate seriously and to make their demands reasonable.[9] Of course, this presumes a judiciary that is independent and fairly activist about cultural accommodation matters.

What is most important is the willingness among all those involved in the policy process and in the broader political system to consider and respect legitimate claims for accommodations.

Dealing with Claims for Accommodation

The question of how claims for accommodations should be dealt with can be addressed by drawing together conclusions and observations made in the last two chapters. Let us first consider the form claims should take, and then principles to govern the process by which such claims should be negotiated.

Three points stand out concerning the form claims for accommodations should take. First, in making its claim, a group must provide evidence and arguments to satisfy the three conditions for justifying claims for accommodation (discussed in Chapter 5, pp. 102-15). These are that the community connects its members with a context of value that supports their capacity for situated autonomy and thus meaningful life; that members are threatened with the involuntary loss of access to the community; and that members are unable to make alternative identifications with the communities available to them. Second, those making the claim must describe the specific measures they are demanding. They also must offer a justification for the measures in terms of their account of the community's context of value and the nature of the threats to its viability. Third, and finally, those making the claim must translate their claim and their account of their community as a context of value into a proposed code of membership rights and obligations. This would serve two purposes. The rights or privileges would indicate what the protective measures would mean in practice, and the obligations, along with any criteria for membership, would indicate who would (and who would not) be eligible to join the community and enjoy the rights and privileges.

The claim having been made, the parties would begin to negotiate. To be consistent with the foundations of meaningful life, the process of negotiation must be guided by three principles, which would apply no matter what forum claims were being made in (legislative committee, town council, courtroom, and so on). The first principle is that everyone with a legitimate interest in the process be permitted to have input. Such interests would include those who would enjoy the protection, as suggested by the proposed membership code; those who would be excluded by the proposed membership code but believe they should be included; representatives of other cultural communities whose viability may be affected by the proposed accommodations (this could include the dominant community); non-members who have an interest in minimizing the burdens they will bear; and the state itself, whose main interest will be in sustaining the wider political community as a moral tradition (see below, pp. 155-57). A corollary principle is that to facilitate such participation, the group's claim must be publicized.

The second principle is that in reaching its decision the state body show equal respect for individuals' interests in meaningful life. The third principle is that the final binding decision on the claim rests with the relevant state institution. Whether this is a legislature or a court or some other body depends on the constitutional structure of the state. The wider political community must prevail not because it is always likely to be right but because it embodies the moral tradition on which the survival of the many valuable sub-communities and traditions depends. This suggests a strong reason for all members of the political community, majority and minority alike, to engage in the wearying and often frustrating dialogues such cultural claim-making requires: these dialogues represent not the granting of concessions to minorities as some form of charity or the crass negotiation of unprincipled modus vivendi but the articulation and enhancement of the moral tradition that makes meaningful life possible for all members of the political community.

A Role for International Adjudication?
There is good reason to be concerned about the principle that the decisions

of state institutions on minorities' claims for accommodation be binding. For instance, it raises all the concerns attributed to minorities in the discussion of the status of states and their boundaries in Chapter 1, pp. 33-35. These concerns are that the best reason minorities have to engage in dialogue is to protect themselves from majorities; that dialogue will be conducted in the language of the majority, a language that usually presupposes the majority's values and conceptions of justice; and that intercultural dialogue will usually be conducted in the context of an imbalance in power.

The combined force of these factors is likely to make it difficult for the majority to resist the tendency "to assert their own perspectives as universal."[10] Thus, there is good reason to suspect that even the most well-meaning majority will not always have the capacity to reach optimal decisions from the perspective of equal respect for meaningful life. For this reason, I explore the possibility that justice might be promoted by incorporating an element of international adjudication.[11]

What I am thinking of here is an international adjudicatory body similar to the United Nations Human Rights Committee, to which those who initiated claims for accommodations could appeal after having exhausted domestic remedies.[12] The legitimacy of decisions the institution rendered would be based on, and limited to, appeal to the universal value of meaningful life. Such an institution would work best if *not* empowered to issue decisions that were binding on states. To see why this is so, let us consider the potential benefits and drawbacks of international adjudication.

The benefit of allowing cultural minorities to pursue their claims at the international level is that it could help address the arbitrary imbalances in power that follow from acceptance of the territorial boundaries of states. It would do so by reducing the advantages that accrue to the majority at the state level. Both the minority and the majority would be required to defend and offer reasons for their positions. This differs significantly from dialogue at the state level, where the status quo, which tends to favour the majority's interests, is usually treated as the default position. As well, if the international adjudicatory system were properly structured, both parties would have to abandon arguments that appeal to values specific to the state-level community's moral tradition and make new arguments appealing directly to the value of meaningful life. Given that the values in the state-level moral tradition likely privilege the majority, this would tend to reduce its advantage.

While these are all good reasons for endorsing international appeal, the role that has been recognized for the wider political community as a moral tradition in helping to sustain meaningful lives suggests reasons for caution. These involve the possible effects of international judgments on state-level politics. Allowing minorities to appeal internationally may jeopardize intercultural dialogue by undermining the spirit of cooperation and compromise on which it depends. If minorities believe that they may be able to do better for themselves at the international level, they may be less willing to compromise in negotiations with the majority and perhaps be more likely to challenge bargains to which they have already agreed. Similarly, if majorities believe minorities may not respect their bargains, they may also be less likely to compromise. This seems more likely to generate mutual suspicion than goodwill.

In addition, the solutions that international adjudicators recommend may prove corrosive to the very values and institutions that have allowed the society to work as well as it has. These values and institutions are often the product of earlier iterations of the intercultural dialogue, "hammered out in difficult negotiations and embodying such consensus as is thrown up by the parties involved."[13] The inner logic and even justice of such agreements, influenced as they are likely to be by contextual factors and sometimes reflecting more compromise than principle, are not likely to be transparent to outsiders adopting a universal perspective. This suggests three dangers. One is that solutions international adjudicators proffer may be incongruent with the often idiosyncratic compromises that enable societies to function. A second is that, whatever the shortcomings of a society's moral tradition, it is usually at least partly constitutive of its members' identities. Any harm that may be done to it by the imposition of outsiders' decisions is likely to have a negative impact on their ability to pursue meaningful lives. As Parekh said of what he calls a society's operative public values, which are relevantly similar to our idea of the state-level moral tradition, they "cannot be radically revised without causing considerable moral and social disorientation."[14] Finally, the possibility that appeals by minorities to international adjudicators might threaten the moral tradition that sustains communities the majority values could give the majority further reason to resent its minorities.

And so, there seems to be good reason to believe that allowing appeals to an international body may chip away at the goodwill that makes possible the dialogue, compromise, and, ultimately, unity, on which the functioning of the state-level community depends. Herein lies the reason such a body should not issue binding decisions. Where international decisions threaten intercultural dialogue, the state-level moral tradition, or the pragmatic compromises that make the community work, it is essential that states retain the freedom to protect these interests by refusing to implement the decision.

This position will surely raise the question, what advantage can there be to insisting on a right to appeal to international adjudicators if the adjudicators' decisions are not binding? The answer, I suggest, is that issuing decisions that will not necessarily be implemented is not the same as leaving the position of the communicants unaltered. If the state loses but refuses to implement the decision, the minority returns to the dialogue armed with the confirmation that a disinterested international body has affirmed its position and found the majority's arguments unpersuasive. The majority, one hopes, returns with the desire to remove a blemish from its international record.[15] If the minority loses, it will have difficulty sustaining the belief that the only reason its claims have not been accepted is that the state is biased against it.

This reminds us that the power of such views lies not so much in their enforcement as in their legitimacy. And this legitimacy is secured to no small extent by the fact that the body issuing the decisions is less susceptible to the biases experienced within the context of the state. By employing adjudicators who have no stake in the conflict and by insisting that arguments appeal directly to the value of meaningful life, a more universal perspective may be adopted and the arbitrary inequalities of power that can be so decisive within the bounds of the state can be moderated. This is as close as we can hope to come to evening the balance of power between majorities and minorities within the state while showing sufficient respect for the state-level moral traditions that contribute to the meaningfulness of people's lives and play a vital role in sustaining social unity.

Mi'kmaq Logging and Fishing Rights

The recent struggles of the Mi'kmaq people of Atlantic Canada to achieve recognition of logging and fishing rights provide an excellent opportunity to illustrate what this claim-making process might look like in practice and to discuss issues to which it draws our attention.

The Mi'kmaq are an Aboriginal people who have lived in what are now Canada's Atlantic provinces since before the first arrival of Europeans. At present they consist of less than 24,000 people, approximately two-thirds of whom live on-reserve.[16] Their story is a familiar one of first being treated as trading partners and military allies, then slowly being marginalized, pushed on to small unproductive plots of land, and generally excluded from the mainstream economy. Relations between the Canadian state and the Mi'kmaq have typically been characterized by domination and subordination and not equal respect of any sort for at least 150 years, as witnessed by a petition sent to the lieutenant governor of Nova Scotia in 1849.[17] At present, conditions on reserves in Atlantic Canada are deplorable compared with those of the mainstream Canadian community, and unemployment among Aboriginal people has run at over twice the regional average.[18]

In this context it not surprising that the Mi'kmaq have attempted to attain accommodations to protect and promote their communities. The claims that lie behind this case study were initiated independently by individuals arrested for logging and fishing without proper licences. In both cases, these individuals claimed the arrests were unlawful because, as Mi'kmaq, their right to engage in these activities was secured under centuries-old treaties with the British Crown.

The defence of liberal multiculturalism developed in this book is intended neither to supplement nor to replace treaty-based arguments for Aboriginal rights. Each should be viewed as a distinct and independent basis for justifying cultural accommodations. While I recognize the importance of treaties to the contemporary struggles of Aboriginal peoples in Canada and I believe that treaty commitments should be honoured, this has no bearing on the present consideration of the Mi'kmaq case. Rather, my interest is to examine the accommodations being claimed and the context in which they arise in order to consider how the claims the Mi'kmaq have made on the basis of treaties would proceed if made instead on the basis of respect for meaningful life. Viewed from this perspective, the treaties take on a different importance: they represent a catalyst for dragging a sometimes well-meaning but almost always complacent majority into negotiations.

I have already identified the three features that a claim should include. The first is that the group making the claim provide evidence that it satisfies the three conditions for justifying a claim for special accommodation. The Mi'kmaq appear to have little difficulty making such a case. Regarding the first condition, reserve communities appear to provide important contexts of value for their members. This is suggested by reports that despite conditions on the reserves, "talented Mi'kmaq tend to stay in the region to seek work among their people"; "Mi'kmaq people continue to view their present and their future in local and regional terms"; and "many of the communal values and assumptions that underpin indigenous culture remain in evidence." As for the second condition, that members are threatened with the involuntary loss of access to their community, economic and social conditions on reserves clearly pose a challenge to the long-term viability of these communities. Thus there is at least the basis for a preventative, if not a remedial, case for protective measures. Finally, the third condition, that members are unable to make alternative identifications with the communities available to them, is supported by the refusal of many Mi'kmaq to abandon their communities "despite years of hardship and discouraging results from their negotiations and protests."[19] While the evidence presented here is insufficient in itself to justify a claim, it indicates what a successful claim might look like.

The second feature a claim should include is a description of the protective measures being demanded and a justification of these measures in terms of the community's context of value and the threats it faces. In this case, the Mi'kmaq are demanding the right to engage in fishing and forestry in their traditional lands on a commercial basis. These measures appear well suited to the communities they are intended to protect. One of the greatest threats to the viability of these communities is their lack of economic opportunity and their relative isolation from other communities in which resident members could find work. Access to fishing and forestry could address this threat because many of the jobs they provide can be mastered by people without high levels of education and training and do not require relocating from the reserves. While not all community members would be able to participate in these industries, the income provided by those who did would be a vital boost to reserve economies.

The third feature of a claim for accommodation is an explanation of how the protection demanded could be translated into a code of membership rights and obligations. For the Mi'kmaq, this might be achieved simply by requiring that access to logging and fishing privileges be limited to those who reside on-reserve. Such an obligation would reflect that the fishing and logging privileges are being justified as a means to preserve valuable communities and not as a means to benefit particular individuals.

So we can see how the Mi'kmaq claim would need to be presented to satisfy the requirements of our approach. Now let us consider the case from the perspective of the three principles that were suggested to guide the process of negotiation. The first is that everyone with a legitimate interest in the process be permitted to have input; the second, that the state body be guided in reaching its final decision by showing equal respect for meaningful life; and the third, that the authority to reach a binding decision on the claim rests with the relevant state institution.

In the Mi'kmaq case, there are five sets of legitimate interests, each with implications for a just outcome. The first involves those of members of Mi'kmaq communities themselves. Their primary concern seems to be with whether the fishing and logging privileges will be extended to and thus controlled by individual Mi'kmaq or by the communities as collectivities. Although there can be no doubt that giving control to the community would bring with it all the problems of corruption, patronage, and favouritism that plague some reserves, extending these rights to individuals, who might take them with them to live in, and thus contribute to the viability of, non-Aboriginal communities is inconsistent with the goal of preserving Aboriginal communities.[20]

A second set of legitimate interests consists of those individuals who believe they had been wrongly excluded from membership and therefore access to these privileges. This group consists primarily of off-reserve and non-status Indians. Status Indians are those who are recognized by the federal government as Indians for the purposes of its Indian Act. One of the privileges of status is the right to live on-reserve. This means that off-reserve status Indians have the right to live on-reserve but have either chosen to not exercise it or been prevented from doing so for reasons such as a lack of adequate housing. Non-status Indians are people who identify as Indians and often share ancestry with status Indians but who have lost their status for any of a variety of reasons. Without status, they have no right to live on-reserve (unless their band has taken control of its membership code and adopted provisions that include them). What both groups have in common is that, not residing on-reserve, they would be excluded from the privileges associated with the cultural accommodation. In New Brunswick, these people have organized as the Aboriginal Peoples Council to promote their interests.[21] From the perspective of equal respect for meaningful life, any demand they might make for participation could not be satisfied, at least if it required extending fishing and logging privileges to individuals residing off-reserve. If, however, their claim were that they are excluded from these privileges because they had been unjustly excluded from the right to participate in reserve communities, they might have a case, but the question of the justice of their exclusion is distinct from the matter at hand.

A third set of legitimate interests includes those associated with non-Aboriginal communities whose economies, and thus survival, are dependent on their members finding work in fishing or logging. Equal respect for meaningful life requires that the interests of these communities not be taken lightly, for many of them, like Aboriginal communities, provide their members with contexts of value. Davis and Jentoft capture this quality of non-Aboriginal fishing communities: "It is a way of life that embodies their families' and communities' generations-deep engagement with making a living from the sea. It is what they are and what they do. Of course, few would have ever thought, at least until recently, of fishing in terms of either 'rights' or 'privileges.' Your people fished and you fished, likely on the same grounds, out of the same harbours, and in the same fisheries."[22] In fact, Ken Coates' description of these communities suggests that they could probably make legitimate claims in their own right: "Most of the fishers in these towns and villages ... are people with firm roots in their communities and industry, only occasionally with skills that can be marketed locally or regionally, and with a deep cultural commitment to the fishery."[23] Concern about the impact of the Aboriginal demands among members of these communities has been expressed in protests and acts of vigilantism. From the perspective of meaningful life, this anger (but not the violence) is perfectly reasonable. Residents of these communities were concerned that the government might satisfy the Mi'kmaq's demands by giving away the economic bases of their communities. This concern is perhaps best reflected in the comments of a non-Aboriginal fisher: "We're just here to protect our rights. We're here to make a living. If we don't protect our rights, Baie St. Anne is over. Miramichi is over, New Brunswick is over, and we may as well get out of Canada. We got nothing left."[24]

Clearly, if our concern is really with equal respect for meaningful life, any solution dismissing the interests of the non-Aboriginal fishers and their communities would be unjust. This being said, I think it is fair to also say that while both communities deserve respect, the claims of the Mi'kmaq would be stronger. Unlike the Mi'kmaq, whose identifications will likely have led them to develop significant purposes that can be pursued only within their reserve communities, the non-Aboriginal fishers are in a better position to sustain meaningful lives if forced to leave their communities. I say this on the presumption that most of the non-Aboriginal fishers and loggers identify directly with the Canadian moral tradition as well as with other communities whose purposes could be pursued in many other Canadian or even English-speaking communities.

A fourth set of interests includes those of non-members at large who might have to bear less direct burdens as a result of an accommodation. In matter of fact, these interests were predominantly represented by business corporations and conservationist groups. They had legitimate interests in pressuring the government to ensure that any accommodations extended to the Mi'kmaq claims did not place excessive burdens on their purposes.

The fifth and final set of interests is represented by the federal and provincial governments. Both governments were implicated because of the constitutional division of powers: the federal government has jurisdiction over offshore fisheries, the provincial governments over forests. From our perspective, both governments had an interest in maintaining respect for key elements of the state-level moral tradition. In this case, what was primarily at stake was respect for the rule of law and, more specifically, the maintenance of respect for the regulatory regimes each had established within its jurisdiction.

How might an accommodation of the Mi'kmaq claims be made consistent with equal respect for meaningful life? The first thing to note is that, viewed from this perspective, this situation does appear open to reconciliation. This is possible if ensuring the sustainability of all relevant communities, Aboriginal and non-Aboriginal alike, is made the primary objective of any accommodation. I believe that if all parties could be convinced that this was indeed the government's objective, much of the anxiety that drives the conflicts of these situations would dissipate. And such solutions do seem practical, at least in the cases of logging and the lobster fishery.[25] Even if allowing the Mi'kmaq into the fishery did amount to a zero-sum game, this could be accommodated in a respectful manner by acquiring quota for Aboriginal communities through voluntary buyouts from non-Aboriginal fishers, a policy the federal government has in fact pursued. Finally, a satisfactory solution would have to include respect for the federal and provincial governments' regulatory authority as a manifestation of the state-level moral tradition. I see no reason, however, why such respect need be inconsistent with the determination of regulations through dialogue and consultation.

Summary
The initiation of claims for cultural accommodation consistent with the foundations of meaningful life involves several key factors. Claims should be initiated by groups that self-organize in response to perceived threats. Such

claims should explain how their situation satisfies the three conditions for justifying accommodation; they should describe the specific accommodations being sought; and they should include a proposed set of communal rights and obligations. In evaluating claims, the state should consider input from all interested parties; it should be guided by the principle of equal respect for meaningful lives in reaching its decision; and its decision should be binding. Given that this process is likely to favour the interests of majority communities, a non-group-specific constitutional right to communal protection and an international adjudicatory process to which aggrieved minorities could appeal are desirable. While reducing disparities in power between majority and minority in intercultural dialogues is an important objective, this should not be achieved at the expense of undermining state-level moral traditions; that is, the decisions of an international adjudicatory body should not be binding on states.

Intervention in the Internal Affairs of Cultural Communities

A second aspect of state-community relations involves state intervention in the internal affairs of sub-state communities. The foundations of meaningful life can be applied to four aspects of state-community relations: reasons for refraining from coercive intervention, intervention to protect "minimal conditions of meaningful life," intervention to enforce obligations to the state-wide community's moral tradition, and principles to govern the process of intervention. In this discussion I try to illustrate that the foundations of meaningful life do not need to be supplemented to defend positions on these matters.

A Preference for Persuasion

Given the foundational role that respect for meaningful life plays in our theory, any decision to intervene in the internal practices of communities cannot be taken lightly. Only in cases where meaningful life itself is at risk can coercive intervention be justified; otherwise, it is usually counterproductive and cannot be countenanced. There are several reasons for such caution. One is simply respect for the fact that people may find meaning in their present way of doing things and see no reason to change. A second, as argued in Chapter 4, is that intervention might actually threaten meaning in people's lives by preventing them from pursuing their significant purposes or by undermining communities on which they rely for meaning. Third, the desire to engage in coercive intervention may be more reflective of differences in power between communities than of real threats to meaning. Being in a position to effect change makes it much easier to convince oneself that aspects of another community that one finds offensive are actually dangerous. Thus, where meaningful life is not at stake, tolerance is in order.

Respect for meaningful life is always consistent, however, with non-coercive forms of intervention such as argument, exhortation, and persuasion. As long as those who object to a community's practices do not force anyone to listen to their arguments and no one inside the community is compelled to ignore them, any resulting changes should reflect the appeal of arguments to the listener's governing assumptions and not differences in wealth or power.

Minimal Conditions of Meaningful Life

One of the grounds on which the foundations of meaningful life can justify intervention is respect for the minimal conditions of meaningful life. These conditions are justified as a limitation on the relationship between communities and their members since communities are valuable only to the extent that they support and promote meaningful lives. If, and to the extent that, communities impede the enjoyment of meaningful lives, they have no value. On this basis, I identify minimal conditions that all communities must respect.

In thinking about minimal conditions we must be cognizant of the difference between the interests of children and adults that was first noted in Chapter 2. This is reflected in Richard Arneson's observation that, unlike adulthood, childhood occurs "before the individual has much experience of the world and a fully formed set of preferences in response to it."[26] Meaningful lives presuppose situated autonomy and identifications with communities that connect people with contexts of value, which together enable them to form and pursue significant purposes. In terms of this conception of meaningful life, it is useful to think of childhood as the time when people's greatest interest is in developing secure identifications and adulthood as a time when people's greatest interest is in exercising situated autonomy.

Minimal conditions of meaningful life will vary according to this distinction. Manipulation and coercion are always inconsistent with respect for the situated autonomy of adults, yet their exercise may be consistent with the goal of socializing children to make the identifications that can support their capacity for situated autonomy in adulthood. And although respect for the situated autonomy of adults may require us to stand aside when, for instance, Dinka spear-masters allow themselves to be buried alive (discussed in Chapter 3), the killing of children is never tolerable. The key difference between children and adults in terms of intervention, then, is that our main concern with adults is their ability to pursue meaningful lives, while our main concern with children is developing their capacity to lead meaningful lives.

Minimal Conditions: Children

The relationship between the pursuit of meaningful lives by adults and the development of significant identifications by their children is generally non-coercive and indivisible. Kenneth Henley illustrates this in his discussion of religious socialization:

In the early years of the child's socialization, he will be surrounded by the religious life of his parents. Since the parents have a right to live such religious lives, and on the assumption that children will normally be raised by their parents, parental influence on the child's religious life is both legitimate and unavoidable ... at such an early stage it can hardly be said that coercion is involved; the child simply lives in the midst of a religious way of life and comes to share in it.[27]

To intervene in this relationship poses a double danger to meaningful lives. It threatens to interfere with the adult socializers' significant purposes – for instance, a personal purpose, such as parenting, or a transcendent collective enterprise, such as perpetuating a community. It also may prevent children from establishing secure identifications with communities, which they need to develop a capacity for situated autonomy. Here again, non-intervention appears to be a good general policy.

One interest that can justify intervention, however, is the children's interest in receiving socialization that respects their capacity for meaningful lives. Socialization does this when it helps children develop moral starting points that can inform their exercise of situated autonomy when they become adults. This interest can justify intervention when parents, in pursuing their own purposes or for any other reason, fail to promote it.

Socialization that respects children's capacity for meaningful life has two characteristics: it is sincere, and it respects children's capacity to exercise meta-agency in the future. Sincere socialization is veracious and non-exploitive. Where socialization is veracious, the contexts of value with which children are encouraged to identify reflect the actual beliefs of those who socialize them: they reflect the best accounts of objective reality the socializers possess – the ones they actually try to live by. Veracity is expressed in reasoning such as: "This way of life has proven meaningful to me. I pass it on to you." Socialization that lacks veracity fails to respect children's capacity for meaningful life. It occurs, for instance, when socializers raise children to accept values they know to be false, as, say, where children are denied an education at least roughly equivalent to that which their socializers received.[28] This failure of respect does not occur, as suggested in the discussion of the life of open-minded conviction in Chapter 4, where only outsiders know the content to be false.

The requirement that socialization be non-exploitive applies to the intent of socializers, not the effects of socialization. It is less a matter of what people are socialized to believe than why they are socialized to believe it. Socialization that results in behaviour others consider strange or oppressive is sincere so long as it reflects a way of life the socializers find meaningful for themselves. If, however, it is intended to create preferences in the young merely for the pleasure, or some other benefit, of the socializers, it is exploitive and thus insincere.

The value of sincere socialization cannot be that it ensures that the contexts of value with which children identify will embody true representations of "objective reality." Instead, it lies in the respect it shows for meaningful life. By ensuring that children receive the best account of objective reality consistent with the development of secure identifications, children are protected from the pain of discovering not only that their contexts of value generate dissonance or lead to inescapable contradictions but also that they were set up for this by the contempt or indifference of those who raised them.[29]

An interesting puzzle this discussion suggests concerns how we should deal with those who have been sincerely socialized by people who were insincerely socialized. Suppose that the founder of a religious sect had been a fraud. Should the state intervene to prevent contemporary members of this sect from socializing their young to accept their beliefs? The answer must be a qualified no, so long as the present-day believers have good reasons for continued adherence. The possibility that their beliefs are based on a lie is something that, when brought to their attention, autonomous agents should take seriously, but the decision not to renounce their beliefs is not decisive evidence of a failure of autonomy; it may be that they have reasons for retaining their beliefs that are not undermined by this information.[30]

Socialization that respects children's capacity to lead meaningful lives must also show respect for the possibility that they may exercise meta-agency in the future to reject or abandon their inherited communities. For this reason, children need to be socialized in ways that are both capable of being renounced and forthright about real alternatives. When socialization is capable of being renounced, children are not subjected to practices in ways that permanently limit their physical or mental capacities.[31] Such practices include foot binding, the elongation of necks, female circumcision, the refusal of life-saving blood transfusions, and those that permanently lower Native intelligence. These are inconsistent with respect for children's capacity for meaningful life because they are not necessary to help the child develop secure identifications, and they may make it impossible for the child to pursue purposes consistent with identifications he or she may adopt in the future. Such practices cannot be saved by the fact that children who have been subjected to them may come to prefer not being able to do what they are prevented from doing. Such "adaptive preferences"[32] result in a person's purposes, not in being her own, and thus significantly undermine her ability to self-govern. This requirement does not preclude the inculcation of values that may lead children to choose to engage in such practices in adulthood. It does, however, preclude practices that make sense only when conducted in childhood.

Socialization that is forthright about alternatives ensures that children do not fail to exercise meta-agency as adults simply because they are unaware that they have options. As Rawls suggests, they should not do so out of "ignorance of their basic rights or fear of punishments for offenses that do not exist."[33] While children need not be "exposed" to other ways of life, as proponents of the examined life and some theories of liberal education suggest, they must learn that other ways of life exist in the wider community and that they are free to leave the community to pursue any of them. This does not require that their education prepare them to pursue those ways of life or that it "require or strongly invite [them] to become skeptical or critical of their own ways of life."[34] This is also consistent with informing them that if they do leave the community they may not be allowed to rejoin it in the future.

Where socialization is veracious, non-exploitive, capable of being renounced, and forthright about alternatives, socializers help children develop secure identifications without, in their zeal for their own purposes, undermining their children's capacity for meaningful lives. Where these conditions are not met, intervention by the wider community may be justified.

Minimal Conditions: Adults
Another source of minimal conditions of meaningful life is the interest of adults in the ability to pursue meaningful lives. This draws attention to two of the potential sources of conflict that were associated with the relationship between communal definition and criteria of membership in previous chapters: the questions of whether membership in a community is voluntary and whether the nature of the community has been defined too narrowly.

Concerns about the voluntary nature of membership can provide a number of justifications for intervention. One is that people should not be exposed to subjectively meaningless threats to their life or security. This permits us to concur with Kymlicka when he says that intervention is warranted in cases of "slavery or genocide or mass torture and expulsions."[35] Our position differs, however, to the extent that threats to life and security can(not) justify intervention where those so threatened are adults who, having received socialization that respected their capacity to lead meaningful lives, voluntarily place themselves in jeopardy as part of their pursuit of significant purposes. Thus, for instance, while intervention to protect Dinka spear-masters from the live burial they accept would not be justified, intervention to protect unwilling initiates to the spirit dance could be.

A second justification for intervention follows from the fact that in exercising meta-agency, people may decide to reject and replace their present identifications. For this reason, people need to be free to exit their communities (for example, Pueblos must not be prevented from moving off reservation; Ontarian Muslims must be able to withdraw from arbitration agreements before settlement procedures have been initiated) and to shed the community's obligations (for example, ex-Coast Salish should not be subjected to grabbing). Beyond these formal requirements, freedom of exit also has substantive elements.[36] Any reasonable account of such requirements,

I believe, is satisfied by the minimal conditions attached to socialization. These ensure that when children become adults they are aware that there are alternative ways of life, they know that they face no legal barriers to pursuing them, they have not been irreversibly prevented from exercising them, and they have been equipped with contexts of value that have proven successful for their parents.

A related minimal condition that follows from the freedom to exit is that adults should not be prevented from learning about other ways of life if they so choose. Thus, communities cannot oblige their members to act in ways that have this effect. This is violated, for instance, by the Amish practice of *Bann und Meidung* (excommunication and shunning) which, in its stricter forms, requires members to extremely limit their interactions with those who have been shunned.[37] This is problematic not because ex-members have a right to even such minimal participation in the community but because it may have the effect of denying members an important source of information about the outside world.[38]

The concern that membership not be defined too narrowly suggests that no one should be excluded from communities with which they identify so long as they satisfy membership criteria and fulfil membership obligations. Thus, intervention may be justified where members who are willing to fulfil their obligations are expelled or denied benefits of membership or where non-members who satisfy membership criteria are prevented from joining.

The violation of such minimal conditions would justify state intervention to preserve equal respect for meaningful life. What this might mean in practice varies with circumstances. In the Salish grabbing case, for instance, where membership was over-inclusive, the charging of the defendants with assault seems sufficient. In the Sawridge case (discussed in Chapter 6), reasonable intervention could involve adjudicating disputes over who rightly belongs in the community. In the hypothetical case of a woman who shares Miriam Wilngal's displeasure at being offered to another tribe as compensation for a killing (pp. 128-29) but lacks the requisite identifications or significant purposes that would enable her to exercise her freedom of exit, intervention could be justified because the involuntary and subjectively meaningless nature of her situation undermines her capacity to exercise situated autonomy. This might occur if, despite her disgust at being given as compensation, she is prevented from leaving because everything she knows, including her friends, family, and means of livelihood, is bound up in the cultural community.[39]

So far I have suggested that the wider community may legitimately intervene in the internal affairs of sub-communities where such communities fail to respect the minimal conditions of meaningful life in their relations with their members. For children, these conditions include socialization that is veracious, non-exploitive, capable of being renounced, and forthright about alternatives. For adults, these conditions include respect for situated autonomy, not being exposed to subjectively meaningless threats to life and security, freedom to exit their community, not being prevented from accessing information about other ways of life, and the right to participate in the community so long as they fulfil obligations of membership. Minimal conditions of meaningful life, however, do not exhaust the possible justifications for state intervention.

Obligations to the Wider Community as a Moral Tradition

The core value of meaningful life can also justify intervention in the internal affairs of communities where this is necessary to enforce legitimate obligations that the wider community as a moral tradition can require of its members. This reflects the interest that all citizens share in the wider community as a moral tradition either because they identify with its context of value directly or because the tradition sustains other communities that contribute meaning to their lives. This gives all citizens an interest in the wider political community's being able to fulfil its functions, whether they acknowledge this or not.[40]

At a minimum, the wider community requires the development of citizens who will not imperil its functioning and stability. This requirement has two facets that will be pursued here, although there are probably others. First, as a social union of individuals to facilitate the pursuit of meaningful lives, the wider community requires children to be socialized in ways that are compatible with this purpose. Second, as a democratic polity, the wider political community requires citizens to develop the ability to negotiate and reach mutual understandings.

A politics of liberal multiculturalism depends on general acceptance of the equal right of all people to pursue subjectively meaningful lives. Ensuring that children develop this commitment requires the inculcation of three values. One is toleration. By toleration, I do not mean the now popular sense that requires embracing and celebrating the projects of one's co-citizens. Instead, I mean it as William Galston defines it: "The principled refusal to use coercive state instruments to impose one's views on others, the commitment to competition through recruitment and persuasion alone."[41] The second value, justificatory reciprocity, refers to the willingness to consider the arguments of others and to present one's own arguments in light of the beliefs and values that those others hold. Toleration and justificatory reciprocity, as defined here, do not require people to stop thinking that their own beliefs are true or that other people's beliefs are wrong. They do require, however, that people accept the empirical fact that their own way of life is not universally accepted, as well as the moral commitment to treat other citizens as persons who, like themselves, have deep commitments to their own beliefs and wish to be free to live according to them. Any community that cannot accept these commitments is incompatible with equal respect for meaningful life and will probably find it difficult to survive in a society structured according to liberal multiculturalism.

The third value is recognition of the wider community as a valuable moral tradition. This follows from the discussion in Chapter 3 suggesting that this is a basis of unity in culturally diverse states. This value draws support from the moral commitment to treat other individuals with equal respect as well as from the pragmatic assessment that, in most cases, one's own way of life will be secure only so long as members of other communities are similarly secure.

The requirement that children be prepared to act as citizens of a democratic polity is partially met by the veracity principle: in the process of socializing children with their subjectively veracious beliefs, socializers will normally teach their children the political skills they have developed in promoting their community's interests in the past. The veracity principle, however, cannot be relied on to promote this interest by itself. The wider community may require that, at a minimum, communities teach their children their political rights, along with the principles, workings, and history of its political institutions.

Other interests that have been suggested as grounds for intervention cannot be justified by this theory of liberal multiculturalism. For example, and not surprisingly, we cannot accept Arneson and Shapiro's suggestion that the wider community can intervene to require children to be educated to lead rationally autonomous lives.[42] Similarly, we cannot accept David Miller's suggestion that the wider community can intervene by outlawing sectarian schools in communities and making schools into places "where members of different ethnic groups are thrown together and taught in common" on the grounds that it has an interest in using the education system to reproduce a "common national identity."[43] Besides undermining the ability of many parents to raise their children to identify with valued and legitimate communities, such intervention goes beyond what is required to generate tolerance and a common identification with the community as a moral tradition. Finally, we cannot go along with Galston's suggestion that the state can require children to be equipped to perform as members of a liberal economy and society.[44] This is unnecessary since people who are meaningfully motivated to move to liberal societies from traditional societies are able, albeit with difficulty, to successfully integrate.[45] It is excessive to the extent that preparation for participation in a liberal market economy may undermine valuable premodern and traditional communities that are not highly integrated into the market economy. This theory could support, however, Feinberg's suggestions that the state intervene to prevent children from becoming "criminal or hopeless dependants on state welfare support" and out of "concern that children not be a source of infection to others."[46]

In sum, a limited number of obligations are associated with the wider community as a moral tradition that may justify state intervention in the internal affairs of sub-state communities. These include the obligations to ensure that children practice toleration, that they develop a capacity for justificatory reciprocity, that they learn to value the wider community as a valuable moral tradition, and that they develop the capacity to act as citizens of a democratic policy.

Illustrative Case Studies

State intervention in the internal affairs of communities can be justified in keeping with our core value of meaningful life where it is required to sustain respect for the minimal conditions of meaningful life and to enforce obligations arising from the wider political community's status as a moral tradition. Let us now consider two cases and how it would apply in each. *Wisconsin v. Yoder* is a case where intervention would not be justified. The demand for Sharia arbitration in Ontario is a case where it could be.

Wisconsin v. Yoder

The *Yoder* case arose when the state of Wisconsin decided to require all children, including those from Amish communities, to attend school to age sixteen rather than age fourteen. Besides the two extra years of education, this would require the Amish children to be bussed to larger urban schools. The Amish argued against this policy, saying that high school education "tends to emphasize intellectual and scientific accomplishments, self-distinction, competitiveness, worldly success, and social life with other students." This, they suggested, made high school education inconsistent with "Amish society[, which] emphasizes informal learning-through-doing; a life of 'goodness,' rather than a life of intellect; wisdom rather than technical knowledge, community welfare, rather than competition; and separation from, rather than integration with, contemporary society." Testimony at the hearing suggested that "compulsory high school attendance could not only result in great psychological harm to Amish children, because of the conflicts it would produce, but would also ... ultimately result in the destruction of the [community]."[47] Our interest in this case concerns whether Wisconsin's intervention in the Amish community could be justified.

We can begin our analysis by identifying the various interests at play. This approach allows us to acknowledge and supplement the interests Joel Feinberg identified in his discussion of the case. Feinberg's analysis focuses on one of the key values we derived from the core value of meaningful life: personal autonomy. He argues that the goal of autonomous selves should be to achieve self-fulfilment by developing "one's chief aptitudes into genuine talents in a life that gives them scope ... and an active realization of the universal human propensities to plan, design and make order." This is the basis of his claim that children have a right-in-trust to an "open future." Viewed through Feinberg's lens, *Yoder* is about balancing autonomy interests: those of the parents to exercise religious freedom and those of their children to safeguard their "open futures."[48] Feinberg concludes that *Yoder* was decided correctly because the two additional years of elementary education at issue would have little impact on the children's future opportunities and could not justify intervention with the parents' religious freedom. Had the case turned on a more significant degree of education, however, "no amount of harm to the parents' interest in the religious upbringing of their children could overturn the children's right-in-trust to an open future."[49]

Our approach recognizes the autonomy interests of the parents and the children, but appeal to the underlying value of meaningful life also enables us to recognize interests associated with the parents' and children's identifications with their community. From our perspective, both Amish parents and their children had good reasons to resist the intervention. For Amish parents, the legislation threatened two significant purposes: their desire to achieve personal salvation – the parents believed "that their own prospects of salvation are tied to raising their own children properly, which means assuring their salvation, which in turn means raising them so that they in due course become loyal and conforming members of the traditional Amish society";[50] and their desire to preserve a community that sustains an important context of value. As for the children, by imperilling the survival of the community, the legislation threatened their interest in developing secure identifications and thus situated autonomy.

Given this account of the interests at play, we can see that two justifications for intervention are relevant: the preservation of the minimal conditions of meaningful life – especially the children's interest in socialization that respects their capacity for meaningful life – and the enforcement of obligations arising from membership in the wider political community.

Regarding the children's interests, no one has ever suggested that Amish socialization is insincere. Indeed, Justice Burger wrote that "the Amish have demonstrated the sincerity of their religious beliefs, the interrelationship of belief with their mode of life, the vital role that belief and daily conduct play in the continuing survival of the Old Order Amish communities."[51] Similarly, it has never been suggested that the post-elementary education the Amish provide their children (basically, vocational training for life in the community) is exploitive or lacks veracity. While Amish education is designed to prepare children for life in the community and to shield them from influences that would lead them away from it, it does not appear to mislead them about their alternatives or to be incapable of being renounced. Arneson and Shapiro's suggestion that "Amish youth do not enjoy a genuine choice as to whether or not to enter the community" because they "have been 'so thoroughly immersed in a total ethnic world with its own language, symbols, and world view' that to leave would involve a traumatic severing of all their significant friendships" is belied by their own claim that "more than a fifth of the children leave the community before adulthood."[52] Thus, as Amish socialization does not appear to violate the minimal conditions of meaningful life, intervention could not be legitimized on this basis.

The case is much the same for the obligations arising from membership in the wider community. Amish socialization is compatible with respect for other people's pursuit of meaningful lives. Children are not raised to be intolerant of outsiders' ways of life. Further, Amish beliefs appear compatible with justificatory reciprocity: one of the reasons they are said to value public education is that it prepares children "to be able to deal with non-Amish people when necessary in the course of daily affairs."[53] Compatibility with justificatory reciprocity is also suggested by the *Yoder* case itself: the Amish demonstrated their ability to successfully couch their position in terms of the First Amendment right to free exercise of religious beliefs. Finally, their commitment to the wider community as a context of value is suggested by their willingness to work through the American judicial system and to have their children educated in its public schools.

The only minimal condition of meaningful lives the Amish may fail to meet is the requirement that children be prepared to act politically as citizens. This, however, does not appear to be the case. Eight years of public school education should be enough to ensure that Amish children are aware of their political rights, and the principles, workings, and history of the political institutions of the wider political community. Although their values discourage active participation in worldly politics, the Amish do seem to accept the necessity to be good citizens. As was noted in the *Yoder* decision, the Amish "do not object to elementary education through the first eight grades as a general proposition because they agree that their children must have basic skills in the 'three R's' in order to read the Bible, [and] to be good farmers and citizens."[54]

Besides demonstrating how our principles might apply in practice, this analysis of *Yoder* illustrates the capacity of our approach to address difficult practical issues without invoking principles or values external to the theoretical framework.[55]

Sharia Arbitration in Ontario

Chapters 5 and 6 suggest that the claim by some Ontarian Muslims for Sharia arbitration in matters of family and inheritance law is compatible with concern for meaningful life. Concerns have been raised about this accommodation that, I argue, could justify state intervention. The most serious focus on the types of decisions that could be made by such tribunals and the quality of the consent of those, primarily women, who agree to be governed by them. In discussing this, I wish to illustrate three points: that these are serious concerns, that the principles suggested here for governing intervention provide a useful language for assessing such concerns, and that the interests at stake can be safeguarded without abandoning the cultural accommodation.

The main concerns about decisions that may result from Sharia arbitration are that they may fail to respect the equality of women and that they may result in undue burdens being placed on non-members. Translated into the language of our approach, the possibility that Sharia-based decisions will fail to respect the women's equality raises the issue of minimal conditions of meaningful life. The first thing that can be said in favour of the arbitration procedure in this regard is that, as it is limited to matters of civil disputes and does not touch on criminal law, issues such as slavery, torture, or cruel or unusual punishments will not be at stake. This said, however, the Canadian Council of Muslim Women has criticized the design of the procedure because, it says, "even plainly illegal activities may occur unless state authorities find out about them in some way."[56] Although a serious concern, this problem can be addressed while retaining the substance of the accommodation: Marion Boyd has suggested changing the regulations to require arbitrators to provide the parties with written copies of their decisions, including their reasons, and to provide to the government an anonymized summary of all decisions reached.[57]

Where minimal conditions of meaningful life are not at stake, a decision that appears to treat men and women unequally cannot in itself justify intervention. Take, for instance, the fact that under Sharia primary custody of children is given to the husband in most cases.[58] Many people would consider this unfair or even unjust, but if we are serious about respecting individuals' situated autonomy by allowing them to live according to their moral commitments, we must refrain from intervening when they consent to being governed by such rules (subject, of course, to the various grounds for intervention). In such matters, I concur with Boyd, who writes: "Just because we may disagree with the manner in which this alternative is used by some individuals does not mean we are allowed to deprive them of the right to use it, as long as they [use] it in an appropriate manner." To do otherwise, she suggests, is to assume that there is a correct choice in such matters that anyone "who is fully informed of her rights and obligations would make" and that some people are "unable to understand how to make ... the right choices for themselves."[59] Further, as Bakht has suggested, to make such assumptions is to engage "in the very infantilizing of Muslim women that one accuses patriarchal culture of."[60] As has likely been anticipated, these arguments against intervention stand or fall on the assumption that the woman involved truly consented to be governed by these rules. If she did not, these arguments do not apply. I return to this question below.

Marion Boyd points to a particular aspect of Sharia family law that may provide a legitimate basis for state intervention. This concerns arbitration settlements. A purported Sharia principle is that husbands are required to support their ex-wives only "for three menstrual cycles or until the birth of a child already conceived at the time of the divorce." As Boyd notes, in countries such as Canada where the state provides social assistance to the destitute, this principle would probably have the effect of placing an unfair burden on non-members, who will have to bear this cost through their taxes.[61] In this case, state intervention could be justified to reconcile the equally legitimate interests of members and non-members in being able to pursue their significant purposes. I say *could* because I suspect that the cumulative impact of such settlements, were they to be made, would be negligible and certainly no more significant than the monetary impact of many other personal decisions we feel people are entitled to make.

In considering concerns about the quality of women's consent to use Sharia arbitration, we find three bases for questioning the legitimacy of this consent: the possibility of spousal abuse, communal pressure to consent, and the special case of new immigrants.[62] The concern that women may consent to the use of unfair arbitration principles because they are being abused by their spouses is reasonable but not one that should be limited to Muslims. Where women consent because they are being abused, this clearly represents a failure of respect for situated autonomy. As such, state intervention is justified. Here again, though, intervention does not require abandoning the accommodation; it can take the form of the introduction of a safeguard to the procedure. Boyd, for example, recommends that arbitrators be trained and required to screen parties to identify issues of power imbalance and domestic violence.[63]

The possibility that women may sign Sharia arbitration agreements in response to communal pressure raises more complex issues. The concern here is not so much with the structure of Sharia arbitration as a cultural accommodation but with the uses to which this accommodation might be put within certain segments of the Muslim community. For example, women who refuse to sign such agreements may be threatened with exclusion from the life and institutions of the community. This concern has been described succinctly by Boyd: "A woman may be told that it is her religious or community duty to accept whichever adjudicative route is chosen for her. Her fear of isolation from her community, the possible negative impact on her children, and concerns of being considered an apostate in her faith may force her into submitting to one form of dispute resolution over another."[64] This situation is especially troubling because the source of the pressure is not derived from some raw coercive force such as spousal abuse. Rather, it emanates from individuals exercising their right to freely associate or not associate with whomever they choose, and from religious institutions, as voluntary associations without the support of criminal law, exercising their right to delineate "who is inside and who is outside the community according to the community's own norms."[65]

This presents a genuine dilemma. On the one hand, the religious community is in a position to exert this pressure on its members only because the state has created the arbitration process. This suggests repeal of the legislation as a solution. The problem with this, however, is that it would deprive all of those individual Muslims who truly want to avail themselves of the purposes the legislation facilitates from doing so.

If the community were using arbitration agreements in this way, and I am not suggesting that this is the case, it would be best to leave the arbitration act in place and allow the kinds of competing tensions identified in the discussion of Pueblo Protestants to play themselves out. If women in the relevant communities decide that signing arbitration agreements is too high a price to pay for membership in the community, they can exercise their freedom to exit the community. Over time this would put pressure on community leaders to drop the requirement as a condition of membership. (Of course, if the women are truly happy with this arrangement as an expression of their religious commitments, they remain free to sign them). The truly regrettable, but I think unavoidable, aspect of this is that some women would be forced to choose between membership in the only communities they know and their right to equal treatment with their husbands in family and inheritance law under regular Ontario law.

The special case of new immigrants involves two distinct issues. One is that women who have immigrated by being sponsored by their husbands will by virtue of this arrangement find themselves in a position of unequal power. This raises the same issues and can be addressed by the same measures as spousal abuse. The second issue is that the ability of these women, as new immigrants, to provide true consent may be hampered by linguistic barriers or ignorance of their rights in Canada.[66] In this case, I think the way to proceed is to treat recent immigrants as being in an analogous position to children in that both are new entrants to the political community. As such, the state can legitimately intervene in the process of integration (as opposed to socialization) to protect their capacity for situated autonomy by ensuring that the information they are provided about Canadian society is veracious and forthright about alternatives. Here again, Boyd's recommendations offer practical guidance. To promote these interests, the state can intervene in the arbitration process by requiring that before signing an agreement both parties receive independent legal advice to ensure that they are aware of and understand their general rights and obligations under Canadian law, the remedies under Ontario family and arbitration law they will be waiving, and the consequences of their waiver.[67] To this I would add that they should specifically be informed that they will face no legal penalties should they refuse to sign. With such safeguards in place, if a recent immigrant chooses to accept a Sharia arbitration agreement, we can reasonably conclude that the decision constitutes true consent and thus should be respected as an exercise of situated autonomy.

The *Yoder* and Sharia case studies demonstrate the ability of our approach to facilitate principled discussions of difficult issues, all within the theoretical framework derived from the foundations of meaningful life. While, as these cases make clear, this approach cannot promise to prevent all dilemmas and difficult choices, its conception of personal autonomy and identification with community as mutually reinforcing values allows us to address conflicts in ways sensitive to interests derived from both values.

The Process of Intervention

To complete the elaboration of this account of liberal multiculturalism something must be said about the process by which intervention should be carried out. Most of the same principles will apply here as applied to the initiation of claims.

As for the initiation of intervention, it is likely to have various sources. For adults, we would expect the initiative to usually rest with the individuals themselves by appealing to legislatures or courts when they believe a community is not respecting their rights. In extreme cases, such as torture, murder, or unlawful confinement, the initiative may lie with organs of the state such police forces or with non-governmental organizations. Regarding the interests of children, concerned relatives or neighbours or any of a variety of institutions, including social services agencies, legislatures, and school inspectors, could initiate intervention.

Five principles seem applicable to the process of intervention. First, equal respect for meaningful lives requires that when the state considers intervening in the internal affairs of a community, it must give community members an opportunity to explain why they believe intervention is unwarranted (if indeed they do). There are good reasons to believe that such interaction may be more than symbolic. Given the wide range of traditions and contexts of value likely to exist within diverse societies, the meaning and purpose of a community's practices and institutions often will not be transparent to state actors. In such cases, dialogue can be mutually educative and may lead the state to change its views.

The other four principles are simply carried over from the discussion of the initiation of claims (pp. 140-44). In deciding whether to proceed with intervention, state actors should consult all affected interests and be guided by the principle of equal respect for individual interests in meaningful life. Although the authority to make binding decisions in these matters should rest with relevant state institutions, aggrieved communities should be able to appeal to international adjudicators to receive non-binding but morally potent opinions.

Summary

As we have seen, the theory of multiculturalism derived from the foundations of meaningful life has the capacity to inform principles that can help answer practical policy questions. Respect for meaningful life provides a range of reasons both for and against intervention that can usefully be invoked when considering what to do in a particular case. These include children's interest in developing the capacity to lead meaningful lives, adults' interests in maintaining the ability to lead meaningful lives, and the state's interest in enforcing obligations associated with its moral tradition. The Amish in Wisconsin and Sharia adjudication in Ontario cases demonstrate the practical applicability of these principles.

Conclusion

This chapter identified principles to govern key elements of state-community relations, as well as principles to guide who should make claims, who should receive them, and how such claims should be negotiated – including the possible use of an international adjudicatory body to balance unequal power relations within the state. A case study of claims for Mi'kmaq logging and fishing rights illustrates the import of these principles. This chapter also addressed state intervention in the internal affairs of communities. While respect for meaningful life is more consistent with the use of persuasion than coercion, coercive intervention can be justified in cases where communities fail to respect the minimal conditions of meaningful life (these differ between dealings with children and those with adults) or to respect obligations to the wider community as a moral tradition. With these considerations, the development of a politics of liberal multiculturalism derived from the foundations of meaningful life is now complete.

Conclusion

You don't understand it, you won't understand it, and, quite
honestly, you don't need to understand it. The point is that we
want it, we consider it important, and we ask you to respect that.

Rabbi Kimche, quoted by Calvin Trillen, "Drawing the Line,"
The New Yorker, 1994

My intervention in the liberal multiculturalism debate can be summarized
thus: by returning to first principles to develop the foundations of meaningful life, I aim to develop a model of just relations in culturally diverse
states, a set of principles for realizing this, and a vocabulary for advocating its
implementation. What are the main accomplishments of this intervention?
As the very appeal to the foundational value of meaningful life suggests, this
book's contribution is more in the nature of innovation or reconfiguration
than of invention. It clearly stands on the shoulders of those who have gone
before it, but in standing on many shoulders, I like to think it has achieved a
novel and useful perspective. Of the insights that have been revealed, I stress
four. Starting with the most theoretical and moving towards the most practical, these are that it is useful to return to first principles to address concerns
about liberal multiculturalism, that the foundations of meaningful life offer
a credible and compelling account of the relationship between individuals
and communities, that these same foundations can provide a coherent
justification for the claims of the liberal culturalist consensus, and that the
terminology developed here is of practical importance to the realization of
just relations in culturally diverse states.

The Importance of First Principles
A key supposition of this book is that much is to be gained by focusing on
first principles or foundational assumptions. This proposition is supported

in two ways. Chapter 1 presents the case negatively by demonstrating how concerns with other theories raises questions that could be answered only by returning to foundational assumptions. The rest of the book presents the case positively by developing such a set of first principles in Part 2 and demonstrating their practical applicability in Part 3.

Relationship between Individuals and Communities

The account of the relationship between individuals and communities embodied in the foundations of meaningful life represents a second contribution. Its importance can be demonstrated in two ways: by its ability to explain why personal autonomy and identification with community should be understood as mutually supportive, rather than inherently conflictual, values; and by the way it enables us to address key issues identified in Chapter 1.

The first key move in the development of the foundations of meaningful life was to identify an underlying value that might explain how various conflicts and tensions – between individual and community, autonomy and identification, modern and premodern cultures – could be reconciled. That value, of course, was meaningful life, defined as the pursuit of subjectively significantly purposes. Once identified and brought to the fore, this conception of meaningful life was used to transform conceptions of personal autonomy and identification with community such that we could see how they actually work together in support of meaningful life. Situated autonomy presumes identifications with communities-as-contexts-of-values that can provide individuals with standards to inform their choices. At the same time, communities-as-contexts-of-value depend for their vitality on the exercise of situated autonomy by which their members, through meta-agency, constantly define and redefine those contexts in response to changing circumstances. So conceived, autonomy and identification work together to enable people to form, pursue, and sustain significant purposes. Neither can do this by itself.

The foundations of meaningful life also inform clear and consistent positions on many of the issues identified in Chapter 1. The general conception of the relationship between individuals and communities is reflected in the idea of self-identity as fluid-yet-fragile. The fragile aspect suggests, contrary to Kukathas and Ronald Dworkin, why some communities should not be treated as merely voluntary associations. The conception of self-identity as fluid and potentially encompassing identifications with multiple communities provides a more compelling conception of the relationship between individuals and communities than that suggested by cultural monism. In fact, the conception of the relationship between individuals and communities is most similar to the fluid identity/constitutive community conception associated in different ways with Iris Marion Young and James Tully.

The association of the value of communities with their ability to function as contexts of value helps clarify other issues. First, it clearly associates cultural interests with individuals, not groups. Second, the emphasis on community-as-context-of-value has implications for the types of community that can warrant accommodation. The point is not that nations or societal cultures cannot warrant accommodation – for they may where they embody valuable contexts of value – but that there is nothing special about their capacity in this regard: other types of communities – ethnic, religious, indigenous; modern, premodern, traditional – may perform the very same functions. Finally, this suggests that valuable communities should be recognized, defined, and protected in terms of the quality for which they are valued: the context of value which they embody.

This approach suggests that conflicts, both intra- and intercommunal, are best addressed by adopting principles reflecting equal respect for meaningful life. In particular, we should ensure that protection is minimal – that is, impermanent and focused on the community's minimal bases – and that membership is defined to allow freedom of exit and according to membership codes that clearly define members' rights and obligations. Where the tensions these principles induce prove insufficient to prevent conflicts, resolution is to be guided by direct appeal to the value of meaningful life. Within communities, those who wish to exercise autonomy in ways that threaten the minimal conditions necessary to sustain the community as a context of value must moderate their claims or leave the community. Between communities, resolution requires identifying conditions that will show equal respect for all citizens' interests in meaningful life. Where no community can demonstrate that meaningful life is at stake, however, resolution should be left to normal political processes. This approach is not intended to ensure identical outcomes across different contexts but to apply consistent and comprehensive principles so that resolutions neither are nor appear to be arbitrary or capricious.

Finally, the foundations of meaningful life inform a clear and principled approach to socialization. Unlike those who would treat socialization as something to be overcome, this approach views it as an essential process by which individuals develop the identifications essential to their capacity to act autonomous adults. That this approach recognizes that children have an interest in socialization does not mean they must be left to the mercy of their socializers; the value of meaningful life that counsels respect for processes of socialization also informs principles that can justify legitimate state intervention in these very same processes.

The Liberal Culturalist Consensus
Besides informing a credible account of the relationship between individuals and communities, the foundations of meaningful life can justify the six

claims associated in the Introduction with the liberal culturalist consensus. First, the idea of communities-as-contexts-of-value facilitates recognition of cultural groups. Second, the idea of the state as a social union of individuals united to facilitate the pursuit of meaningful life provides a basis for recognizing and accommodating such groups. Third, appeal to communities-as-contexts-of-value can justify accommodation of all four types of groups associated with the liberal cultural consensus: both national majorities and national minorities, where they embody valuable moral or purposive traditions; indigenous peoples and traditional or premodern minorities, as the foundations of meaningful life presume neither the inevitability of modernity nor the superiority of the examined life; and ethnic and immigrant groups, since cultural interests are associated with individuals, not any particular type of community, such as the nation or societal culture. Fourth, the substance of recognition or accommodation will vary with context since it must be tailored to the nature of a community's context of value and the particular challenges it faces. Fifth, the foundations of meaningful life suggest two complementary purposes for intercultural dialogue: to discover, articulate, and adjust the moral traditions that often constitute a pre-existing basis of social unity of political communities contained within existing state boundaries; and to function as a mutually educative process through which minorities' appeals for accommodation and proposals for state interventions can be negotiated. Sixth, and finally, accommodating legitimate claims appears likely to enhance social unity since the motivations for doing so, both moral (equal respect for meaningful life) and prudential (desire to preserve the state-level moral tradition) are likely to reinforce in the minds of participants the role the wider political community plays in sustaining meaning in their own lives.[1]

Practical Implications

Finally, and most concretely, by clarifying terminology and the relationship between words, I like to think that the argument advanced in this book provides intellectual resources that will help us imagine and advocate new solutions to the old problem of establishing just relations in culturally diverse states. Without the words to communicate such solutions and explain their advantages, political leaders will never be able to convince citizens to abandon a familiar yet unjust and undesirable status quo.

A key practical problem I believe this argument can help address is that for members of many groups, accepting many of the dominant theories of liberal multiculturalism requires accepting foundational assumptions that deny the legitimacy of their own ways of life. For example, how can members of traditional and premodern cultures accept theories that presume that modernity is inescapable and that illiberal ways of life are inherently unjust? How can ethnic, religious, or indigenous communities accept theories that presume the moral distinctiveness of modern nations? Conversely, how can those who accept these dominant theories not view the accommodation of traditional, premodern, or illiberal groups as arbitrary and unjust? My guiding intuition has been that the way ahead, if indeed there is a way ahead, must involve appeal to some value that can be accepted without compromise from within each of these perspectives. I believe the foundations of meaningful life constitute this way ahead for two reasons: the assumptions on which they are based do not necessarily deny the legitimacy of any way of life – modern or premodern; liberal or illiberal; national, ethnic, or indigenous – and, as the quotation of Rabbi Kimche in the epigraph to this Conclusion suggests, to act on them we do not need to understand, accept, or celebrate other people's contexts of values. We need only recognize that they value them and that they differ from our own.

Final Word: Liberal Multiculturalism

I believe that the theory of multiculturalism developed here represents the most extensive recognition that can be given to cultural diversity while maintaining a commitment to the moral universalism that underlies the very idea of human rights. It is a liberal and universalist theory of multiculturalism, not an anything-goes cultural relativism, because the very same principle of respect for meaningful life that justifies the accommodation of culturally diverse communities also provides a basis for judging, and at times intervening in, the internal practices of these communities. As such, I believe it strikes the balance implicit in Carens' call for "a critical perspective which is at the same time open to the possibility of genuine differences among people's values and commitments" and Eisenberg's call for "an approach that systematically and fairly incorporates the cultural and historical circumstances of different people into analysis, without giving everything away to context."[2] Only such a theory, or another that achieves similar outcomes by different means, can justify the hope of achieving a non-coerced consensus on the nature of justice in relations among the culturally diverse peoples who inhabit the world today.

Notes

Introduction

1 Will Kymlicka, *Liberalism, Community, and Culture* (Oxford: Oxford University Press, 1989).

2 Chandra Kukathas, "Are There Any Cultural Rights?" *Political Theory* 20 (1992): 105-39; Brian M. Barry, *Culture and Equality: An Egalitarian Critique of Multiculturalism* (Cambridge, MA: Harvard University Press, 2001).

3 Bhikhu Parekh, *Rethinking Multiculturalism: Cultural Diversity and Political Theory* (Houndmills, UK: Macmillan, 2000).

4 Desmond M. Clarke and Charles Jones, "Introduction," in *The Rights of Nations: Nations and Nationalism in a Changing World,* ed. Desmond M. Clarke and Charles Jones (New York: St. Martin's Press, 1999), 18.

5 Joseph H. Carens, *Culture, Citizenship, and Community* (Oxford: Oxford University Press, 2000), 235 n. 35.

6 Avigail Eisenberg, "Context, Cultural Difference, Sex and Social Justice," *Canadian Journal of Political Science* 35 (2002): 628.

7 Will Kymlicka, *Politics in the Vernacular: Nationalism, Multiculturalism, and Citizenship* (Oxford: Oxford University Press, 2001), 39-48.

8 The terminology is derived from Charles Taylor, "Cross-Purposes: The Liberal-Communitarian Debate," in *Liberalism and the Moral Life,* ed. Nancy L. Rosenblum (Cambridge, MA: Harvard University Press, 1989), 159-60.

9 Will Kymlicka, *Multicultural Citizenship* (Oxford: Clarendon Press, 1995), 182.

10 Kymlicka, *Politics in the Vernacular,* 9.

11 Carens, *Culture, Citizenship, and Community,* 14.

12 Ibid.

13 John Rawls, *A Theory of Justice* (Cambridge, MA: Belknap, 1971), 5.

Chapter 1: Why Return to Foundational Assumptions?

1 Ronald Dworkin, "What Is Equality? Part 2: Equality of Resources," *Philosophy & Public Affairs* 10 (1981): 288.

2 Ronald Dworkin, "What Is Equality? Part 3: The Place of Liberty," *Iowa Law Review* 73 (1987): 31, emphasis added.

3 Ronald Dworkin, "Liberal Community," *California Law Review* 77 (1989): 503.

4 Ronald Dworkin, "Foundations of Liberal Equality," *The Tanner Lectures on Human Values* 11 (1990): 102.

5 Dworkin, "Liberal Community," 490.

6 Michael Sandel, *Liberalism and the Limits of Justice* (Cambridge: Cambridge University Press, 1982), 62, 20-21.

7 Ibid., 143.

8 Ibid., 142-43, 150, emphasis in original.

9 Will Kymlicka, *Politics in the Vernacular: Nationalism, Multiculturalism, and Citizenship* (Oxford: Oxford University Press, 2001), 307.
10 Will Kymlicka, *Multicultural Citizenship* (Oxford: Clarendon Press, 1995), 76.
11 Ibid., 83.
12 He says this is not a claim "about the limits of human possibility, but about reasonable expectations." Ibid., 86.
13 Will Kymlicka, *Liberalism, Community, and Culture* (Oxford: Oxford University Press, 1989), 190.
14 Kymlicka, *Multicultural Citizenship*, 152, emphasis in original. An exception occurs where the survival of the community is at risk – that is, where "the vast majority of its members [would] end up dead, or in jail, or on skid row." Kymlicka, *Liberalism, Community, and Culture*, 170.
15 Kymlicka, *Liberalism, Community, and Culture*, 167. Of course, much turns on how the character of a community is described. If French Canada is conceived as a linguistic community, its "promotion of the French language does not aim at suffocating individuals under the yoke of community ... Quebec and Acadia can remain liberal in fundamental ways and at the same time endorse policies that promote a particular good, namely the French language." Pierre Coulombe, *Language Rights in French Canada* (New York: Peter Lang, 1995), 154-55. Conceived in terms of the pre-Quiet Revolution Québécois values of faith and tradition, the picture looks much different.
16 Kymlicka, *Multicultural Citizenship*, 113.
17 Ibid., 105.
18 James Nickel, "Liberalism, Community, and Culture" (book review), *Canadian Philosophical Reviews* (Edmonton: Academic Printing and Publishing, January 1990), 415.
19 Similarly, Amelie Oksenberg Rorty writes, criticizing Charles Taylor: "An individual's cultural identity is by no means the sole or even the dominant influence on his or her conception of a good life. Many other groups and associations also shape the habits – the frames of interpretation and categorization, the primary practices, interests, and motivational preoccupations – that express, actualize, and define an individual's identity." "The Hidden Politics of Cultural Identification," *Political Theory* 22 (1994): 154.
20 Kymlicka has tried to contain critiques based on the fact that individuals do select options that originated in other cultures by suggesting that this does not really represent individuals participating in multiple societal cultures but rather options from one societal culture have been incorporated into another. Kymlicka, *Multicultural Citizenship*, 103. Even if accepted, this raises a further question: How did these options enter the shared vocabulary of social life in the first place? Accepting that some people do choose options that are available only outside their societal culture, Kymlicka says he is "only dealing with general trends ... most people, most of the time, have a deep bond to their own culture" (90). This leaves unexplained why some people can do this.
21 Charles Taylor, *Modern Social Imaginaries* (Durham, NC: Duke University Press, 2004), 23.
22 Ibid., 185. As a product of historical development, it was not always so; as a state of consciousness of a particular civilization, not everyone shares it even today.
23 Charles Taylor, "Les Sources de l'identitie moderne," in *Les frontières de l'identité: Modernité et postmodernism au Quebec*, ed. Mikhael Elbaz, Andrée Fortin, and Guy LaForest (Sainte-Foy: Les Presses de L'Université Laval, 1996), 359. He also says that the Quebec state can pursue such "strong collective goals" and still remain "liberal" so long as it respects the diversity of those of its citizens who are not members of the cultural nation. He supports this claim by distinguishing between fundamental liberties, which must always be respected, and "privileges and immunities," such as those concerning the language of commercial signs, which need not. Charles Taylor, "The Politics of Recognition," in *Multiculturalism: Examining the Politics of Recognition*, ed. Amy Gutmann (Princeton, NJ: Princeton University Press, 1994), 59.
24 See, for example, his discussion of Pueblo dissidents. Kymlicka, *Liberalism, Community, and Culture*, 196-98.
25 Taylor, *Modern Social Imaginaries*, 191.
26 For instance, he has written: "What does individual assent mean? Is it agreement by the

individual in an identity quite independent of the community? Or by the individual who has come to live by the community goods? If the former, few communities would ever get started; if the latter, then the exit-veto option can't be everywhere appropriate." Charles Taylor, "A Catholic Modernity," in *A Catholic Modernity? Charles Taylor's Marianist Award Lecture*, ed. James L. Heft (New York: Oxford University Press, 1999), 112.

27 Chandra Kukathas, "Are There Any Cultural Rights?" *Political Theory* 20 (1992): 107 emphasis in original, 116, 117, 116, 126.

28 Ibid., 117, 110, 111, 112, 114.

29 Another example is found in Marilyn Friedman's idea of communities of choice. Communities of choice share communitarian insights about a "social self" that "acknowledges the role of social relationships and human community in constituting both self-identity and the nature and meaning of the particulars of individual lives" but are based not on shared history but on shared values, interests, or backgrounds of similar experience. Marilyn Friedman, "Feminism and Modern Friendship: Dislocating the Community," *Ethics* 99 (1989): 276. Such communities, she says, "may be as deeply constitutive of the identities and particulars of the individuals who participate in them as are the communities of place so warmly invoked by communitarians" (289).

30 I.M. Young, *Justice and the Politics of Difference* (Princeton, NJ: Princeton University Press, 1990), 44-45.

31 Ibid., 9.

32 Ibid., 46, emphasis in original.

33 I.M. Young, "Polity and Group Difference: A Critique of the Ideal of Universal Citizenship," *Ethics* 99 (1989): 260.

34 Kymlicka, *Multicultural Citizenship*, 23.

35 I.M. Young, "Polity and Group Difference," 267, 260.

36 Kukathas, "Are There Any Cultural Rights?" 116.

37 Will Kymlicka, "The Rights of Minority Cultures," *Political Theory* 20 (1992): 143.

38 Kymlicka, *Multicultural Citizenship*, 81.

39 Chandran Kukathas, "Cultural Rights Again: A Rejoinder to Kymlicka," *Political Theory* 20, 4 (November 1992): 677-78.

40 Joseph H. Carens, *Culture, Citizenship, and Community* (Oxford: Oxford University Press, 2000), 57.

41 Will Kymlicka, "Western Political Theory and Ethnic Relations in Eastern Europe," in *Can Liberal Pluralism Be Exported? Western Political Theory and Ethnic Relations in Eastern Europe*, ed. Will Kymlicka and Magda Opalski (Oxford: Oxford University Press, 2001), 34.

42 Taylor, "Politics of Recognition," quotations at 30, 28, 26, 28, 32.

43 Taylor writes: "The projection of an inferior or demeaning image on another can actually distort and oppress, to the extent that the image is internalized." Ibid., 36.

44 Ibid., 61.

45 Charles Taylor, "No Community, No Democracy, Part II," *Responsive Community* 14 (2003-04): 18, emphasis in original.

46 Taylor, *Modern Social Imaginaries*, 189, 190.

47 Ibid., 188-89, 192.

48 Taylor, "No Community, No Democracy, Part II," 20.

49 This is illustrated when, in discussing the place of Quebec in Canada, Taylor writes: "Refusing all mention of this [the promotion and protection of Quebec's distinct society] in the canonical definitions of the Canadian identity can only increase the feeling of many Quebeckers that they have no place in the federation." Charles Taylor, "Democratic Exclusion (and Its Remedies?)," Political theory workshop, University of Chicago, 7 February 2000, http://ptw.uchicago.edu/taylor00.pdf.

50 Charles Taylor, "Nationalism and Modernity," in *The Morality of Nationalism*, ed. Robert McKim and Jeff McMahan (New York: Oxford University Press, 1997), 46.

51 Carens, *Culture, Citizenship, and Community*, 171.

52 Ibid., 86.

53 James Tully, "Introduction," in *Multinational Democracies*, ed. Alain-G. Gagnon and James Tully (Cambridge: Cambridge University Press, 2001), 5.

54 James Tully, *Strange Multiplicity* (Cambridge: Cambridge University Press, 1995), 5-6, 7.
55 Tully, "Introduction," 13.
56 Kymlicka, *Multicultural Citizenship,* 80. More generally, see Kymlicka, ibid., 76-80; and Taylor, "The Politics of Recognition," 25-37.
57 For Taylor, this inescapability is associated with certain "institutional forms" of modernity – "the modern bureaucratic state, market economies, science, and technology." Taylor, *Modern Social Imaginaries,* 195. For a similar account, this time of these institutions' irresistibility, see Taylor, "Nationalism and Modernity," 43. For his part, Kymlicka says of societal cultures that they "did not always exist, and their creation is intimately linked with the process of modernization" and that they are the only type of culture that can survive in the modern world. Kymlicka, *Multicultural Citizenship,* 76, 80.
58 Taylor, *Modern Social Imaginaries,* 18.
59 Ibid., 151, 195.
60 Taylor, "Nationalism and Modernity," 44.
61 Kymlicka, "Western Political Theory," 23-24.
62 There are good reasons to resist assuming that modernity is inescapable. First, and most simply, as an empirical claim it is, at the very least, contestable; for example, all that traditional communities such as the Amish and Hutterites really seem to need to survive is to be left alone. Second, I think Taylor's explanation of why he thinks modernization inevitable is an excellent example of the importance of Carens' caution that "one can accept too readily constraints which, however real, should themselves be subject to criticism." Carens, *Culture, Citizenship, and Community,* 226. Taylor writes: "Whoever fails to take [the economic and bureaucratic processes of modernization] or some good functional equivalent on will fall behind so far in the power stakes as to be taken over and forced to undergo these changes anyway. There are good reasons in the relations of force for the onward march of modernity so defined." Taylor, "Nationalism and Modernity," 43. To treat as a constraint the tendency of powerful modern cultures to do what they want with less powerful premodern ones is to take the question of how we *should* deal with traditional cultures off the table, and thus, to undermine a key reason for thinking about justice and cultural diversity at all.
63 Kymlicka, *Multicultural Citizenship,* 170, 167.
64 Ibid., 120. He describes this as his "view" but declines to elaborate a defence for it.
65 Carens, *Culture, Citizenship, and Community,* 261.
66 Ibid., 7.
67 Ibid., 8, 12, 13.
68 Ibid., 260.
69 Joseph Raz, *The Morality of Freedom* (Oxford: Oxford University Press, 1986), 289-91.
70 Ibid., 301.
71 Ibid., 394, 392.
72 Ibid., 394.
73 Ibid., 392.
74 Joseph Raz, "Facing Up: A Reply," *Southern California Law Review* 62 (1989): 1227.
75 Ibid., Part 5.
76 He writes: "In modern pluralistic societies socialization introduces people ... to the value of choice, and of self-determination ... [If] the range of options actually open to them, unlike those available to others in their society, is disablingly restrictive, they have a legitimate grievance." Raz, "Facing Up: A Reply," 1229.
77 Raz, *The Morality of Freedom,* 424.
78 Ibid.
79 Joseph Raz and Avishai Margalit, "National Self-Determination," in *Ethics in the Public Domain: Essays in the Morality of Law and Politics* (Oxford: Clarendon Press, 1994). Raz's cultural monist assumptions rely heavily on a monological and deterministic conception of the effects of socialization. For instance, he writes: "Only through being socialized in a culture can one tap the options which give life a meaning." Joseph Raz, "Multiculturalism: A Liberal Perspective," in *Ethics in the Public Domain: Essays in the Morality of Law and Politics* (Oxford: Clarendon Press, 1994), 162. And further: "Our

options are limited by what is available in our society." Raz, *The Morality of Freedom*, 394. Similarly, he has described as "failures of socialization" members who are alienated from their culture and unable to find fulfilment in it. Raz, "Multiculturalism," 169.

80 Raz, "Multiculturalism."
81 For measures concerning multicultural groups, see Raz, "Multiculturalism," 174-75. For national self-determination, see Raz and Margalit, "National Self-Determination," 124-27.
82 Tully, *Strange Multiplicity*, 185, 4.
83 Carens, *Culture, Citizenship, and Community*, 61.
84 Tully, *Strange Multiplicity*, 4.
85 Ibid., 4.
86 Ibid., 99.
87 James Tully, "The Crisis of Identification: The Case of Canada," *Political Studies* 42 (1994): 90.
88 Tully, *Strange Multiplicity*, 30.
89 Ibid., 41.
90 Ibid., 43. As I understand this, it applies to Kymlicka's difficulty finding a place for groups that do not constitute (modern) societal cultures.
91 Ibid., 99-100, 14.
92 Ibid., 37, 57.
93 Kymlicka, *Multicultural Citizenship*, 171-72. Carens writes: "My ideal of differentiated citizenship thus entails a dialogue between aboriginal people and non-aboriginal people over the meaning of justice." Carens, *Culture, Citizenship, and Community*, 197.
94 Kymlicka, *Politics in the Vernacular*, 62-63; Carens, *Culture Citizenship, and Community*, 197.
95 Tully, *Strange Multiplicity*, 57.
96 Ibid., 30.
97 See, for example, Taylor, "No Community, No Democracy, Part II," 18-20; and Kymlicka's discussion of English Canadians in *Finding Our Way: Rethinking Ethnocultural Relations in Canada* (Oxford: Oxford University Press, 1998), 161.
98 Kymlicka, *Multicultural Citizenship*, 138-44.
99 Tully, *Strange Multiplicity*, 24.
100 Kymlicka, *Multicultural Citizenship*, 186, emphasis added.
101 Taylor, "No Community, No Democracy, Part II," 20.

Chapter 2: Meaningful Life and the Conception of the Person

1 John Rawls, *A Theory of Justice* (Cambridge, MA: Belknap, 1971), 5.
2 *Webster's Ninth Collegiate Dictionary* (Markham, ON: Thomas Allen and Son, 1990), 597.
3 Alfred Stern, *The Search for Meaning* (Memphis: Memphis State University Press, 197), 86.
4 Bhikhu Parekh, *Rethinking Multiculturalism: Cultural Diversity and Political Theory* (Houndmills, UK: Macmillan, 2000), 142.
5 Robert Nozick, *Philosophical Explanations* (Cambridge, MA: Belknap, 1981), 594.
6 Ibid., 575.
7 Ibid., 596-97.
8 For example, Tolstoy wrote of faith that "no matter how irrational and monstrous the answers that faith gave, they had this advantage that they introduced into each answer the relation of the finite to the infinite, without which there could be no answer." Leo Tolstoy, "My Confession," in *Life and Meaning: A Reader*, ed. Oswald Hanfling (Oxford: Basil Blackwell, 1987), 18.
9 Nozick, *Philosophical Explanations*, 601.
10 Tolstoy, "My Confession," 17-18.
11 Nozick, *Philosophical Explanations*, 610.
12 Ibid., 618.
13 Bernard Williams, "Persons, Character, and Morality," in *The Identities of Persons*, ed. Amelie Oksenberg Rorty (Berkeley: University of California, 1976), 207.
14 Quoted in O. Hanfling, *The Quest for Meaning* (Oxford: Basil Blackwell, 1987), x, emphasis in original.
15 Kurt Baier, "The Purpose of Man's Existence," in *Life and Meaning: A Reader*, ed. Oswald Hanfling (Oxford: Basil Blackwell, 1987), 23.

16 Charles Taylor, "A Catholic Modernity?" in *A Catholic Modernity? Charles Taylor's Marianist Award Lecture,* ed. James L. Heft (New York: Oxford University Press, 1999), 26.

17 Viktor Frankl, *Man's Search for Meaning* (New York: Washington Square Press, 1985), 98.

18 J.S. Mill, "Autobiography," in *Essential Works of John Stuart Mill,* ed. Max Lerner (New York: Bantam Books, 1961), 83.

19 Tolstoy, "My Confession," 11.

20 Emile Durkheim, *Suicide,* trans. John A. Spaulding and George Simpson (Glencoe, IL: The Free Press, 1951), 248.

21 Rawls, *A Theory of Justice,* 440.

22 David Archard, "Autonomy, Character and Situation," in *Liberalism, Citizenship and Autonomy,* ed. David Milligan and William Watts Miller (Aldershot, UK: Avebury, 1992), 158.

23 In I.M. Young, *Justice and the Politics of Difference* (Princeton, NJ: Princeton University Press, 1990), 46.

24 Michael Sandel, *Liberalism and the Limits of Justice* (Cambridge: Cambridge University Press, 1982), 20.

25 This account of persons whose self-identities are derived in part from identifications with communities and whose governing assumptions are subsets of these self-identities is similar to Bhikhu Parekh's suggestion that "human beings are articulated at three different but interrelated levels: what they share as members of a common species, what they derive from and share as members of a cultural community, and what they succeed in giving themselves as reflective individuals." Parekh, *Rethinking Multiculturalism,* 123.

26 Charles Taylor, "The Politics of Recognition," in *Multiculturalism: Examining the Politics of Recognition,* ed. Amy Gutmann (Princeton, NJ: Princeton University Press, 1994), 33-34.

27 While this phrase is borrowed from Alasdair MacIntyre, I do not mean to import his idea that moral starting points are permanently constitutive. Alasdair MacIntyre, *After Virtue,* 2nd ed. (Notre Dame, IN: University of Notre Dame Press, 1984), 220.

28 Sandel, *Liberalism and the Limits of Justice,* 165.

29 Parekh, *Rethinking Multiculturalism,* 145.

30 These descriptions are based on John Kekes' discussion of two types of relationship described by Michael Oakeshott. Kekes gives no name to what we are calling purposive tradition; Oakeshott calls it "enterprise association." Michael Oakeshott, "On the Civil Condition," in *On Human Conduct* (Oxford: Clarendon Press, 1975), 119.

31 John Kekes, "Moral Tradition," in *Life and Meaning: A Reader,* ed. Oswald Hanfling (Oxford: Basil Blackwell, 1985), 237.

32 Ibid., 240.

33 I.M. Young, *Justice and the Politics of Difference,* 186.

34 Ibid., 186.

35 Sandel, *Liberalism and the Limits of Justice,* 80, 143.

36 Charles Taylor, *Sources of the Self* (Cambridge, MA: Harvard University Press, 1989), chap. 2.

37 This is often employed in discussions of tradition and agency. See, for instance, Alasdair MacIntyre's *After Virtue,* esp. chaps. 14 and 15, and *Whose Justice? Which Rationality?* (Notre Dame, IN: Notre Dame University Press, 1988), esp. chaps. 17 and 18.

38 Philyp Rosser, "Growing Through Political Change," in *The National Question Again: Welsh Political Identity in the 1980s,* ed. J. Osmond (Llandysul, UK: Gomer Press, 1985), quotations at 182, 182, 182, 184, 189, 190, 190.

39 John Christman, "Introduction," *The Inner Citadel: Essays on Individual Autonomy,* ed. John Christman (New York: Oxford University Press, 1989), 6-7.

40 Gerald Dworkin, *The Theory and Practice of Autonomy* (Cambridge: Cambridge University Press, 1988), 15.

41 Stanley Benn, "Freedom, Autonomy, and the Concept of a Person," *Proceedings of the Aristotelian Society* 76 (1975-76): 116, 113.

42 Harry G. Frankfurt, "Freedom of the Will and the Concept of a Person," *Journal of Philosophy* 68 (1971): 11.

43 Benn, "Freedom, Autonomy, and the Concept of a Person," 124.

44 I.M. Young, *Justice and the Politics of Difference,* 45; Robert Young, *Personal Autonomy:*

Beyond Negative and Positive Liberty (London: Croom Helm, 1986), 8. Onora O'Neil has also developed an approach that emphasizes coherence and independence. See her "Autonomy, Coherence and Independence," in *Liberalism, Citizenship and Autonomy*, ed. David Milligan and William Watts Miller (Aldershot, UK: Avebury, 1992).

45 In a similar vein, Joseph Raz claims that only over-intellectualized conceptions of autonomy require people to give unity to their lives. Raz, *The Morality of Freedom*, 370-71. He also rejects the "ideal of the perfect existentialist with no fixed biological and social nature who creates himself as he goes along" (155).

46 Dworkin, *The Theory and Practice of Autonomy*, 18.

47 John Christman, "Autonomy: A Defense of the Split-Level Self," *Southern Journal of Philosophy* 25 (1987): 291.

48 Robert Young, "Autonomy and Socialization," *Mind* 89 (1980): 573.

49 Robert Young, *Personal Autonomy*, 40. See also Robert Young, "Autonomy and Socialization," 568; M. Friedman, "Autonomy and the Split-Level Self," *Southern Journal of Philosophy* 24 (1986); Benn, "Freedom, Autonomy, and the Concept of a Person"; and Christman, "Introduction."

50 Benn, "Freedom, Autonomy, and the Concept of a Person," 116.

Chapter 3: Justifying Cultural Accommodation

1 Calvin Trillen, "Drawing the Line," *The New Yorker*, 12 December 1994, 51.

2 I.M. Young, *Justice and the Politics of Difference* (Princeton, NJ: Princeton University Press, 1990), 46.

3 In the following example, at least one identification at each interval provides a link to the earlier identity:

t_1: identity$_{abc}$; given identification b, a is replaced by d.
t_2: identity$_{dbc}$; given identification d, b is replaced by e.
t_3: identity$_{dec}$; given identification d, c is replaced by f.
t_4: identity$_{def}$.

At each interval at least one identification provides a link to the earlier identity.

4 Alasdair MacIntyre, *After Virtue*, 2nd ed. (Notre Dame, IN: University of Notre Dame Press, 1984), 217-18.

5 I thank Richard Vernon for pointing out the similarity between this and Michael Oakeshott's idea that the identity in historical change "may be found in its own coherence; that is, in its character as a passage of differences which touch and modify one another and converge to compose a subsequent difference." Michael Oakeshott, "Historical Change," in *On History and Other Essays* (Oxford: Basil Blackwell, 1983), 114.

6 Will Kymlicka, *Liberalism, Community, and Culture* (Oxford: Oxford University Press, 1989), 170.

7 Charles Taylor, *Sources of the Self* (Cambridge, MA: Harvard University Press, 1989), 27.

8 Joseph Raz, *The Morality of Freedom* (Oxford: Oxford University Press, 1986), 310-11.

9 Stanley Benn, *A Theory of Freedom* (Cambridge: Cambridge University Press, 1988), 218.

10 David Archard, "Autonomy, Character and Situation," in *Liberalism, Citizenship and Autonomy*, ed. David Milligan and William Watts Miller (Aldershot, UK: Avebury, 1992), 167.

11 Benn, *A Theory of Freedom*, 181.

12 Of course, a person with identity$_{hij}$, which prevented him from identifying with l, *might* come to identify with it over the mid- to long term through an indirect process like this:

t_1: identity$_{hij}$; given identification i, h is replaced by k.
t_2: identity$_{ijk}$; given identification k, i is replaced by l.
t_3: identity$_{jkl}$.

13 Harry G. Frankfurt, "The Importance of What We Care About," in *The Importance of What We Care About* (Cambridge: Cambridge University Press, 1988), 86-87, emphasis in original.

14 Ronald Dworkin, "Liberal Community," *California Law Review* 77 (1989): 490.

15 Ralph Linton, "The Distinctive Aspects of Acculturation," in *The Emergent Native Americans*, ed. Deward E. Walker Jr. (Boston: Little, Brown, 1972), 8-9.

16 In a very relevant article, Chandler and Lalonde use statistical data for First Nations in British Columbia to argue for a connection between self-continuity, cultural continuity, and suicide. Michael J. Chandler and Christopher Lalonde, "Cultural Continuity as a Hedge against Suicide in Canada's First Nations," *Transcultural Psychology* 35 (2): 191-219. Ronet Bachman documents that Indians in the United States suffer the worst levels of poverty of any group, have homicide rates second only to blacks, and have had the highest suicide rate. Ronet Bachman, *Death and Violence on the Reservation: Homicide, Family Violence, and Suicide in American Indian Populations* (New York: Auburn House, 1992). Others have made the case, in studying the Pueblo, Navajo, and Apache, that level of acculturation seems to be an important factor in explaining suicide rates. Nancy Westlake Van Winkle and Philip A. May, "Native American Suicide in New Mexico, 1957-1979: A Comparative Study," *Human Organization* 45 (1986): 306-7.

17 Joel Feinberg, "The Child's Right to an Open Future," in *Whose Child? Children's Rights, Parental Authority, and State Power*, ed. William Aiken and Hugh LaFollette (Totowa, NJ: Rowman and Littlefield, 1980), 148-49.

18 Brian Fay, *Contemporary Philosophy of Social Science* (Oxford: Blackwell, 1996), chap. 1.

19 John Kekes, *The Morality of Pluralism* (Princeton, NJ: Princeton University Press, 1993), 125-32.

20 A practice that does not match this description is a rural African ritual in which a widow is expected to have sex with one of her dead husband's relatives "to break the bond with his spirit and, it is said, save her and the rest of the village from insanity and disease." Where the widow does not choose to practice this ritual, as was the case in the *Times* story, the facts that it posed serious risks for her (especially given the prevalence of AIDS) and that it constituted part of a way of life that appeared designed to exploit her without offering any compensatory benefits, provide good reasons to resist accommodating it. I discuss the issues raised by such cases more thoroughly in Chapters 6 and 7. Sharon LaFraniere, "AIDS Now Compels Africa to Challenge Widows' Cleansing," *New York Times*, 11 May 2005.

21 Will Kymlicka, *Multicultural Citizenship* (Oxford: Clarendon Press, 1995), 173.

22 Charles Taylor, "Shared and Divergent Values," in *Reconciling the Solitudes*, ed. Guy LaForest (Montreal: McGill-Queen's University Press, 1993), 183; John Rawls, *Political Liberalism* (New York: Columbia University Press, 1993), 329.

23 Kymlicka, *Multicultural Citizenship*, 173, 176.

24 David Miller, *On Nationality* (Oxford: Clarendon Press, 1995), 93, 92.

25 Ibid., 138-42; Kymlicka, *Multicultural Citizenship*, 176-81.

26 Kymlicka, *Multicultural Citizenship*, 182.

27 Miller, *On Nationality*, 140. While Miller directs this comment at "radical multiculturalists," it surely applies to all groups that reject identification with the wider community.

28 Ibid., 108-15. Kymlicka also accepts that there may be circumstances in which secession is a legitimate solution. Kymlicka, *Multicultural Citizenship*, 186.

29 Miller, *On Nationality*, 84-85.

30 Ibid., 116-17.

31 Kymlicka, *Multicultural Citizenship*, 188, 191.

32 Ibid., 191, referring to Taylor.

33 Bhikhu Parekh, *Rethinking Multiculturalism: Cultural Diversity and Political Theory* (Houndmills, UK: Macmillan, 2000), 98.

34 Kymlicka, *Multicultural Citizenship*, 189.

35 Will Kymlicka, *Finding Our Way: Rethinking Ethnocultural Relations in Canada* (Oxford: Oxford University Press, 1998), 175.

36 James Tully, *Strange Multiplicity* (Cambridge: Cambridge University Press, 1995), 24-25.

37 Jeremy Webber quoted in Kymlicka, *Finding Our Way*, 176.

38 Ibid., 177.

39 Joseph H. Carens, *Culture, Citizenship, and Community* (Oxford: Oxford University Press,

2000), 98.
40 In particular, the majority, in its use of the state, will have to respect the same principles as suggested in Chapter 6 for minorities in administering their communities. Similarly, to justify special measures to protect its community, a majority, just like a minority community, would have to demonstrate that it is threatened with destruction. Given its dominant position, this would be a difficult but not necessarily impossible requirement to meet.
41 Taylor, "Shared and Divergent Values," 183.

Chapter 4: Situated Autonomy and Socialization

1 Gerald Dworkin, *The Theory and Practice of Autonomy* (Cambridge: Cambridge University Press, 1988), 20.
2 Ibid., 47.
3 Ibid., 36.
4 Ibid., 12.
5 Marilyn Friedman, "Autonomy and the Split-Level Self," *Southern Journal of Philosophy* 24 (1986): 25.
6 Dworkin, *The Theory and Practice of Autonomy*, 20.
7 John Christman, "Introduction," *The Inner Citadel: Essays on Individual Autonomy*, ed. John Christman (New York: Oxford University Press, 1989), 9.
8 Friedman, "Autonomy and the Split-Level Self," 26, emphasis in original.
9 J.P. Sartre, mentioned in Dworkin, *The Theory and Practice of Autonomy*, 36.
10 Stanley Benn, *A Theory of Freedom*, (Cambridge: Cambridge University Press, 1988), 179, 175.
11 Stanley Benn, "Freedom, Autonomy, and the Concept of a Person," *Proceedings of the Aristotelian Society* 76 (1975-76): 126.
12 Ibid., 117.
13 Thomas Hurka, "Why Value Autonomy?" *Social Theory and Practice* 13 (1987): 366.
14 Ibid., 361-62.
15 In a similar way, Raz's conception of well-being also allows him to reject the idea that all good lives must involve choice: "I do not see that the absence of choice diminishes the value of human relations or the display of excellence in technical skills, physical ability, spirit and enterprise, leadership, scholarship, creativity, or imaginativeness, which can all be encompassed in such lives." Joseph Raz, "Facing Up: A Reply," *Southern California Law Review* 62 (1989): 1227.
16 Jon Elster, "Sour Grapes – Utilitarianism and the Genesis of Wants," in *Utilitarianism and Beyond*, ed. Amartya Sen and Bernard Williams (Cambridge: Cambridge University Press, 1982), 228, emphasis added.
17 Benn, "Freedom, Autonomy, and the Concept of a Person," 122, 123, 129, 124, 129.
18 Ibid., 123.
19 Ibid., 126.
20 While Benn may deny this — for example, he claims that autonomy requires only that a person "be alive to, and disposed to resolve by rational reflection and decision, incoherences in the complex tradition which he has internalized" (*A Theory of Freedom*, 182) – this does not bear scrutiny. Someone who was merely "alive to and disposed to" resolve incoherences but never actually experienced any could not become autonomous on this account since she would never have made her standards her own. Without such experiences she cannot discover "who she really is." Benn, "Freedom, Autonomy, and the Concept of a Person," 127.
21 John Stuart Mill, "Utilitarianism," in *Utilitarianism, On Liberty and Considerations on Representative Government*, ed. H.B. Acton (London: Dent, 1972), 10.
22 On "progressive beings" and the "higher faculties," see Mill, "On Liberty," in *Utilitarianism, On Liberty and Considerations on Representative Government*, ed. H.B. Acton (London: Dent, 1972), 79; and Mill, "Utilitarianism," 9-10, respectively. Progressive beings pursue the utilitarian goal of discovering "more and more effective means for the diminution of evils and the multiplication of higher pleasures." Mill, "On Liberty," 459n8. The list of examples is found in "On Liberty," 126.

23 Mill, "On Liberty," 128, 124.

24 E.G. West, "Liberty and Education: John Stuart Mill's Dilemma," *Philosophy* 40 (1965): 136.

25 Mill, "On Liberty," 86.

26 Ibid., 176-77, emphasis added.

27 Will Kymlicka, *Multicultural Citizenship* (Oxford: Clarendon Press, 1995), 92, 82.

28 Kenneth Henley, "The Authority to Educate," in *Having Children: Philosophical and Legal Reflections on Parenthood,* ed. Onora O'Neill and William Ruddick (New York: Oxford University Press, 1979), 261.

29 Amy Gutmann, "Undemocratic Education," in *Liberalism and the Moral Life,* ed. Nancy L. Rosenblum (Cambridge, MA: Harvard University Press, 1989), 82, 77-79.

30 Richard Arneson and Ian Shapiro, "Democratic Autonomy and Religious Freedom: A Critique of *Wisconsin v. Yoder,*" in *Democracy's Place,* ed. Ian Shapiro (Ithaca, NY: Cornell University Press, 1996), 171.

31 Ibid., 162, 174, emphasis added.

32 Will Kymlicka, *Liberalism, Community, and Culture·*(Oxford: Oxford University Press, 1989), 53, emphasis in original.

33 William Galston, "Civic Education in the Liberal State," in *Liberalism and the Moral Life,* ed. Nancy L. Rosenblum (Cambridge, MA: Harvard University Press, 1989), 101.

34 Imagine a medical school that gave equal time to the claims of modern medicine, phrenology, and witchcraft.

35 As Galston notes, proposals like Gutmann's "can have corrosive consequences for political communities in which it is allowed to take place. The pursuit of truth – scientific, historical, moral, or whatever – can undermine structures of unexamined but socially central belief." Galston, "Civic Education in the Liberal State," 90.

36 Quoted in Joel Feinberg, "The Child's Right to an Open Future," in *Whose Child? Children's Rights, Parental Authority, and State Power,* ed. William Aiken and Hugh LaFollette (Totowa, NJ: Rowman and Littlefield, 1980), 134.

37 Benn, *A Theory of Freedom,* 190-91, 183.

38 Canada, Royal Commission on Aboriginal Peoples, *Overview of the First Round – Public Hearings,* prepared for the Commission by Michael Cassidy, Ginger Group Consultants (Ottawa: Royal Commission on Aboriginal Peoples, 1992), 19.

39 Galston, "Civic Education in the Liberal State," 100.

40 One argument they might make is based on Mill's defence of the "higher pleasures." The argument is that the *majority* of those who have experienced both higher and lower pleasures prefer the higher (Mill, "Utilitarianism," 9-11). Even were this true, it cannot justify compelling people to live examined lives. First, this evidence would demonstrate only that this way of life was preferred by more people, not that it was superior. Second, the comparison may not be neutral: it may be that people's characters are changed in the process of learning to enjoy higher pleasures and what is in their interest changes with it Richard Lindley, *Autonomy* (London: Macmillan Education, 1986), 60-61. For example, while people may come to prefer Robert Nozick's "experience machine" after they have been hooked up to it, this cannot be an argument for hooking them up now against their will. Robert Nozick, *Anarchy, State, and Utopia* (New York: Basic Books, 1974), 42. Third, even were the life of higher pleasures objectively superior, respect for meaningful lives requires that people be left to choose or reject it for themselves.

41 Lindley, *Autonomy,* 50.

42 For instance, Gregg Easterbrook writes:

Suppose you accept the Big Bang theory ... Here's what you believe, roughly, according to the model proposed by Alan Guth, a physicist at the Massachusetts Institute of Technology:

You believe that, once upon a time, all the potential of the cosmos – ... a firmament of 40 billion galaxies at last count – was packed into a point smaller than a proton. You believe that within this incipient cosmos was neither hypercompressed matter nor superdense energy nor any tangible substance. It was a "false vacuum" through which coursed a weightless, empty quantum-mechanical probability framework called a "scalar field" ...

Next, you believe that, when the Big Bang sounded, the universe expanded from a pinpoint to cosmological size in far less than one second – space itself hurtling outward in a torrent of pure physics, the bow wave of the new cosmos moving at trillions of times the speed of light.

Further, you believe that, as subatomic particles began to unbuckle from the inexplicable proto-reality, both matter and antimatter formed. Immediately, these commodities began to collide and annihilate themselves, vanishing as mysteriously as they came. The only reason our universe is here today is that the Bang was slightly asymmetrical, its yield favouring matter over antimatter by about one part per 100 million. Because of this, when the stupendous cosmic commencement day ended, a residue of standard matter survived, and from it the galaxies formed ...

It's wise to take the Big Bang hypothesis seriously, since considerable evidence weighs in its favour ...

Yet, for sheer extravagant implausibility, nothing in theology or metaphysics can hold a candle to the Bang. Surely, if this description of the cosmic genesis came from the Bible or the Koran rather than the Massachusetts Institute of Technology, it would be treated as preposterous myth.

Gregg Easterbrook, "Is God at the End of the Scientific Rainbow?" *Globe and Mail,* 24 October 1998, D5.

43 Gerald Dworkin also challenges the distinction between autonomy of moral principles and autonomy of scientific principles, in *The Theory and Practice of Autonomy,* ch. 4.

44 Diana Meyers, "Personal Autonomy and the Paradox of Feminine Socialization," *Journal of Philosophy* 84, 10 (1987): 625-26.

45 K. Pyne Addelson, "Personal Autonomy and the Paradox of Feminine Socialization," *Journal of Philosophy* 84, 10 (1987): 629.

46 Henley, "The Authority to Educate," 262.

47 Mill, "On Liberty," 125.

48 Lindley, *Autonomy,* 52. Similarly, Robert Young speaks of "true motivations," discovered through critical reflection, which are "central or important to who one is and what one wants to be." Robert Young, *Personal Autonomy: Beyond Negative and Positive Liberty* (London: Croom Helm, 1986), 39-40.

49 Feinberg, "The Child's Right to an Open Future," 149.

50 Lindley, *Autonomy,* 52.

51 Henley, "The Authority to Educate," 256, emphasis in original.

52 Feinberg, "The Child's Right to an Open Future," 143, 149-51, emphasis in original.

53 Diana Meyers, *Self, Society and Personal Choice* (New York: Columbia University Press, 1989), 96, 207, 262.

54 Ibid., 20, 44.

55 Ibid., 20.

56 Ibid., 92.

57 Diana Meyers, "The Socialized Individual and Individual Autonomy: An Intersection between Philosophy and Psychology," in *Women and Moral Theory,* ed. Eva Feder Kittay and Diana T. Meyers (Totowa, NJ: Rowman and Littlefield, 1987), 151.

58 Meyers, *Self, Society and Personal Choice,* 81.

59 Ibid., 76.

60 Ibid., 95.

61 Ibid., 54.

62 Ibid., 215, 233.

63 Ibid., 193

64 John Christman, "Autonomy: A Defense of the Split-Level Self," *Southern Journal of Philosophy* 25 (1987): 287.

65 Benn, *A Theory of Freedom,* 179, 182.

66 Ibid., 183. Similarly, as we have seen, Kymlicka associates the genesis and basis of "societal cultures" with modernization. Kymlicka, *Multicultural Citizenship,* 76.

67 Benn, *A Theory of Freedom*, 180.
68 Benn, "Freedom, Autonomy, and the Concept of a Person," 118, 124, emphasis in original.
69 Since differences between people leading open-minded lives and those leading dogmatic lives become pronounced only when and if they experience dissonance, by sustaining conditions in which people can lead lives of situated autonomy, we necessarily permit others to lead dogmatic and wanton lives. This cannot be avoided.
70 This idea is influenced by Dworkin, *The Theory and Practice of Autonomy*, 38.
71 David O. Brink, *Moral Realism and the Foundations of Ethics* (Cambridge: Cambridge University Press, 1989), 103, emphasis in original.
72 Harry G. Frankfurt, "Identification and Wholeheartedness," in *The Importance of What We Care About* (Cambridge: Cambridge University Press, 1988), 168-69.
73 Alasdair MacIntyre, *Whose Justice? Which Rationality?* (Notre Dame, IN: Notre Dame University Press, 1988), 400.
74 John Kekes, "Moral Tradition," in *Life and Meaning: A Reader,* ed. Oswald Hanfling (Oxford: Basil Blackwell, 1985), 245.
75 Harry G. Frankfurt, "Freedom of the Will and the Concept of a Person," *Journal of Philosophy* 68 (1971): 16-17.
76 Harry G. Frankfurt, "The Importance of What We Care About," in *The Importance of What We Care About*, 80-94 (Cambridge: Cambridge University Press, 1988), 88.
77 Hanna Papanek, "To Each Less than She Needs, from Each, More than She Can Do: Allocations, Entitlements, and Value," in *Persistent Inequalities: Women and World Development,* ed. Irene Tinker (Oxford: Oxford University Press, 1990), 176.
78 In using this example, I am not endorsing Young's account of why this should be considered autonomous. R. Young, *Personal Autonomy*, 16-17.
79 Dworkin, *The Theory and Practice of Autonomy*, 38.
80 Susan Moller Okin, "Gender Inequality and Cultural Differences," *Political Theory* 22 (1994): 19, emphasis in original.
81 Marlise Simons, "France Moves to Stem Polygamy," *Globe and Mail,* 1 February 1996, A18.
82 Joseph H. Carens, *Culture, Citizenship, and Community* (Oxford: Oxford University Press, 2000), 235.
83 Frankfurt, "The Importance of What We Care About," 87.

Chapter 5: Defining Communities and Justifying Accommodation

1 Amelie Oksenberg Rorty, "The Hidden Politics of Cultural Identification," *Political Theory* 22 (1994): 161.
2 Bhikhu Parekh, *Rethinking Multiculturalism: Cultural Diversity and Political Theory* (Houndmills, UK: Macmillan, 2000), 137.
3 Rorty, "The Hidden Politics of Cultural Identification," 158.
4 Anne Phillips, "Dealing with Difference: A Politics of Ideas or a Politics of Presence?" *Constellations* 1 (1994): 85.
5 Robert Matas, "Religious Ruling Comes as Blow to Liberal Sikhs," *Globe and Mail,* 28 April 1998, A2.
6 Pierre Coulombe, *Language Rights in French Canada* (New York: Peter Lang, 1995), 123.
7 Emory Sekaquaptecco Jr., in US Congress, Senate, Subcommittee on Constitutional Rights of the Committee of the Judiciary, *Amendments to the Indian Bill of Rights,* 91st Cong., 1st sess., 1969, 121.
8 Coulombe, *Language Rights in French Canada,* 123.
9 Canada, House of Commons, *Minutes of the Proceedings and Evidence of the Standing Committee on Aboriginal Affairs and Northern Development* (Ottawa: Canadian Government Publishing Centre), issue no. 39 (27 April 1988), 56.
10 US Congress, Senate, 121.
11 *R. v. Powley,* [2003] 2 S.C.R. 207, 2003 SCC 43. All parenthetical citations are to paragraph numbers from the decision.
12 John Borland, Ralph Fevre, and David Denney, "Nationalism and Community in North West Wales," *Sociological Review* 40 (1992), 56, emphasis in original.

13 Ibid., 61, 62.
14 Ibid., 63.
15 Ibid., 65-66.
16 *Ford v. Quebec (Attorney General),* [1988] 2 S.C.R. 712 at 749.
17 Rorty, "The Hidden Politics of Cultural Differentiation," 155.
18 Edward P. Dozier, *The Pueblo Indians of North America* (New York: Holt, Rinehart and Winston, 1970), 43.
19 Joseph H. Suina and Laura B. Smolkin, "The Multicultural Worlds of Pueblo Indian Children's Celebrations," *Journal of American Indian Education* 34 (1995): 19.
20 Dozier, *The Pueblo Indians of North America,* 151.
21 Edward P. Dozier, "Factionalism at Santa Clara Pueblo," *Ethnology* 5 (1966): 174-75.
22 Dozier, *The Pueblo Indians of North America,* 50, 67.
23 Ibid., 75.
24 Ibid., 68.
25 Will Kymlicka, *Liberalism, Community, and Culture* (Oxford: Oxford University Press, 1989), 196; Frances Svensson, "Liberal Democracy and Group Rights: The Legacy of Individualism and Its Impact on American Indian Tribes," *Political Studies* 27 (1979): 431.
26 Alfonso Ortiz, "The Dynamics of Pueblo Cultural Survival," in *North American Indian Anthropology,* ed. Raymond J. Demallie and Alfonso Ortiz (Norman: University of Oklahoma Press, 1994), 296.
27 Suina and Smolkin, "Multicultural Worlds," 20.
28 US Congress, Senate, 20.
29 Quoted in Barry Osborne, "Cultural Congruence, Ethnicity, and Fused Biculturalism: Zuni, and Torres Strait," *Journal of American Indian Education* 28 (1989): 11.
30 US Congress, Senate, 38, 7.
31 Ortiz, "The Dynamics of Pueblo Cultural Survival," 298.
32 Alfonso Ortiz, *The Tewa World* (Chicago: University of Chicago Press, 1969), 70.
33 J. Wunder, *"Retained by the People": A History of American Indians and the Bill of Rights* (Oxford: Oxford University Press, 1994), 163.
34 Ortiz, "The Dynamics of Pueblo Cultural Survival," 304.
35 Jill D. Sweet, "Burlesquing the Other in Pueblo Performance," *Annals of Tourism Research* 16 (1989): 67-73.
36 Ortiz, "The Dynamics of Pueblo Cultural Survival," 303.
37 Suina and Smolkin, "Multicultural Worlds," 21.
38 Ibid., 20.
39 Ibid., 23.
40 US Congress, Senate, 55, 58.
41 Wayne Suttles, "Spirit Dancing and the Persistence of Native Culture among the Coast Salish," in *Coast Salish Essays* (Vancouver: Talon Books, 1987), 204.
42 Ibid., 207-8.
43 Pamela Amoss, *Coast Salish Spirit Dancing: The Survival of an Ancestral Religion* (Seattle: University of Washington Press, 1978), 142-44.
44 Suttles, "Spirit Dancing," 208.
45 Reliance on summer work made the traditional potlatch festival inconvenient. Suttles, "Spirit Dancing," 207-8.
46 Ibid., 200-6.
47 Amoss, *Coast Salish Spirit Dancing,* 152.
48 Ibid., 158, 163.
49 Benedict Anderson, *Imagined Community* (London: Verso, 1983), chap. 4; Amoss, *Coast Salish Spirit Dancing,* 159.
50 Amoss, *Coast Salish Spirit Dancing,* quotations at 145, 147, 151.
51 Will Kymlicka, *Multicultural Citizenship* (Oxford: Clarendon Press, 1995), 23.
52 Suttles, "Spirit Dancing," 204. In fact, this has often been associated with the socialization of deviants. For instance, Amoss writes, "If a young adult is drinking heavily, is involved in a romantic affair of which his family disapproves, or simply is being difficult and rebellious, he may find himself 'grabbed' and initiated as a dancer for the express purpose

of correcting his behavior." Amoss, *Coast Salish Spirit Dancing,* 143. The process "is commenced by the initiate being 'grabbed,' by his or her initiators, and taken to a Long House and there detained for a number of days ... While in the Long House, the initiate undergoes a process which includes being lifted horizontally to shoulder or head height, by eight or so initiators who, among other things, blow on the body of the initiate to help the initiate 'bring out' or sing his or her song ... During the process the initiate participates in rituals including a ceremonial bath, dressing in clean clothes, fasting and sleeping in a blanket tent set up in the House." *Thomas v. Norris,* [1992] 2 C.N.L.R. 139, 34.

53 *Thomas v. Norris,* [1992] 2 C.N.L.R. 139, 8.

54 Tim Schouls, *Shifting Boundaries: Aboriginal Identity, Pluralist Theory, and the Politics of Self-Government* (Vancouver: UBC Press, 2003), 120.

55 In a recent article, Kymlicka provides an interesting example of an identity, Cossack, that probably couldn't warrant special accommodation for this reason. Of the Cossack identity, he writes: "It appears as if the right to rule over others has become part and parcel of the very idea of 'Cossack-ness' ... Were this claim to dominance given up, it is not clear that Cossacks would have any basis or reason to distinguish themselves from other Russians, or to continue to mobilize for ethnic minority rights." Will Kymlicka, "Western Political Theory and Ethnic Relations in Eastern Europe," in *Can Liberal Pluralism Be Exported? Western Political Theory and Ethnic Relations in Eastern Europe,* ed. Will Kymlicka and Magda Opalski (Oxford: Oxford University Press, 2001), 81.

56 *Wisconsin v. Yoder,* 92 S. Ct. 1526 (1972), 1530.

57 For further discussion of this case, see Natasha Bakht, "Family Arbitration Using Sharia Law: Examining Ontario's Arbitration Act and Its Impact on Women," *Muslim World Journal of Human Rights* 1 (2004), http://www.bepress.com/mwjhr; and Marion Boyd, *Dispute Resolution in Family Law: Protecting Choice, Promoting Inclusion* (Toronto: Ministry of the Attorney General, 2004).

58 Bakht, "Family Arbitration Using Sharia Law," 3-5.

59 Ibid., 10, emphasis in original removed.

60 Marion Boyd, "Executive Summary," *Dispute Resolution in Family Law: Protecting Choice, Promoting Inclusion* (Toronto: Ministry of the Attorney General, 2004), 1-2.

61 Boyd has noted one possible state interest. In countries such as Canada where the state accepts responsibility to provide social assistance to the destitute, the state has interest in ensuring that settlements in dissolution of marriages provide adequate support for wives and children. Boyd, *Dispute Resolution in Family Law,* 102. I discuss this in Chapter 7, pp. 159-63.

62 CBC News, "Relocated Innu community plagued by social problems," 1 October 2004, http://www.cbc.ca/canada/story.

63 *Ford v. Quebec (Attorney General),* [1988] 2 S.C.R. 712 at 777-78.

64 The population of Welsh speakers in Wales has declined from approximately 930,000, or 50 percent of the population in 1901, to 508,098, or 18.6 percent in 1991. The 1901 figure is cited in Charlotte Aull Davies, *Welsh Nationalism in the Twentieth Century: The Ethnic Option and the Modern State* (New York: Praeger, 1989), 39; the 1991 figure in Janet Davies, "The Welsh Language," in *Post-War Wales,* ed. Trevor Herbert and Gareth Elwyn Jones (Cardiff: University of Wales Press, 1995), 58.

65 J. Aitchison and H. Carter, quoted in J. Davies, "The Welsh Language," 68.

66 Fiona Bowie, "Wales from Within: Conflicting Interpretations of Welsh Identity," in *Inside European Identities,* ed. Sharon Macdonald (Providence, RI: Berg, 1993), 183. In 1989, the "percentage of such [holiday] homes, which were unoccupied for most of the year, was so high as to virtually destroy the social life of many Welsh-speaking communities." C. Davies, *Welsh Nationalism,* 48.

67 Gareth Elwyn Jones, *Modern Wales: A Concise History* (Cambridge: Cambridge University Press, 1994), 316.

68 J. Wunder, *Retained by the People.*

69 *Thomas v. Norris,* [1992] 2 C.N.L.R. 139, 40.

70 Justice Hood concluded that it is not clear whether grabbing is integral to the practice. Ibid., 43.

71   Joseph Raz, "Multiculturalism: A Liberal Perspective," in *Ethics in the Public Domain: Essays in the Morality of Law and Politics* (Oxford: Clarendon Press, 1994), 174.

72   M. Estellie Smith, "The Process of Sociocultural Continuity," *Current Anthropology* 23 (1982): 130.

73   A contemporary example of such an approach was the Atlantic Groundfish Strategy in Canada, intended primarily to help members of Newfoundland outport communities adjust to the end of a way of life that had depended on the Atlantic cod. A similar point is made by Joseph Raz when he advocates gradual change in communities to protect "vested interests," since "denying a person the possibility of carrying on with his projects, commitments and relationships [prevents] him from having the life he has chosen." Joseph Raz, *The Morality of Freedom* (Oxford: Oxford University Press, 1986), 411.

74   Amoss, *Coast Salish Spirit Dancing*, 163-64.

Chapter 6: Designing Cultural Accommodation

1   I.M. Young, "Gender as Seriality: Thinking about Women as a Social Collective," *Signs: Journal of Women in Culture and Society* 19 (1994): 724, 725.

2   Ibid., 723-24, 725.

3   Bhikhu Parekh, *Rethinking Multiculturalism: Cultural Diversity and Political Theory* (Houndmills, UK: Macmillan, 2000), 148.

4   The case of refugees is different because they did not choose to leave their homelands and thus they may lack meaningful reasons for having come to their new community. Since they presumably want either to move back to their homeland or to immigrate to some other community, temporary accommodations may be in order.

5   Roger Gibbins, *Conflict and Unity: An Introduction to Canadian Political Life*, 3rd ed. (Scarborough, ON: Nelson Canada, 1994), 139.

6   *Ford v. Quebec, (Attorney General)*, [1988] 2 S.C.R. 712 at 717.

7   Gibbins, *Conflict and Unity*, 139-41.

8   This policy was recently upheld by the Supreme Court of Canada. Kirk Makin and Rheal Seguin, "Supreme Court Averts Quebec Language Fight," *Globe and Mail*, 1 April 2005, A10.

9   Michelle Ryan, "Blocking the Channels," in *Wales: The Imagined Nation*, ed. Tony Curtis (Bridgend, Mid Glamorgan: Poetry Wales Press, 1986), 185.

10   S4C has been described as "the most subsidized television channel in the world." Hugh MacKay and Hugh Powell, "Wales and Its Media: Production, Consumption, and Regulation," in *Contemporary Wales*, vol. 9, ed. Graham Day and Dennis Thomas (Cardiff: University of Wales Press, 1996), 24.

11   R. Brinley Jones, "Education in a New Era," in *The New Wales*, ed. David Cole (Cardiff: University of Wales Press, 1990), 195.

12   J. Davies, "The Welsh Language," 73-74nB15.

13   See, for instance, David Blackaby and Stephen Drinkwater, "Welsh-Speakers and the Labour Market," in *Contemporary Wales*, vol. 9, ed. Graham Day and Dennis Thomas (Cardiff: University of Wales Press, 1996), 158-59; and Anthony Alcock, "The Protection of Regional Cultural Minorities and the Process of European Integration: The Example of South Tyrol," *International Relations* 11 (1992): 23.

14   South Tyrol has a policy of official bilingualism but avoids favouring Germans, who are typically bilingual, over Italians, who typically are not, by insisting that employment in the public service be proportionate to each group's share of the population. See A. Alcock, "The Protection of Regional Cultural Minorities," and "South Tyrol," in *Minority Rights in Europe*, ed. Hugh Miall (New York: Council for Foreign Relations Press, 1994).

15   Clive James and Colin H. Williams, "Language and Planning in Scotland and Wales," in *Nationality and Planning in Scotland and Wales*, ed. Roderick Macdonald and Huw Thomas (Cardiff: University of Wales Press, 1997), 286, 288.

16   Florence Hawley, "The Keresan Holy Rollers: An Adaptation to American Individualism," *Social Forces* 26 (1947-48): esp. 273-74. This pattern of conflict became prominent on two occasions. On the first, several Pueblo Indians went to court claiming that the governing body of their village had "subjected them to indignities, threats and reprisals

because of their religious faith." The court dismissed the case on the ground that it had no jurisdiction. *Toledo v. Pueblo de Jemez,* 119 F. Supp. 429 (DNM, 1954), 429-30. On the second, a US Senate subcommittee heard submissions on a bill to exempt the Pueblo from the Indian Bill of Rights (which had become law in 1968). Many Pueblo feared that the bill would lead to the disestablishment of their theocratic institutions and prevent the eviction of Protestants. US Congress, Senate, Subcommittee on Constitutional Rights of the Committee of the Judiciary, *Amendments to the Indian Bill of Rights,* 91st Cong., 1st sess., 1969. See also Warren Weston, "Freedom of Religion and the American Indian," in *The American Indian: Past and Present,* ed. Roger L. Nichols and George R. Adams (Waltham, MA: Xerox College Publishing, 1971).

17 I say few, because Kymlicka does recognize "that there can be some legitimate restrictions on the internal activities of minority members, where those activities would *literally threaten* the existence of the community." Will Kymlicka, *Liberalism, Community, and Culture* (Oxford: Oxford University Press, 1989), 199, emphasis added.

18 Will Kymlicka, *Multicultural Citizenship* (Oxford: Clarendon Press, 1995), 113.

19 Kymlicka, *Liberalism, Community, and Culture,* 196.

20 Frances Svensson, "Liberal Democracy and Group Rights: The Legacy of Individualism and Its Impact on American Indian Tribes," *Political Studies* 27 (1979): 434, emphasis in original.

21 Ibid., 437. While Svensson believes there may be cases where the claims of individual rights outweigh group rights, this is not one of them. Ibid., 436.

22 US Congress, Senate, Subcommittee on Constitutional Rights of the Committee of the Judiciary, *Amendments to the Indian Bill of Rights,* 91st Cong., 1st sess., 1969.

23 Erin Anderssen, "How the Sawridge Millions Tore apart a Native Community," *Globe and Mail,* 31 October 1998, A1, 8-9.

24 This is the basis of a criticism Charles Taylor has made of Kymlicka's argument. Charles Taylor, "The Politics of Recognition," in *Multiculturalism: Examining the Politics of Recognition,* ed. Amy Gutmann (Princeton, NJ: Princeton University Press, 1994), 41 n. 16.

25 Gerald Tulchinsky, "Is Jewish History Ending?" (book review), *Globe and Mail,* 12 July 1997, D11.

26 Marion Boyd, "Executive Summary," *Dispute Resolution in Family Law: Protecting Choice, Promoting Inclusion* (Toronto: Ministry of the Attorney General, 2004), 4.

27 Carens makes a similar point when he says that the claim that Fijians "want" their present system gains validity from the facts that Fijians have free, democratic, contested elections and they are free to leave. Joseph H. Carens, *Culture, Citizenship, and Community* (Oxford: Oxford University Press, 2000), 249.

28 Seth Mydans, "Woman Defies Tribal Tradition," *Globe and Mail,* 7 May 1997, A16.

29 Kukathas says that after the Maori gained real freedom of exit, their identity became "much more a matter of individual personal choice." Chandra Kukathas, "Are There Any Cultural Rights?" *Political Theory* 20 (1992): 128.

30 Clearly, the happy outcome in this case was facilitated in no small measure by Ms Wilngal's having developed significant purposes that could facilitate her transition from her traditional community to a more modern society in Port Moresby. I consider the more challenging possibility of women who are both unhappy with the community's practices and lack the requisite identifications or purposes to join a different community in Chapter 7, p. 154.

31 Michael Sandel, "Freedom of Conscience or Freedom of Choice?" in *Articles of Faith, Articles of Peace,* ed. James Davidson Hunter and Os Guinness (Washington, DC: The Brookings Institution, 1990), 89.

32 Ibid., 89.

33 US Congress, Senate, 87.

34 Melissa S. Williams, "Group Inequality and the Public Culture of Justice," in *Group Rights,* ed. Judith Baker (Toronto: University of Toronto Press, 1994), 39.

35 On the difficulties of choosing between identifications, see Avigail Eisenberg, "Diversity and Equality: Three Approaches to Cultural and Sexual Difference," *Journal of Political Philosophy* 11 (2003): 55-62. I would like to thank one of the manuscript's anonymous

readers for bringing this article to my attention.

36   Schouls expresses a similar idea very nicely when he writes that "the core of an Aboriginal community is not to be found in its cultural or national identity but in the commitment of its members to remain together, as a community, over time." Tim Schouls, *Shifting Boundaries: Aboriginal Identity, Pluralist Theory, and the Politics of Self-Government* (Vancouver: UBC Press, 2003), 172.

37   Edward P. Dozier, "Factionalism at Santa Clara Pueblo," *Ethnology* 5 (1966): 177-83, quotations at 177 and 178.

38   Anderssen, "How the Sawridge Millions Tore Apart a Native Community."

Chapter 7: State-Community Relations

1   Anne Phillips, "Dealing with Difference: A Politics of Ideas or a Politics of Presence?" *Constellations* 1 (1994): 75-91, esp. 76; I.M. Young, "Polity and Group Difference: A Critique of the Ideal of Universal Citizenship," *Ethics* 99 (1989)," 260.

2   I.M. Young, "Polity and Group Difference," 262.

3   Roger Gibbins and Loleen Youngman, "The Institutional Expression of Multiple Identities: The Electoral Reform Debate," in *Braving the New World*, ed. Thomas M.J. Bateman, Manuel Mertin, and David M. Thomas (Toronto: Nelson Canada, 1995), 215-17, quotation at 217.

4   For instance, Ian Brodie suggests that the extension of constitutional protection to specific groups can perpetuate problems of group conflict within the political system. He concludes, in reference to Canada, that "trying to resolve group-based conflict by conferring constitutional status on the groups promotes, not political stability, but rather damaging group competition." Ian Brodie, "The Market for Political Status," *Comparative Politics* 28 (1996): 267.

5   Anne Phillips, "Democracy and Difference: Some Problems for Feminist Theory," *Political Quarterly* 63 (1992): 85-86.

6   I.M. Young, *Justice and the Politics of Difference* (Princeton, NJ: Princeton University Press, 1990), 190.

7   Vernon Van Dyke, "Collective Entities and Moral Rights: Problems in Liberal-Democratic Thought," *Journal of Politics* 44 (1982): 36. This is also similar to Tully's suggestion that popular sovereignty be revised to mean that "culturally diverse peoples here and now seek to reach constitutional agreements from time to time by means of negotiations in which the conventions of recognition, continuity and consent are honoured." James Tully, "The Crisis of Identification: The Case of Canada," *Political Studies* 42 (1994): 95.

8   I thank Richard Vernon for pointing out this distinction.

9   Kathy Brock says of attempts by North American Indians to secure rights through the courts that "while the political arena allows for compromise and negotiation, the legal forum forces issues into a zero sum situation with winners and losers." Kathy Brock, "The Issues of Self-Government: Canadian and American Aboriginal Policy Compared," in *Canada and the United States: Difference That Count*, ed. David Thomas (Peterborough, ON: Broadview Press, 1993), 263. See also Melissa Williams, "Political and Judicial Approaches to Justice toward Groups," in *Citizenship and Rights in Multicultural Societies*, ed. Michael Dunne and Tiziano Bonazzi (Keele, Staffordshire: Keele University Press, 1995).

10   I.M. Young, "Polity and Group Difference," 262.

11   This idea has been broached but not explored by some of the theorists discussed in Chapter 1. For instance, Kymlicka raises the possibility of international adjudication when he writes: "It would be preferable if all governments – majority and minority – are subject to some form of international scrutiny." Will Kymlicka, *Politics in the Vernacular: Nationalism, Multiculturalism, and Citizenship* (Oxford: Oxford University Press, 2001), 87. Similarly, Tully has written: "Therefore, minorities need to be able to appeal to other decision-taking institutions at the end of the dialogue, such as courts, parliaments, international human rights regimes, non-partisan adjudicators or mediators, global transnational networks and so on. These too are imperfect and need to be open to challenge in turn, but they provide indispensable checks and balances on the powers of the dominant groups to manipulate the dialogue and manufacture agreement." James

Tully, "Recognition and Dialogue: The Emergence of a New Field," *Critical Review of International Social and Political Philosophy* 7 (2004): 102.

12 For a more thorough discussion of this proposal, see Andrew M. Robinson, "Would International Adjudication Enhance Contextual Theories of Justice? Reflections on the UN Human Rights Committee, Lovelace, Ballantyne and Waldman," *Canadian Journal of Political Science* 38 (2): 271-91.

13 Bhikhu Parekh, *Rethinking Multiculturalism: Cultural Diversity and Political Theory* (Houndmills, UK: Macmillan, 2000), 207.

14 Ibid., 273.

15 This, of course, draws attention to another contextual matter. As Joseph Carens and Marc Doucet reminded me, this is most likely to be true in countries such as Canada where the state cares about how it is seen by the UN.

16 Ken Coates, *The Marshall Decision and Native Rights* (Montreal and Kingston: McGill-Queen's University Press, 2000), 51.

17 An excerpt of the petition is quoted in Ken Coates, *The Marshall Decision*, 36-37. I reproduce part of it because of its relevance to the discussion:

Before the white people came, we had plenty of wild roots, plenty of fish, and plenty of cord. The skins of the Moose and Cariboo were warm to our bodies, we had plenty of good land, we worshipped "Kesoult" the Great Spirit, we were free and we were happy.

Good and Honorable Governor, be not offended at what we say, for we wish to please you. But your people had not land enough, they came and killed many of our tribe and took from us our country. You have taken from us our lands and trees and have destroyed our game ...

In our old times our wigwams stood in the pleasant places along the sides of the rivers. These places are now taken from us, and we are told to go away. Upon our camping grounds you have built towns and the graves of our fathers are broken by the plow and harrow. Even the ash and maple are growing scarce. We are told to cut no trees upon the farmer's ground, and the land you have give us is taken away every year ...

All your people say they wish to do us good, and they sometimes give, but give a beggar a dinner and he is a beggar still. We do not like to beg. As our game and fish are nearly gone and we cannot sell our articles, we have resolved to make farms, yet we cannot make farms without help. What more can we say? We will ask our Mother the Queen to help us. We beg your Excellency to help us in our distress, and help us that we may at last be able to help ourselves.

18 Ibid., 55-62.

19 Ibid., 52, 54.

20 Whether the historical treaties can support such an individual right is an entirely separate matter.

21 Coates, *The Marshall Decision*, 118.

22 Anthony Davis and Svein Jentoft, "The Challenge and the Promise of Indigenous Peoples' Fishing Rights – from Dependency to Agency," *Marine Policy* 25 (2001): 234.

23 Coates, *The Marshall Decision*, 155.

24 Quoted in ibid., 140.

25 Coates describes an arrangement New Brunswick has made to transfer 5 percent of the allowable logging cut to Aboriginal control. Ibid., 112. As for the lobster fishery, Davis and Jentoft suggest that Aboriginals were taking less than 5 percent of the non-Aboriginal catch. Davis and Jentoft, "The Challenge and the Promise," 227 n. 9. Coates suggests any increase would be marginal and sustainable (128-29). Also of note, Davis and Jentoft suggest that Aboriginal and non-Aboriginal fishers might find a common ground in uniting to manage the coast zone fishery and protect it from unsustainable large-scale fishing (235). This strikes me as an example of the kind of creative solutions that could be identified if we started thinking about these issues in terms of equal respect for meaningful life.

26 Richard Arneson, "Autonomy and Preference Formation," in *In Harm's Way: Essays in*

Honor of Joel Feinberg, ed. Jules L. Coleman and Allen Buchanan (Cambridge: Cambridge University Press, 1994), 59.

27   Kenneth Henley, "The Authority to Educate," in *Having Children: Philosophical and Legal Reflections on Parenthood,* ed. Onora O'Neill and William Ruddick (New York: Oxford University Press, 1979), 260-61.

28   This distinction is nicely illustrated by Goldwin Emerson's comments on a conversation he overheard between a grandmother, a mother, and a four-year-old girl in which the child was told: "Santa [Claus] does see everything you do – he's just like God ... He keeps track of everything you do." Of this Emerson writes: "Perhaps the mother and grandmother were sincere in their belief that God sees everything you do – if so, they were simply passing along a belief that they themselves genuinely accepted as reality. But surely they did not believe that Santa Claus keeps track of all children's behaviour." Goldwin Emerson, "It's no fun to threaten kids with Santa-spy," *London (Ontario) Free Press,* 6 December 1997, F7.

29   Carens makes a similar point when he suggests that the legitimacy of actual traditions and systems of authority cannot be undermined by their reliance to some degree on their reproduction of processes of socialization involving myths and political rule involving power. The question, it seems, is whether this is all they rely on. If this is the case, their legitimacy should last no longer than the lies and coercion. Joseph H. Carens, *Culture, Citizenship, and Community* (Oxford: Oxford University Press, 2000), 239.

30   Carens has made a similar point about contemporary Amish identity being shaped in part by the historical experience of persecution in Europe. He thinks that their continuing affirmation of their culture in the absence of persecution gives their choice legitimacy. Ibid., 99.

31   To this extent, I agree with Feinberg's "child's right to an open future," which is violated by conduct that "guarantees *now* that when the child is an autonomous adult, certain key options will already be closed to him." Joel Feinberg, "The Child's Right to an Open Future," in *Whose Child? Children's Rights, Parental Authority, and State Power,* ed. William Aiken and Hugh LaFollette (Totowa, NJ: Rowman and Littlefield, 1980), 126, emphasis in original.

32   Jon Elster, "Sour Grapes – Utilitarianism and the Genesis of Wants," in *Utilitarianism and Beyond,* ed. Amartya Sen and Bernard Williams (Cambridge: Cambridge University Press, 1982).

33   John Rawls, *Political Liberalism* (New York: Columbia University Press, 1993), 199.

34   William Galston, "Two Concepts of Liberalism," *Ethics* 105 (1995): 529.

35   Will Kymlicka, *Multicultural Citizenship* (Oxford: Clarendon Press, 1995), 169.

36   See, for instance, the discussion of Kymlicka's criticism of Kukathas' account of the freedom to exit in Chapter 1 and Galston's description of four elements of a substantive freedom of exit in "Two Concepts of Liberalism," 533.

37   John A. Hostetler, *Amish Society* (Baltimore: Johns Hopkins Press, 1963), 62-65.

38   The case would be different if the community only counselled but did not enforce the ban.

39   The situation would be more complicated if the woman's participation appeared to be voluntary. Even if it did, we would have to ask whether the socialization she had received that led her to accept this treatment was non-exploitive. On the assumption that the obligations and benefits a culture assigns to its members must be examined as a whole rather than one at a time to get a true picture of whether a practice is exploitive or not, I am willing to entertain the possibility that such participation might be truly voluntary. In such cases, and even where we are not entirely certain about exploitation, respect for meaningful life requires that we defer to the woman's stated preferences in the matter. Of course, we would also want to be sure that the other principles governing the socialization of children had been met, particularly that these women knew they were free to leave their community. If it did turn out that the women's participation was either non-voluntary or based on illegitimate socialization, intervention would be justified.

40   I realize this will not sit well with those who have criticized Alan Cairns for insisting that thinking about Aboriginal/non-Aboriginal relations in Canada must start from the

assumption that both sides share a common citizenship. Alan C. Cairns, *Citizens Plus: Aboriginal Peoples and the Canadian State* (Vancouver: UBC Press, 2000).

41 Galston, "Two Concepts of Liberalism," 528.

42 Richard Arneson and Ian Shapiro, "Democratic Autonomy and Religious Freedom: A Critique of *Wisconsin v. Yoder*," in *Democracy's Place*, ed. Ian Shapiro (Ithaca, NY: Cornell University Press, 1996), 158ff.

43 David Miller, *On Nationality* (Oxford: Clarendon Press, 1995), 142.

44 Galston, "Two Concepts of Liberalism," 528.

45 An interesting though non-academic exploration of the success of young adults raised in Bountiful, British Columbia – a colony of the Fundamentalist Church of Jesus Christ of Latter Day Saints that, among other things, does not encourage education beyond grade 10 – discusses the possibility and challenges of such transitions. Jane Armstrong, "Making a Break from Bountiful," *Globe and Mail*, 9 April 2005, A7.

46 Feinberg, "The Child's Right to an Open Future," 128.

47 *Wisconsin v. Yoder*, 92 S. Ct. 1526 (1972), 1530-31.

48 Feinberg, "The Child's Right to an Open Future," 143, 126, 128.

49 Ibid., 135-37, quotation at 137.

50 Arneson and Shapiro, "Democratic Autonomy and Religious Freedom," 152.

51 *Wisconsin v. Yoder*, 92 S. Ct. 1526 (1972), 1528.

52 Arneson and Shapiro, "Democratic Autonomy and Religious Freedom," 141, citing Donald Kraybill, *The Riddle of Amish Culture* (Baltimore: Johns Hopkins University Press, 1989), 140.

53 *Wisconsin v. Yoder*, 92 S. Ct. 1526 (1972), 1531.

54 Ibid.

55 By comparison, Kymlicka defends accommodations for Amish and Hutterites even though he recognizes that the internal restrictions they place on their members conflict with personal autonomy. He justifies this position by appealing to reasons outside his theoretical framework, such as honouring agreements: "We may now regret these historical exemptions, but they were granted, and we cannot entirely dismiss them, unless they are unconscionably unjust." Kymlicka, *Multicultural Citizenship*, 170.

56 Quoted in Natasha Bakht, "Family Arbitration Using Sharia Law: Examining Ontario's Arbitration Act and Its Impact on Women," *Muslim World Journal of Human Rights* 1 (2004): 6. http://www.bepress.com/mwjhr.

57 Marilyn Boyd, "Executive Summary," *Dispute Resolution in Family Law: Protecting Choice, Promoting Inclusion* (Toronto: Ministry of the Attorney General, 2004), 8-9.

58 Marion Boyd, *Dispute Resolution in Family Law: Protecting Choice, Promoting Inclusion* (Toronto: Ministry of the Attorney General, 2004), 101.

59 Ibid., 75.

60 Bakht, "Family Arbitration Using Sharia Law," 22 n. 119.

61 Boyd, *Dispute Resolution in Family Law*, 102-3.

62 Bakht, "Family Arbitration Using Sharia Law," 8-10.

63 Boyd, "Executive Summary," 8.

64 Boyd, *Dispute Resolution in Family Law*, 107.

65 Ibid., 89.

66 Bakht, "Family Arbitration Using Sharia Law," 19-20.

67 Boyd, "Executive Summary," 6-7.

Conclusion

1 A corollary to this sixth point is that the idea of a state-level moral tradition that helps sustain meaning in the lives of all citizens also provides a reason for trying to keep multinational states together, even where secession is a viable option.

2 Joseph H. Carens, *Culture, Citizenship, and Community* (Oxford: Oxford University Press, 2000), 235 n. 35; Avigail Eisenberg, "Context, Cultural Difference, Sex and Social Justice," *Canadian Journal of Political Science* 35 (2002): 628.

Bibliography

Addelson, K. Pyne. "Personal Autonomy and the Paradox of Feminine Socialization." *Journal of Philosophy* 84 (1987): 619-29.

Alcock, Anthony. "South Tyrol." In *Minority Rights in Europe,* ed. Hugh Miall, 46-55. New York: Council for Foreign Relations Press, 1994.

–. "The Protection of Regional Cultural Minorities and the Process of European Integration: The Example of South Tyrol." *International Relations* 11 (1992): 17-36.

Amoss, Pamela. *Coast Salish Spirit Dancing: The Survival of an Ancestral Religion.* Seattle: University of Washington Press, 1978.

Anderson, Benedict. *Imagined Community.* London: Verso, 1983.

Archard, David. "Autonomy, Character and Situation." In *Liberalism, Citizenship and Autonomy,* ed. David Milligan and William Watts Miller, 157-70. Aldershot, UK: Avebury, 1992.

Arneson, Richard. "Autonomy and Preference Formation." In *In Harm's Way: Essays in Honor of Joel Feinberg,* ed. Jules L. Coleman and Allen Buchanan, 42-75. Cambridge: Cambridge University Press, 1994.

Arneson, Richard, and Ian Shapiro. "Democratic Autonomy and Religious Freedom: A Critique of *Wisconsin v. Yoder.*" In *Democracy's Place,* ed. Ian Shapiro, 137-74. Ithaca, NY: Cornell University Press, 1996.

Bachman, Ronet. *Death and Violence on the Reservation: Homicide, Family Violence, and Suicide in American Indian Populations.* New York: Auburn House, 1992.

Baier, Kurt. "The Purpose of Man's Existence." In *Life and Meaning: A Reader,* ed. Oswald Hanfling, 20-33. Oxford: Basil Blackwell, 1987.

Bakht, Natasha. "Family Arbitration Using Sharia Law: Examining Ontario's Arbitration Act and Its Impact on Women." *Muslim World Journal of Human Rights* 1 (2004). http://www.bepress.com/mwjhr.

Barry, Brian M. *Culture and Equality: An Egalitarian Critique of Multiculturalism* (Cambridge, MA: Harvard University Press, 2001).

Benn, Stanley. *A Theory of Freedom.* Cambridge: Cambridge University Press, 1988.

–. "Freedom, Autonomy, and the Concept of a Person." *Proceedings of the Aristotelian Society* 76 (1975-76): 109-30.

Blackaby, David, and Stephen Drinkwater. "Welsh-Speakers and the Labour Market." In *Contemporary Wales,* vol. 9, ed. Graham Day and Dennis Thomas, 158-70. Cardiff: University of Wales Press, 1996.

Borland, John, Ralph Fevre, and David Denney. "Nationalism and Community in North West Wales." *Sociological Review* 40 (1992): 49-72.

Bowie, Fiona. "Wales from Within: Conflicting Interpretations of Welsh Identity." In *Inside European Identities: Ethnography in Western Europe,* ed. Sharon Macdonald, 167-93. Providence, RI: Berg, 1993.

Boyd, Marion. *Dispute Resolution in Family Law: Protecting Choice, Promoting Inclusion.* Toronto: Ministry of the Attorney General, 2004.

–. "Executive Summary." *Dispute Resolution in Family Law: Protecting Choice, Promoting Inclusion.* Toronto: Ministry of the Attorney General, 2004.

Brink, David O. *Moral Realism and the Foundations of Ethics.* Cambridge: Cambridge University Press, 1989.

Brock, Kathy. "The Issues of Self-Government: Canadian and American Aboriginal Policy Compared." In *Canada and the United States: Difference That Count,* ed. David Thomas, 252-70. Peterborough, ON: Broadview Press, 1993.

Brodie, Ian. "The Market for Political Status." *Comparative Politics* 28 (1996): 253-71.

Cairns, Alan C. *Citizens Plus: Aboriginal Peoples and the Canadian State.* Vancouver: UBC Press, 2000.

Canada. House of Commons. *Minutes of the Proceedings and Evidence of the Standing Committee on Aboriginal Affairs and Northern Development.* Ottawa: Canadian Government Publishing Centre, issue no. 39 (27 April 1988).

–. Royal Commission on Aboriginal Peoples, *Overview of the First Round – Public Hearings.* Prepared for the Commission by Michael Cassidy, Ginger Group Consultants. Ottawa: Royal Commission on Aboriginal Peoples, 1992.

Carens, Joseph H. *Culture, Citizenship, and Community: A Contextual Exploration of Justice as Evenhandedness.* Oxford: Oxford University Press, 2000.

Chandler, Michael J., and Christopher Lalonde. "Cultural Continuity as a Hedge against Suicide in Canada's First Nations." *Transcultural Psychology* 35 (2): 191-219.

Christman, John. "Autonomy: A Defense of the Split-Level Self." *Southern Journal of Philosophy* 25 (1987): 281-94.

–. "Introduction." In *The Inner Citadel: Essays on Individual Autonomy,* ed. John Christman, 3-23. New York: Oxford University Press, 1989.

Clarke, Desmond M., and Charles Jones. "Introduction." In *The Rights of Nations: Nations and Nationalism in a Changing World,* ed. Desmond M. Clarke and Charles Jones, 1-25. New York: St. Martin's Press, 1999.

Coates, Ken. *The Marshall Decision and Native Rights.* Montreal and Kingston: McGill-Queen's University Press, 2000.

Cohen, M.J. *The New Penguin Dictionary of Quotations.* London: Penguin, 1992.

Coulombe, Pierre. *Language Rights in French Canada.* New York: Peter Lang, 1995.

Davies, Charlotte Aull. *Welsh Nationalism in the Twentieth Century: The Ethnic Option and the Modern State.* New York: Praeger, 1989.

Davies, Janet. "The Welsh Language." In *Post-War Wales,* ed. Trevor Herbert and Gareth Elwyn Jones, 55-77. Cardiff: University of Wales Press, 1995.

Davis, Anthony, and Svein Jentoft. "The Challenge and the Promise of Indigenous Peoples' Fishing Rights – from Dependency to Agency." *Marine Policy* 25 (2001): 223-37.

Dozier, Edward P. "Factionalism at Santa Clara Pueblo." *Ethnology* 5 (1966): 172-85.

–. *The Pueblo Indians of North America.* New York: Holt, Rinehart and Winston, 1970.

Durkheim, Emile. *Suicide.* Translated by John A. Spaulding and George Simpson. Glencoe, IL: The Free Press, 1951.

Dworkin, Gerald. *The Theory and Practice of Autonomy.* Cambridge: Cambridge University Press, 1988.

Dworkin, Ronald. "Foundations of Liberal Equality." *The Tanner Lectures on Human Values* 11 (1990): 1-120.

–. "Liberal Community." *California Law Review* 77 (1989): 479-504.

–. "What Is Equality? Part 3: The Place of Liberty." *Iowa Law Review* 73 (1987): 1-54.

–. "What Is Equality? Part 2: Equality of Resources." *Philosophy & Public Affairs* 10 (1981): 283-345.

Eisenberg, Avigail. "Context, Cultural Difference, Sex and Social Justice." *Canadian Journal of Political Science* 35 (2002): 613-28.

–. "Diversity and Equality: Three Approaches to Cultural and Sexual Difference." *Journal of Political Philosophy* 11 (2003): 41-64.

Elster, Jon. "Sour Grapes – Utilitarianism and the Genesis of Wants." In *Utilitarianism and Beyond,* ed. Amartya Sen and Bernard Williams, 219-38. Cambridge: Cambridge University Press, 1982.

Fay, Brian. *Contemporary Philosophy of Social Science*. Oxford: Blackwell, 1996.

Feinberg, Joel. "The Child's Right to an Open Future." In *Whose Child? Children's Rights, Parental Authority, and State Power*, ed. William Aiken and Hugh LaFollette, 124-53. Totowa, NJ: Rowman and Littlefield, 1980.

Ford v. Quebec (Attorney General), [1988] 2 S.C.R. 712.

Frankfurt, Harry G. "Freedom of the Will and the Concept of a Person." *Journal of Philosophy* 68 (1971): 5-20.

–. "Identification and Wholeheartedness." In *The Importance of What We Care About*, 58-68. Cambridge: Cambridge University Press, 1988.

–. "The Importance of What We Care About." In *The Importance of What We Care About*, 80-94. Cambridge: Cambridge University Press, 1988.

Frankl, Viktor. *Man's Search for Meaning*. New York: Washington Square Press, 1985.

Friedman, Marilyn. "Autonomy and the Split-Level Self." *Southern Journal of Philosophy* 24 (1986): 19-36.

–. "Feminism and Modern Friendship: Dislocating the Community." *Ethics* 99 (1989): 275-90.

Galston, William. "Civic Education in the Liberal State." In *Liberalism and the Moral Life*, ed. Nancy L. Rosenblum, 89-101. Cambridge, MA: Harvard University Press, 1989.

–. "Two Concepts of Liberalism." *Ethics* 105 (1995): 516-34.

Gibbins, Roger. *Conflict and Unity: An Introduction to Canadian Political Life*. 3rd ed. Scarborough, ON: Nelson Canada, 1994.

Gibbins, Roger, and Loleen Youngman. "The Institutional Expression of Multiple Identities: The Electoral Reform Debate." In *Braving the New World*, ed. Thomas M.J. Bateman, Manuel Mertin, and David M. Thomas, 210-22. Toronto: Nelson Canada, 1995.

Gutmann, Amy. "Undemocratic Education." In *Liberalism and the Moral Life*, ed. Nancy L. Rosenblum, 71-88. Cambridge, MA: Harvard University Press, 1989.

Hanfling, Oswald. *The Quest for Meaning*. Oxford: Basil Blackwell, 1987.

Hawley, Florence. "The Keresan Holy Rollers: An Adaptation to American Individualism." *Social Forces* 26 (1947-48): 272-80.

Henley, Kenneth. "The Authority to Educate." In *Having Children: Philosophical and Legal Reflections on Parenthood*, ed. Onora O'Neill and William Ruddick, 254-64. New York: Oxford University Press, 1979.

Hostetler, John A. *Amish Society*. Baltimore: Johns Hopkins Press, 1963.

Hurka, Thomas. "Why Value Autonomy?" *Social Theory and Practice* 13 (1987): 361-82.

James, Clive, and Colin H. Williams. "Language Planning in Scotland and Wales." In *Nationality and Planning in Scotland and Wales*, ed. Roderick Macdonald and Huw Thomas, 264-302. Cardiff: University of Wales Press, 1997.

Jones, Gareth Elwyn. *Modern Wales: A Concise History*. Cambridge: Cambridge University Press, 1994.

Jones, R. Brinley. "Education in a New Era." In *The New Wales*, ed. David Cole, 193-204. Cardiff: University of Wales Press, 1990.

Kekes, John. "Moral Tradition." In *Life and Meaning: A Reader*, ed. Oswald Hanfling, 234-48. Oxford: Basil Blackwell, 1985.

–. *The Morality of Pluralism*. Princeton, NJ: Princeton University Press, 1993.

Kukathas, Chandran. "Are There Any Cultural Rights?" *Political Theory* 20 (1992): 105-39.

–. "Cultural Rights Again: A Rejoinder to Kymlicka." *Political Theory* 20, 4 (November 1992): 674-80.

Kymlicka, Will. *Finding Our Way: Rethinking Ethnocultural Relations in Canada*. Oxford: Oxford University Press, 1998.

–. *Liberalism, Community, and Culture*. Oxford: Clarendon Press, 1989.

–. *Multicultural Citizenship*. Oxford: Clarendon Press, 1995.

–. *Politics in the Vernacular: Nationalism, Multiculturalism and Citizenship*. Oxford: Oxford University Press, 2001.

–. "The Rights of Minority Cultures." *Political Theory* 20 (1992): 140-46.

–. "Western Political Theory and Ethnic Relations in Eastern Europe." In *Can Liberal*

Pluralism Be Exported? Western Political Theory and Ethnic Relations in Eastern Europe, ed. Will Kymlicka and Magda Opalski, 13-105. Oxford: Oxford University Press, 2001.

Lindley, Richard. *Autonomy.* London: Macmillan Education, 1986.

Linton, Ralph. "The Distinctive Aspects of Acculturation." In *The Emergent Native Americans,* ed. Deward E. Walker Jr., 6-19. Boston: Little, Brown, 1972.

MacIntyre, Alasdair. *Whose Justice? Which Rationality?* Notre Dame, IN: Notre Dame University Press, 1988.

–. *After Virtue.* 2nd ed. Notre Dame, IN: University of Notre Dame Press, 1984.

MacKay, Hugh, and Hugh Powell. "Wales and Its Media: Production, Consumption, and Regulation." In *Contemporary Wales,* vol. 9, ed. Graham Day and Dennis Thomas, 8-39. Cardiff: University of Wales Press, 1996.

Meyers, Diana. "Personal Autonomy and the Paradox of Feminine Socialization." *Journal of Philosophy* 84 (1987): 619-28.

–. *Self, Society and Personal Choice.* New York: Columbia University Press, 1989.

–. "The Socialized Individual and Individual Autonomy: An Intersection between Philosophy and Psychology." In *Women and Moral Theory,* ed. Eva Feder Kittay and Diana T. Meyers, 139-53. Totawa, NJ: Rowman and Littlefield, 1987.

Mill, John Stuart. "Autobiography." In *Essential Works of John Stuart Mill,* ed. Max Lerner. New York: Bantam Books, 1961.

–. "On Liberty." In *Utilitarianism, On Liberty and Considerations on Representative Government,* ed. H.B. Acton, 69-185. London: Dent, 1972.

–. "Utilitarianism." In *Utilitarianism, On Liberty and Considerations on Representative Government,* ed. H.B. Acton, 1-67. London: Dent, 1972.

Miller, David. *On Nationality.* Oxford: Clarendon Press, 1995.

Nickel, James. "Liberalism, Community, and Culture." (Book review.) *Canadian Philosophical Reviews,* 413-15. Edmonton: Academic Printing and Publishing, January 1990.

Nozick, Robert. *Anarchy, State, and Utopia.* New York: Basic Books, 1974.

–. *Philosophical Explanations.* Cambridge, MA: Belknap, 1981.

Oakeshott, Michael. "Historical Change." In *On History and Other Essays,* 97-118. Oxford: Basil Blackwell, 1983.

–. "On the Civil Condition." In *On Human Conduct,* 108-84. Oxford: Clarendon Press, 1975.

Okin, Susan Moller. "Gender Inequality and Cultural Differences." *Political Theory* 22 (1994): 5-24.

O'Neil, Onora. "Autonomy, Coherence and Independence." In *Liberalism, Citizenship and Autonomy,* ed. David Milligan and William Watts Miller, 203-25. Aldershot, UK: Avebury, 1992.

Ortiz, Alfonso. "The Dynamics of Pueblo Cultural Survival." In *North American Indian Anthropology,* ed. Raymond J. Demallie and Alfonso Ortiz, 296-306. Norman: University of Oklahoma Press, 1994.

–. *The Tewa World: Space, Time, Being, and Becoming in a Pueblo Society.* Chicago: University of Chicago Press, 1969.

Osborne, Barry. "Cultural Congruence, Ethnicity, and Fused Biculturalism: Zuni, and Torres Strait." *Journal of American Indian Education* 28 (1989): 7-20.

Papanek, Hanna. "To Each Less than She Needs, from Each, More than She Can Do: Allocations, Entitlements, and Value." In *Persistent Inequalities: Women and World Development,* ed. Irene Tinker, 162-84. Oxford: Oxford University Press, 1990.

Parekh, Bhikhu. *Rethinking Multiculturalism: Cultural Diversity and Political Theory.* Houndmills, UK: Macmillan, 2000.

Phillips, Anne. "Dealing with Difference: A Politics of Ideas or a Politics of Presence?" *Constellations* 1 (1994): 74-91.

–. "Democracy and Difference: Some Problems for Feminist Theory." *Political Quarterly* 63 (1992): 79-90.

Rawls, John. *A Theory of Justice.* Cambridge, MA: Belknap, 1971.

–. *Political Liberalism.* New York: Columbia University Press, 1993.

Raz, Joseph. "Facing Up: A Reply." *Southern California Law Review* 62, 3/4 (1989): 1153-235.

–. "Multiculturalism: A Liberal Perspective." In *Ethics in the Public Domain: Essays in the Morality of Law and Politics,* 155-76. Oxford: Clarendon Press, 1994.

–. *The Morality of Freedom.* Oxford: Oxford University Press, 1986.

Raz, Joseph, and Avishai Margalit. "National Self-Determination." In *Ethics in the Public Domain: Essays in the Morality of Law and Politics,* 110-32. Oxford: Clarendon Press, 1994.

Rorty, Amelie Oksenberg. "The Hidden Politics of Cultural Identification." *Political Theory* 22 (1994): 152-66.

Rosser, Philyp. "Growing Through Political Change." In *The National Question Again: Welsh Political Identity in the 1980s,* ed. J. Osmond, 180-91. Llandysul, UK: Gomer Press, 1985.

R. v. Powley. [2003] 2 S.C.R. 207, 2003 SCC 43.

Ryan, Michelle. "Blocking the Channels." In *Wales: The Imagined Nation,* ed. Tony Curtis, 181-96. Bridgend, Mid Glamorgan: Poetry Wales Press, 1986.

Sandel, Michael. "Freedom of Conscience or Freedom of Choice?" In *Articles of Faith, Articles of Peace,* ed. James Davidson Hunter and Os Guinness, 74-92. Washington, DC: The Brookings Institution, 1990.

–. *Liberalism and the Limits of Justice.* Cambridge: Cambridge University Press, 1982.

Schouls, Tim. *Shifting Boundaries: Aboriginal Identity, Pluralist Theory, and the Politics of Self-Government.* Vancouver: UBC Press, 2003.

Smith, M. Estellie. "The Process of Sociocultural Continuity." *Current Anthropology* 23 (1982): 127-42.

Stern, Alfred. *The Search for Meaning: Philosophical Vistas.* Memphis: Memphis State University Press, 1971.

Suina, Joseph H., and Laura B. Smolkin. "The Multicultural Worlds of Pueblo Indian Children's Celebrations." *Journal of American Indian Education* 34 (1995): 18-27.

Suttles, Wayne. "Spirit Dancing and the Persistence of Native Culture among the Coast Salish." In *Coast Salish Essays,* 199-208. Vancouver: Talon Books, 1987.

Svensson, Frances. "Liberal Democracy and Group Rights: The Legacy of Individualism and Its Impact on American Indian Tribes." *Political Studies* 27 (1979): 421-39.

Sweet, Jill D. "Burlesquing the Other in Pueblo Performance." *Annals of Tourism Research* 16 (1989): 62-75.

Taylor, Charles. *A Catholic Modernity? Charles Taylor's Marianist Award Lecture,* ed. James L. Heft. New York: Oxford University Press, 1999.

–. "Cross-Purposes: The Liberal Communitarian Debate." In *Liberalism and the Moral Life,* ed. Nancy L. Rosenblum, 159-83. Cambridge, MA: Harvard University Press, 1989.

–. "Democratic Exclusion (and Its Remedies?)." Political theory workshop, University of Chicago, 7 February 2000. http://ptw.uchicago.edu/taylor00.pdf.

–. "Les sources de l'identité moderne." In *Les frontières de l'identité: Modernité et postmodernism au Quebec,* ed. Mikhael Elbaz, Andrée Fortin, and Guy LaForest, 347-63. Sainte-Foy: Les Presses de L'Université Laval, 1996.

–. *Modern Social Imaginaries.* Durham, NC: Duke University Press, 2004.

–. "Nationalism and Modernity." In *The Morality of Nationalism,* ed. Robert McKim and Jeff McMahan, 31-55. New York: Oxford University Press, 1997.

–. "No Community, No Democracy, Part II." *Responsive Community* 14 (2003/2004): 15-25.

–. "Shared and Divergent Values." In *Reconciling the Solitudes,* ed. Guy LaForest, 155-86. Montreal: McGill-Queen's University Press, 1993.

–. *Sources of the Self.* Cambridge, MA: Harvard University Press, 1989.

–. "The Politics of Recognition." In *Multiculturalism: Examining the Politics of Recognition,* ed. Amy Gutmann, 25-74. Princeton, NJ: Princeton University Press, 1994.

Thomas v. Norris, [1992] 2 C.N.L.R. 139.

Toledo v. Pueblo de Jemez, 119 F. Supp. 429 (DNM, 1954).

Tolstoy, Leo. "My Confession." In *Life and Meaning: A Reader,* ed. Oswald Hanfling, 9-19. Oxford: Basil Blackwell, 1987.

Trillen, Calvin. "Drawing the Line." In *The New Yorker,* 12 December 1994, 50-62.

Tully, James. "Recognition and Dialogue: The Emergence of a New Field." *Critical Review of International Social and Political Philosophy* 7 (2004): 84-106.

–. "Introduction." In *Multinational Democracies,* ed. Alain-G. Gagnon and James Tully, 1-33. Cambridge: Cambridge University Press, 2001.

–. *Strange Multiplicity.* Cambridge: Cambridge University Press, 1995.

–. "The Crisis of Identification: The Case of Canada." *Political Studies* 42 (1994): 77-96.

US Congress. Senate. Subcommittee on Constitutional Rights of the Committee of the Judiciary. *Amendments to the Indian Bill of Rights.* 91st Cong., 1st sess., 1969.

Van Dyke, Vernon. "Collective Entities and Moral Rights: Problems in Liberal-Democratic Thought." *Journal of Politics* 44 (1982): 21-40.

West, E.G. "Liberty and Education: John Stuart Mill's Dilemma." *Philosophy* 40 (1965): 129-42.

Westlake Van Winkle, Nancy, and Philip A. May. "Native American Suicide in New Mexico, 1957-79: A Comparative Study." *Human Organization* 45 (1986): 296-309.

Weston, Warren. "Freedom of Religion and the American Indian." In *The American Indian: Past and Present,* ed. Roger L. Nichols and George R. Adams, 263-68. Waltham, MA: Xerox College Publishing, 1971.

Williams, Bernard. "Persons, Character, and Morality." In *The Identities of Persons,* ed. Amelie Oksenberg Rorty, 197-216. Berkeley: University of California, 1976.

Williams, Melissa. "Group Inequality and the Public Culture of Justice." In *Group Rights,* ed. Judith Baker, 34-65. Toronto: University of Toronto Press, 1994.

–. "Political and Judicial Approaches to Justice toward Groups." In *Citizenship and Rights in Multicultural Societies,* ed. Michael Dunne and Tiziano Bonazzi, 53-66. Keele, Staffordshire: Keele University Press, 1995.

Wisconsin v. Yoder, 92 S. Ct. 1526 (1972).

Wunder, J. *"Retained by the People": A History of American Indians and the Bill of Rights.* Oxford: Oxford University Press, 1994.

Young, Iris Marion. "Gender as Seriality: Thinking about Women as a Social Collective." *Signs: Journal of Women in Culture and Society* 19 (1994): 713-38.

–. *Justice and the Politics of Difference.* Princeton, NJ: Princeton University Press, 1990.

–. "Polity and Group Difference: A Critique of the Ideal of Universal Citizenship." *Ethics* 99 (1989): 250-74.

Young, Robert. "Autonomy and Socialization." *Mind* 89 (1980): 565-76.

–. *Personal Autonomy: Beyond Positive and Negative Liberty.* London: Croom Helm, 1986.

Index

Printed and bound in Canada by Friesens
Set in Stone by Blakeley
Copy editing: Judy Phillips
Proofreading: Heather Lange
Indexing: Clive Pyne